SEAN O'CASEY
Politics and Art

SEAN O'CASEY
Politics and Art

by

C. Desmond Greaves

LAWRENCE AND WISHART
LONDON

Lawrence and Wishart Ltd
39 Museum Street
London WC1

First published 1979
Copyright © C. Desmond Greaves

Printed and bound in Great Britain at
The Camelot Press Ltd, Southampton

CONTENTS

PREFACE

You've really caught the very note
Of how he spits and clears his throat.
F. Schiller, *Wallenstein's Camp*, Sc. 6

The purpose of this book is to investigate the political evolution of the great Irish dramatist Sean O'Casey in order to throw light on his work. It is in no sense a biography, though its method is historical. It is certainly not intended as an essay in literary criticism, though it touches upon questions of aesthetics when these appear relevant. The plays are examined with a view to their content. The status of the content is of course dependent on its presentation, but I am not concerned with technique for the sake of technique, important as that may be to the critic. It is the development of O'Casey, not the development of his technique, that most concerns me.

Opinions are divided over O'Casey. In Ireland it is widely held that his Dublin plays are his greatest and that he should have stayed at home and written more. With that view I am in sympathy. But it was not quite so easy as it sounds. It is harder to sympathize with those who deny all value to the later plays and argue that his talent withered once he touched foreign soil.

But there are others who take up a completely different position. O'Casey professed to regard his Dublin plays as little more than juvenilia. Critics fiercely loyal to O'Casey regard him as first and foremost an expressionist. To my mind they accept uncritically his own view of himself and his work. But what is important is that the choice between the two critical positions is not merely literary. It is political. The Irish are quite clear about this. But some of the non-Irish writers appear to believe that their judgement is based solely on artistic considerations.

They are mostly American academics. Since so much essential material has found its way across the Atlantic, they enjoy facilities for research that do not exist in Ireland, and while not sharing their conclusions, I fully appreciate the debt of gratitude that is due to them for making so much generally available. The future may, however, demand more than a choice between schools of thought. It may demand a synthesis. This would be greatly facilitated if some friendly millionaire would have all the O'Casey papers copied on microfilm and deposited in the National Library. For Dublin is the natural centre for O'Casey studies. In the meantime, however, in the interest of an ultimate synthesis, I have carried further the work of ascertaining historical facts and have suggested certain lines of thought that arise from them.

The subject is beset with difficulties. What is the political content of a play? Does it remain constant, or does it take on fresh aspects with changing time and changing audiences? If it does so change, dare a historian take account of any significance but the contemporaneous? I have held that he is allowed some slight license to trespass.

As regards sources I have used Mr Margulies's invaluable *Early Life of Sean O'Casey** and Mr Gabriel Fallon's *Sean O'Casey – The Man I Knew*. The first volume of Dr David Krause's monumental collection of O'Casey's letters has been of great value. Sean McCann's *World of Sean O'Casey* contains *inter alia* Anthony Butler's work on O'Casey's early life. The real difficulty begins when we examine what should be the richest mine of all, the six volumes of O'Casey's recollections.

O'Casey lived two lives which were separated by the revolution and counter revolution that gave us his three 'blazing masterpieces'. The second O'Casey looked back at the first across a pit filled with smoke. To live through a revolution is to witness the remoulding of the minds of millions of people and to have one's own mind reshaped in the midst of it.

Dr Krause describes the autobiography as 'expressionist'. The Dublin wits called it 'the books in which Sean O'Casey invented his life story'. Mr R. Ayling defended it by saying that it was a work of art in its own right. That may be, but may it not then be history in its own wrong? For this reason Mr Margulies excluded from his book any statement contained in the life story that was not independently corroborated. I have extended that principle by actively seeking corroboration of events described in the autobiography. But I have not excluded from consideration material that lacks corroboration, provided it is intrinsically probable. This involves a degree of personal judgement, but I do not imagine the reader will find difficulty in distinguishing what is corroborated from what is not. I have used the present tense when describing the contents of O'Casey's writings. The task of finding out what really happened has not always been successfully accomplished, for the life story is a chronological farrago.

There has grown up, particularly in the USA, something approaching a cult of O'Casey based on the uncritical acceptance of the life story. The intention is to exalt, though the effect is to diminish the man. O'Casey was warm, kindly, shrewd, generous, and possessed

* See Select Bibliography (p. 197) for particulars of works mentioned in the text and notes.

unshakable integrity, personal, political and artistic. His family adored him and have cherished his memory. But like many artists he was a man of the heart. He was given to enthusiasms. He could nourish resentments. And he wrote at the top of his voice. As an actor is said never to leave off acting, so the dramatist never stopped dramatising himself. In his younger days he was subjected to humiliations which he recalled with bitterness. He developed his talents in the face of mountainous obstacles. Hence he was not content merely to remember the past across intervening time. He must wrestle with the memory. He did this in the brief autobiographical sketches that grew into the life story, and also in his plays.

His own countrymen who knew him and were familiar with the material he made use of, betimes took what he said with a grain of salt, and he threw at his 'bum Irish critics' a volley of words that hurt nobody. But during the last years of his life when he was passing into the canon, he was visited by worshipping young men, sophomores let loose, so to speak, among the foothills of Parnassus. These recognised his dramatic genius, but lacked his sympathy with Ireland. They had no instinctive grasp of what was likely and what was not. Nor could they attempt to distinguish what O'Casey said because he meant it, from what he said for 'divilment'. Yet some, despite these deficiencies, constituted themselves O'Casey's posthumous defenders, when in fact he needs none. His reputation is safe while there is a stone of Dublin standing.

From the too literal reading of the life story, false history has been derived. It is widely believed that O'Casey was born in a slum tenement, received virtually no formal education, and because of his origins, rejected nationalism and became a socialist. For example, the dust cover of Dr Krause's *Sean O'Casey and His World* carries the legend: 'His poverty-stricken upbringing in the Dublin slums, made him suspect the fanatical idealism of the nationalists.'

This is a gross over simplification, and it is not true to O'Casey's own vocabulary. He uses the word 'nationalist' to mean Redmond's party, the United Irish League, successor to Parnell's Irish National League. He himself belonged to the much more nationalistic Irish Republican Brotherhood. He continued to support Republican policies until he was nearly thirty-nine. The supposititious poverty-stricken upbringing was of remarkably delayed action. Would it not be better to ascribe his socialism to more mature experience, beginning with the great lock-out of 1913? For he was not born in the slums. His upbringing was not all poverty-stricken.

The same cover described O'Casey as 'a working-class rebel who put socialism first'. But when did he put it first? Very late in life. He had little

or no connection with the Socialist Party of Ireland or its successor the
Communist Party of Ireland. He told Lady Gregory that he 'had been' a
socialist, but referred only to a producer cooperative society. During
the last three decades of his life he professed communism. Dr Krause
hastily brushes this aside by explaining that it was 'more emotional than
political'. Those who read his contributions to the *Daily Worker* over
the years certainly thought they were about politics. Is a thing to be
disregarded if it is accompanied by emotion?

Dr Krause can enter the field of emotive politics on his own behalf.
He writes that O'Casey 'consistently disaffiliated himself from, and
mocked his excessively nationalistic countrymen'. He never disaffiliated
himself from his countrymen. Nor did he 'mock' even the most
fanatically nationalistic among them. When in 1939 Republicans were
convicted of causing explosions in England, he protested at the
excessive sentences imposed on them and subsequently supported the
movement for an amnesty. Dr Krause may have accepted the opinion
of the 'western' establishment that the independence of small nations is
something to be treated with disrespect. But he has no right to ascribe it
to O'Casey.

A group of able young men in the United States have been publishing
a magazine called the *Sean O'Casey Review*. Its writers are so much
O'Casey enthusiasts that one sometimes catches them echoing the
master's mannerisms. Their work is very much to be applauded, and
'lang may their lums reek'. But sometimes even they voice sentiments
which derive from the reverse side of O'Casey's ultra-leftism. They fail
to recognise the progressive side of Irish nationalism.

In a symposium of essays on the subject of O'Casey's *The Plough
and the Stars*, writers have permitted themselves a certain
superciliousness when discussing the Rising of Easter 1916. It is
recognised of course that the play is a negative comment on it. It is
likewise recognized that O'Casey told Lady Gregory that it had been a
'terrible mistake'. O'Casey was over half-way to that conclusion as
early as the summer of 1919 when he published his *History of the Irish
Citizen Army*.

But what is the historical status of this opinion? In the life story he
attempts to show that he knew an insurrection was being planned and
tried to prevent it. There is no independent evidence whatsoever for this
assertion. But there is evidence from 1917. In a pamphlet published in
that year, O'Casey *glorifies* the Rising. When did he change his mind? I
believe in 1919. In December 1918 he was still supporting Sinn Fein.
But in the early part of 1919 the revolutionary government, Dail
Eireann, abandoned its 'Democratic Programme' and reverted to the

policy of Arthur Griffith. In the bitterness of disillusionment, O'Casey condemned the Rising retrospectively.

The fact that he had taken no part in it made this easy for him. It justified his inaction. When he spoke to Lady Gregory the counter-revolution had triumphed. There is all the difference in the world between an Irishman's repudiating his past convictions in the anguish of betrayal and defeat and the postprandial tut tuttings of academics in a far-off land, who never had the slightest stake in the matter. Many worthy but easy-minded people cannot understand that the fact that he was not 'out' in 1916, may have demanded a process of self-justification, and troubled O'Casey's political conscience for the rest of his life.

At the present time propagandists for the international companies never cease telling the Irish people to forget their national identity, abandon the quest for a united Ireland, and ignore the socialist objectives Connolly taught could be best achieved by their own efforts, made in their own good time. It is therefore regrettable that O'Casey should be used against Connolly by people who have not appreciated O'Casey's position and what gave rise to it.

Ira facit poetam: the great artist creates out of his inner turbulence. The components of that turbulence are derived from experience. The act of creation orders it afresh, so that through art the artist becomes a different person, even becoming as if he had had a different past. In this sense Mr Ayling is quite right to call the autobiography art. But until we cease treating it as fact and find out as far as possible what actually happened, we shall never be able to examine O'Casey as a whole, as a phenomenon of Irish society.

While he is solely responsible for the opinions expressed in this work, and any accompanying deficiencies, the author would like to express his indebtedness to the many friends who assisted with information or encouragement. Special thanks are due to the ever-helpful officials of the National Library of Ireland.

Perhaps it should be added that despite a considerable delay between completion and publication the author has not had the advantage of Dr Krause's second volume of O'Casey correspondence. Whether its contents affect his conclusions we shall see when it appears.

PROTESTANTS AND CATHOLICS

The words I speak, the written line,
These are not uniquely mine,
For in my heart and in my will
Old ancestors are warring still.
Richard Rowley (1887–1947)

Sean O'Casey was born in Dublin on 30 March 1880 and baptised John Casey at St Mary's Protestant church on 28 July. His birthplace, 85 Upper Dorset Street, was in an area not far from the Royal Canal, then the virtual boundary of the city proper. It was in a district that belonged to the unpretentious but studiously respectable lower middle class. Thom's Directory lists the premises at the decent valuation of £20, and Michael Casey, Sean's father, was registered as the rate-paying tenant. It is sheer speculation that he acted in the capacity of caretaker. O'Casey described the premises as an 'apartment house' run by his father, adding characteristically that it nearly ruined him. That Michael Casey was a person of standing is shown by the fact that during the time he was at 85 Dorset Street, his name appeared in the list of 'nobility, gentry, merchants and traders' of the City of Dublin. He was the possessor of capital.

Any investigation into the background of O'Casey must begin with this interesting man. The more that can be discovered or inferred about him, the deeper our insight into his gifted family. Successive vital documents register his occupations as commercial clerk (1863), assistant accountant (1865), merchant's clerk (1867 and 1869), law clerk (1871), mercantile clerk (1874), clerk ICM, presumably Irish Church Missions (1876) and finally again mercantile clerk (1880). Sean, presumably relying on his mother, believed him to be a native of Limerick City. But Christopher Casey, who had his information from Sean's eldest brother Michael, believed he came from Cahersiveen in Co. Kerry, and stated that he was told of a family tradition that either two brothers or two uncles had been Catholic priests.

Casey is indeed a Catholic name, commonest in the south-west of Ireland. How then did Michael Casey come to be a Protestant? According to the life story he was the youngest son of a Catholic father and a Protestant mother. The father, John Casey whose name we know

from the registration of Michael's marriage, was a farmer. According to
the life story he died while Michael was an infant. His mother insisted on
bringing up her youngest in the Protestant faith. After her death he left
for Dublin in order to escape quarrels over religion with his brothers
and sisters.

Perhaps something like this might have happened in Limerick City.
In the rural setting (not necessarily Cahersiveen) indicated by the
father's occupation, it would seem very doubtful. In the early nineteenth
century mixed marriages were not unusual. The boys followed the
religion of the father, the girls of the mother. The widow Casey, unless
she had money, must have been a very strong-minded woman to defy
established custom in 1836–37 when the Tithe War was scarcely over.
And surely the quarrels would have been more likely when she was still
alive. Then again, O'Casey writes of quarrels with sisters. But these
would be his co-religionists. It cannot be said, therefore, that O'Casey
knew anything definite about his father's origins.

When there are bitter feelings one suspects a *change* in religion. The
so-called famine devastated the countryside in 1846–48. Protestant
zealots sought converts with a bowl of free soup in one hand and the
bible in the other, whence the name 'soupers'. Whether such
proselytizers invaded the Casey family may one day be discovered.
Some scrap of tradition may linger somewhere in the country. It is one
possibility, but there is another. O'Casey says that his father was a fine
Latin scholar and possessed a copy of the Vulgate. Now this was within
O'Casey's own knowledge. What would a man want with Latin on a
Limerick or Kerry farm? Nothing, unless he was studying for the
priesthood. Michael Casey may have been a 'spoiled priest' who turned
Protestant and married a Protestant girl.

Certainly nothing about Michael Casey indicates the peasant. Of his
opinions O'Casey knew only what the family told him, for he died when
the boy was only six. But he recorded the titles of a number of books in
his library. There were several versions of the bible besides the Vulgate,
a concordance, Josephus's *Wars of the Jews*, d'Aubigny's *History of
the Reformation*, and polemical works against Roman Catholicism.
There was Gibbon's *Decline and Fall of the Roman Empire*, a fine
swashbuckling story, best appreciated by those who regard the
misfortunes of other ages as a penalty for their not attaining the
enlightenment of eighteenth-century England.

There were English novels. O'Casey mentions the works of Dickens,
Scott, Eliot, Meredith and Thackeray. Michael Casey was thus
interested in the contemporary novel of conscience. As far as George
Eliot and Meredith were concerned he must have purchased their works
quite soon after publication. Justin McCarthy in his reminiscences of

nineteenth-century Cork, made it clear that middle class Irish families used customarily to follow the literature *dont on parle* in London. But Michael Casey had deeper interests. He had the English and Scottish poets, Shakespeare, Burns, Keats, Milton, Gray and Pope. O'Casey lists nothing whatever belonging to Irish tradition, no Lover, no Lever, not even Swift or Maria Edgeworth. And Trollope, the only contemporary English novelist in positive sympathy with Ireland, is also absent.

Michael Casey is a stern figure in the autobiography. His opinions are recorded, but no jests or aphorisms. He wanted his children to work hard and get on. One can imagine his sympathy with Adam Bede: 'My children will receive the best education my means will allow.' These words, which O'Casey puts into his father's mouth, do not seem to fit a slum tenement. He wanted his eldest son to be an architect. He rejected the parish school at St Mary's, and paid the fees required for sending his children to the Central Model Schools in Marlborough Street. Here Protestant Unionism was given a liberal veneer. We have a picture of a family of hardworking puritans pushing discreetly up the social ladder, its newspaper the *Daily Express*, mouthpiece of the landlords, described by W. B. Yeats as 'the most conservative paper in Ireland'.

Michael Casey married Susan Archer at St Catherine's Church, Thomas Street, on 27 January 1863, Thomas and Anna Hall standing witness. Susan's name was at times written Susanna or even Susannah. Such uncertainty can imply illiteracy in the parents. But her father is described as an auctioneer. Both stated that they resided in Chamber Street, Michael at no. 22, Susan giving no number. Chamber Street was situated between the Coombe and what was then open country, and therefore in the part of Dublin where incomers from the south-west would be most likely to settle.

It has been suggested that the auctioneer's family considered themselves a cut above the Caseys. This may explain the inclusion of the name Archer in those of two of the children. O'Casey's surviving sister, Ella of the autobiography, was christened Isabella Archer (one document substitutes Charlotte) and was presumably called after the Isabella Archer who registered Sean's birth. Whatever her social position she was certainly illiterate.

The first child, Susan, did not survive. Isabella was born in 1865. The eldest son was called Michael Harding. There was a Reverend David Harding who from 1860 officiated at Zion Chapel in Kings Inn Street, not far distant from the Caseys' home in Wellington Street. His name disappears from the record in 1866 and Michael was born in 1867. There may be a connection. Thomas, born in 1869, was probably called after Thomas Hall. If this man is the uncle of that name mentioned in the life story, then Anna would be Susan's sister. He is described as an Orangeman who fought at Balaclava.

But now there was a change. What circumstances occasioned it – death, reconciliation, enlightenment – we do not know. Michael Casey decided that his next son should be called after his father.

The established custom was that the first son should be called after the father's father, the second after the father. The Caseys had broken this custom as if to declare their intention of living their own lives. They had called their two eldest after themselves. But a boy was born in 1871 and was duly christened John. Then came Isaac Archer in 1873. In a sense he was called after Abraham. According to Margulies he adopted the name Joseph after his conversion to Catholicism in the year 1900. But John lived only four years. The next son, born in 1876, was therefore called John. He lived only six months. O'Casey refers to his mother's understandable trepidation when her husband insisted that their last-born should also be named John. This one lived to translate his name into Irish.

In *Sean O'Casey and his World*, Dr Krause states that O'Casey was one of thirteen children. He presumably took this information from the last volume of the life story. But in the first, O'Casey says he was one of eight, of which three had died. We know the names of the eight; we know when they were born and when they died. But what of the other five? In my opinion they never existed.

The Caseys paid noticeable attention to family names, and it can only mean one thing. They came from families which were accustomed to possessing property. They were no slum-dwellers but saw themselves as members, humble members perhaps, of a privileged caste. But what did this privilege amount to? To understand this, and much of what follows, it is relevant to examine the social and religious scene in nineteenth-century Ireland.

There is nothing either new or particularly Irish in wearing religion as a badge of political allegiance. 'Name your god and I will tell you your king, and to whom the taxes must be paid.' The Saracens are said to have applied this principle when offering their captives the choice of the Koran or the sword. The English did likewise when they decided to impose a new land-owning class on Ireland. The newcomers were alien in language and alien in religion. By this they signalled their allegiance. Much of the failure of the English to understand the Irish arises from the identification of Protestantism with what the reformed religion meant to them. It meant something quite different to the Irish. In England it was the badge of the emancipated; in Ireland it was the mark of the tyrant. Catholicism was the religion of the oppressed people. It is thus pointless to object to its influence on the national character. James Connolly, by no means a devout man, sent his children to a Catholic school because there they would learn to be Irish. The history of the nation and the history of the religion were intertwined.

This fact was well appreciated within the Irish church, as an avowed atheist, P. S. O'Hegarty, explained in his *History of Ireland Under the Union*:

The Catholic church is a universal one, but in Ireland the church is ninety-nine per cent national, and universal only in the very highest realms of church policy. In the eighteenth century it went into outlawry with the people, and the priest, hunted with a price on his head, as he was during a great part of the century, without a dwelling house or a church, was still the only leader the people had. In the end of the eighteenth century people and church entered into the daylight together.[1]

The close reciprocal relations between church and people loosened somewhat after 1829. Efforts were made to assimilate the emancipated English Catholics and to some extent the Irish too. The young Disraeli intimated in his novels that gentlemen of the 'old faith' might safely identify themselves with the new establishment. Lord Melbourne sent Thomas Drummond to Ireland. He reorganized the police along non-sectarian lines and curbed the Orange Order. But when the Irish hierarchy were lulled into accepting the King of England's veto on the appointment of their bishops, the laity revolted and O'Connell ensured the withdrawal of the proposal.

On the continent the Catholic church has been traditionally identified with the latifundia. This was impossible in Ireland. Rather did it serve as the collective conscience of the small bourgeoisie. This is a constantly differentiating class. Yet no class is so devoted to stability. The church encouraged those who extended their links with the more affluent. It discouraged those whose proximity to the working class was liable to weaken their confidence in stability, or pitch them into the arms of Fenianism or socialism.

The economic changes induced by Gladstone's reforms created problems which are reflected in the novels of Canon Sheehan, more than one of whose heroes scent the excitement of new ideas, only to decide that ideas are dangerous, and lock the library door. According to the life story, O'Casey reproved this tendency in the early years of this century. But he does not seem to have traced it to the instinctive Jansenism of a class which could for the first time rise by its own efforts thanks to the possession of land.[2]

To conclude, anybody who imagines that nineteenth-century Irish catholicism was an unchanging monolith, to be characterized in a few trite phrases, vastly oversimplifies. It received nothing from the state, and among its members were the poorest of the poor. Its organizations were called upon to apply to these the only palliative available, charity, itself in short enough supply. With centuries of tradition in their minds, its leaders could not escape a sense that they had been rescued at the last moment, and some, when they surveyed their once populous parishes desolated by famine and emigration, must have consoled themselves that the diaspora of the Irish was in accordance with a divine plan which it was their duty not to upset – the catholicization of the British Empire.

When we turn to the established church we go from the hovel to the big house, to industry, commerce, enterprise, enlightenment and their otiose train. The land functions not as soil but as property, which only an old heretic like St Augustine would describe as theft. The typical class, outside the cities, is that of the landlords who until Drummond's time were all but feudal tyrants, with the sense of responsibility of soldiers on the loot. Their greed and improvidence were castigated by Maria Edgworth in *Castle Rackrent*. Their charming qualities as soldiers of fortune were described by Charles Lever. In the days of their decay, Thackeray showed they could turn out a recognizable bum. Of course there were exceptions; there were 'good landlords' in every county. But on the whole they were an effete class, preserved long after their time to do duty as an economic garrison. Throughout the country there were fine Anglican churches empty but for the squire and his relations, maintained until 1837 by tithes imposed on the overwhelmingly Catholic tenantry, and, until dis-establishment in 1870, by the same people by less direct means. Their incumbents, frequently men of high culture and philanthropy, were the moral prisoners of an indefensible system.

In the cities, and especially Dublin, Anglicanism had other aspects. Here there was an established bourgeoisie which at times made common cause with the Catholic merchants, who had pushed their way up from obscurity. There was nevertheless a pinchbeck quality in many of their establishments. Where they employed Protestants only, they bred a proletariat of unashamed slavishness which nevertheless looked down on the Catholic 'rebels' who did the menial work or lined the gutters. At the same time among Anglicans of the professional classes, there were men of outstanding qualities, especially in the environment of their principal educational institution, Trinity College.

The counter-revolution of 1798 destroyed the United Irishmen. The Act of Union dealt a crushing blow to the patriot party. But it was not annihilated. Something of its tradition lived on within the framework of the establishment. While the question of sovereignty remained in abeyance there were Protestants who began to identify themselves with the Celtic past. The development of nineteenth-century science and criticism assisted this process, as an example will show. A contemporary of Drummond was Captain Larcom, an Englishman entrusted with the inauguration of the ordnance survey of Ireland. Larcom early realized the necessity of learning Irish. He was confronted with a mapful of Irish place names and a population the majority of which could speak nothing else. He enlisted the services of Petrie, O'Donovan, Samuel Ferguson, Eugene O'Curry and the poet Mangan. The result was to help to encourage studies which though not nationalistic were patriotic in effect. It was a patriotism outside politics, arising from the rediscovery of the richest cultural mine in western Europe. Dublin developed an exceptionally brilliant intelligentsia which, while predominantly Protestant, did not exclude Catholics. So weighty was the country's cultural ballast that every attempt to govern it in a new way swung it in a national direction.

It may be of use to mention a few names that enter into the tradition for those who care to go further into the matter. Among the older generation were Bunting (born 1773), Hardiman (1782), and Petrie (1789). Then came O'Donovan (1804), Ferguson (1810), Rowan Hamilton (1805), Sir William Wilde, father of Oscar (1815), Robert Kane (1809) and William Stokes, son of Whitley Stokes the United Irishman. There followed his son, Whitley Stokes (1830), Standish Hayes O'Grady (1832), Standish James O'Grady (1846) who is usually credited with founding the 'literary revival' and the musicologist, Grattan Flood (1859). The above list is of course not confined to Protestants but all made their contributions in a milieu which was predominantly Protestant. It was a short step from the poems of Samuel Ferguson and the popularizations of Standish O'Grady, to the more famous work of Yeats, Synge, Edward Martyn and Lady Gregory.

There is no evidence that this liberal tradition played any part in O'Casey's background, least of all the acceptance of Catholics on grounds of merit. So what kind of Protestant was he? Reference has been made to Orange connections on the mother's side. These were merely peripheral. There was a period during the eighteen-thirties when the supporters of the Duke of Cumberland utilized the Orange Order in their efforts to supplant Victoria. They attempted to subvert the army and Thomas Hall may have been one of their successes. There is no reason for assuming any connection with Ulster. The headquarters of the Orange Order was not in Belfast but in Dublin, and all the autobiography tells us is that O'Casey knew it as a child, and felt it was part of his own environment.

If the Orange Order made war on Catholics' lives and livelihoods, as Drummond speedily discovered, more latterly the Society for Church

Missions assaulted their minds. According to what Captain Larcom told Sir Samuel Ferguson, when he first realized that for the sake of his work he must learn Irish, he chanced upon the premises of the Irish Society in O'Connell Street. The committee explained to him that their purpose was to 'convert the Irish to Protestantism by giving them the Scriptures in their native tongue'. The society languished and was later taken over by the Society for Church Missions with its headquarters in England.

This organization was founded in 1849 by the Reverend Alexander Dallas, Rector of Wonston in Hampshire, an enthusiastic proselytizer. He was known for his efforts to convert the Jews of London, and was invited to preach in Ireland where he was impressed by the size of this new field for evangelism. After the absorption of the Irish Society, the work of conversion began in Connemara. It is of interest that one of O'Casey's teachers at St Barnabas school was a 'middle-aged hard-drinking native Irish speaker from Galway',[3] possibly a product of this campaign. The society's historian, A. E. Hughes, rebuts the charge of 'souperism', asserting that charity was given to all in need. But he provides simultaneous evidence of hard preaching. According to Margulies, Michael Casey worked for the Irish Church missions for a quarter of a century, though this scarcely tallies with his own description of himself as 'merchant's clerk'. How far he was committed to them is not known. That he accepted a low salary because of his beliefs is speculation unsupported by the slightest evidence, and seems to be part of the myth of poverty which is engulfing one by one everybody O'Casey ever spoke to. According to the life story Michael Casey earned £2 a week. A smaller figure is given by Margulies.[4] This amounts to something less than thirty shillings. While not princely it was by no means beggarly in those days. And it is possible that for a period he may have been in receipt of two incomes. For if we can suppose without evidence that he was poorer than he need be, we may also suppose the contrary.

If Michael Casey was from Cahersiveen, then he knew Irish. If he was from Limerick he probably knew it. But O'Casey never makes the slightest suggestion of this. That his father was a farmer we know from his own statement. Is it possible that he knew Irish and refrained from saying so to his wife? All we see is a barrier. Michael Casey may not however have worked for the Church Missions because he knew Irish. By the seventies, thirty years after the famine and in the midst of a wave of evictions, the importance of the language as a means of proselytizing had declined. There was however a proselytizing literature in English with which O'Casey shows signs of being acquainted. One of its objects was to identify St Patrick, who brought Christianity to Ireland, with a species of 'proto-Protestantism'.

The argument may be presented as follows: St Patrick, who came to Ireland from Britain, was in no sense an envoy of Rome, but made his second, voluntary, journey to Ireland solely as a result of the vision described in his *Confessio*. In the record we have of his teaching there is no reference to transubstantiation or purgatory. It was as a result of following a doctrine free from these errors that Ireland became the 'land of saints and scholars', and it was the special disservice of the Anglo-Normans that by their invasion in 1169 they established in Ireland the supremacy of Rome. From this stemmed the country's many misfortunes. But matters could easily be put right, now that the English had abandoned the Roman faith. All the Irish had to do was to follow them, and in the process restore the pure canon of their ancestors.

This is of course historical balderdash and need not detain us. But it is of interest that in the life story,[5] when O'Casey complains to his mother that the local Catholic children have been teasing him by saying that 'Protestants are not really Irish', she replies by quoting his father's belief that 'St Patrick was really as Protestant as Protestant could be' and the Caseys were just as aboriginal as the Kellys who had been teasing him. The second proposition is of course quite correct.

This may have been the extent of Michael Casey's interest in Irish history. He seems to have been extending his knowledge in an exclusively English direction. O'Casey's background was one of lower middle-class Protestant evangelism. It is useful to recall this when pondering his decision to present himself to the Abbey as a labourer who had come up, rather than a clerical worker who had gone down.

NOTES

1. p. 399.
2. Contrary to what many people believe it is quite possible for the clergy to follow the laity in political matters. In the early sixties Mr Sean Redmond and I were driven through a part of the Co. Fermanagh by the late Mr Cahir Healy, MP for the county. When we stopped in a village the local priest would come out to seek his explanation of current events. It is ridiculous to laugh at the old Nationalist Party for being Catholic. The penal laws were still in operation in that part of Ireland, and it could be nothing else.
3. Margulies, *Early Life of Sean O'Casey*, p. 28.
4. op. cit., p. 10.
5. *I Knock at the Door*, p. 258.

[2]

UNIONIST SCHOOLBOY

> I thank the goodness and the grace
> That on my birth have smiled,
> And made me in these Christian days
> A happy English child.
>
> Ann Taylor (1783–1827)
> *Hymns for Infant Minds*

Nobody could mistake the note of querulousness that repeatedly sounds in O'Casey's life story. From what does it arise? Some have replied from the extraordinary hardships of an impoverished childhood in a Dublin slum tenement. They have then quoted the Dublin housing statistics. But people do not usually grow plaintive when they come up in the world. And as we have seen, O'Casey's early childhood was spent in comfort and security according to the standards of the time. Perhaps the utmost he had to complain of would be an element of puritan frugality against which the older children were learning to rebel.

Of these, Isabella was a school teacher at St Mary's. She had learned French. She could play the piano, an accomplishment requiring lengthy tuition not obtainable for nothing, undisturbed application and an entourage where it is appreciated. Michael and Thomas worked in the Post Office, and could expect to attain to comfortable positions by automatic promotion. Between O'Casey and his next older brother there was a gap of seven years. O'Casey was thus very much the baby. He may not always have relished this position, but no doubt took what spoiling came his way. He was an exceptionally bright child. He told Gabriel Fallon that his mother taught him to read at a very early age.[1]

He started his schooling in May 1885, not at the Central Model Schools but at St Mary's. There is no reason to suspect that the family could not afford the fees. These were days of prosperity. The probable explanation is that he had already been struck by the painful eye disease which troubled him throughout his life and which it was his remarkable achievement to overcome. His sister could take him to school and indeed she was his teacher for a number of years.

After attempting some old wives' cures, Mrs Casey took him to St Mark's Ophthalmic Hospital and he was forbidden to attend school.[2] Margulies ascertained that his attendance was irregular for the first two years, but not so afterwards. The eye disease alone would be adequate to explain the sense of insecurity O'Casey recollected when writing of his childhood.

In September 1886 his father died after a lingering illness. From the entry in the register of deaths, 'bronchitis, anasarca', one suspects lung cancer. In the life story O'Casey describes the funeral 'on a very cold day'. But the meteorological records show that the day was by no means cold for early September. He records Isabella's satisfaction at the hiring of a 'closed-in hearse' necessary for 'anybody who is anything' and Michael's at the presence of three carriages, twenty-six cabs and six side-cars. Now, when beggars die there are no carriages seen. The funeral had indeed been announced two days previously in the *Daily Express*. In other words it was an event likely to interest members of the respectable classes who possessed carriages. O'Casey's numbers are, one assumes, without precise significance. But there were carriages there.

In his description of the funeral, O'Casey introduces the character of Bugler Benson, whom he treats as an embodiment of original sin, a sort of Heathcliff whose intrusion betokens the ruin of the family. O'Casey may have had reasons for disliking him, but there is no justification for Mr Herbert Goldstone's describing him[3] as an 'insane, cruel and selfish dreamer'. Nicholas Beaver, as his name was, served as a drummer in the King's Liverpool Regiment. He was then aged eighteen, was friendly with the elder Casey boys and even more friendly with Isabella. This circumstance must have occasioned Mrs Casey's early antagonism towards him. It can hardly have been due to the reason O'Casey puts into her mouth, namely that her husband would never sanction a soldier, for he had already sanctioned Thomas Hall. Possibly there was a touch of snobbery. The family had come up in the world since 1863. This is illustrated in the autobiography where O'Casey has Isabella warn him that if he does not study he will be no more than a 'common labourer'.[4] Labourers, like 'other ranks', were thought 'common' by members of the Casey household.[5]

Beaver was born in Dungarvan, Co. Waterford, in June 1868, of a Catholic family and the son of an army pensioner. At the age of thirteen he presented himself at Clonmel, enlisted, and was sent to join the Liverpool Regiment at Bradford. At that time he was 4 ft $9\frac{1}{2}$ in. in height, and $28\frac{1}{2}$ in. in chest measurement. One would not think him much good for fighting. But the army had faith in Providence. On one part of the form they entered his 'declared age' (fifteen) and elsewhere his 'apparent age' and left it to nature to bring the two into accord.

For a time he was in poor health. He was treated for bronchitis, 'palpitations' and the skin diseases common among soldiers. By the time his battalion was posted to the Curragh in 1885, he had turned into a very presentable young fellow in the scarlet uniform of a regimental drummer.

In the life story O'Casey described the events surrounding Victoria's jubilee of 22 June 1887 when, embellished with a red white and blue rosette, he was taken to see the illuminations. From the description of the route taken by the tram on which he and his mother travelled, it appears that the family were still living at Innisfallen Parade where Michael Casey had died. O'Casey tells of the antagonism of Catholic children to Protestants who flaunted their Unionism, and remarks that he liked to have Protestant schoolfellows around him for protection. He names Ecret and Middleton. But Margulies established that Ecret was a pupil at St Mary's, whereas Middleton belongs to a later period.

The status of the political conversation on the tram is not easy to decide. The republican tram conductor and the genteel looking man 'with the watery mouth and drooping moustache' have appeared in a previous chapter. Benstock[6] takes this man to be Middleton's father. But in 1887 O'Casey would not know Middleton or his father. Nor does the text demand any such identification. A statement that an 'unbelieving Protestant' was not fit to lead the Irish people could scarcely come from the mouth of a Unionist. What then is the purpose of the episode? O'Casey wished to work in his mother's defence of Parnell, but, surrounding it with fictitious accompaniments, brings doubt upon it.

Mrs O'Casey's politics moreover seem to have undergone an evolution. The first time they meet the conductor she tells her son to murmur 'God Save the King' (O'Casey carelessly forgets that this had not been sung since 1837) whenever he heard a Fenian song. But on the way to the jubilee celebration two years later, at a time when one would expect loyalist sentiment to be at its strongest, she says that a Fenian active enough to have had to flee the country, lived in the same house as herself and Michael Casey, and that he and Michael were great friends. As evidence she mentions a 'little table' with a drawer that was bought from him. But in an earlier chapter this is a 'two leaved mahogany table' and is the only table in a list of household possessions. The earlier chapter however refers to a later period. It is tempting to connect the Fenian's flight with the Dublin raids of 1863, for this is just the time when the couple might have been buying furniture. But O'Casey may be doing no more than creating symbols of the tensions affecting people who did not know whether they should be Irish or British.

Mother and son witnessed the riot which started outside Trinity College. O'Casey's account tallies with that in the newspapers next day, though they made little of it. For the first time O'Casey was brought face to face with the reality of nationalism and the brutality of imperialism. But where were the other children? Perhaps the answer is to be found in the fact that providing music for the festivity was the band of the Liverpool Regiment, in which Nicholas Beaver would be playing his spectacular part. It must surely have been as a result of his influence that Michael and Thomas decided to quit their safe employment and become soldiers themselves. They enlisted, Michael in the Royal Engineers and Thomas in the Dublin Fusiliers. This was in February 1888.

Their departure must have reduced the family income by some £4 a week. According to Margulies, O'Casey told Krause that towards the end of the eighties the family joined Isabella in a flat attached to her school in Dominick Street. The Liverpool Regiment left for Aldershot in February 1889, but by then Isabella had agreed to marry Beaver, who returned for the ceremony. It was performed on 7 March, Mrs Casey disapproving, as was natural in view of its economic implications, and refusing to attend the church. Thomas Casey gave away the bride. Beaver described himself as a Protestant born in Dublin.

Presumably Isabella's employment shortly ceased, and with it her accommodation. It has been suggested that she finished out the school year and that the family then moved to 25 Hawthorn Terrace. Over eighteen months a very substantial income had been lost. Apart from anything the three soldiers could spare, and anything Isabella might earn on an irregular basis, for this need not be excluded in the case of a teacher who knew music and French, the family was dependent on the earnings of Isaac. He was employed by the *Daily Express* and was paid fifteen shillings a week. This was a good wage, for he was not sixteen years old until November 1889. Indeed it was a man's wage by the standards of manual workers. In *Pictures in the Hallway* O'Casey gives instances of vanmen who were paid only fourteen shillings. Poverty is not penury. But to the young O'Casey the family's decline must have seemed catastrophic.

The period of greatest hardship may well have been that immediately before the move from Innisfallen Parade. Whether at once or after a period with Isabella, the family found cheaper accommodation at 25 Hawthorn Terrace. O'Casey describes Isabella's bringing his mother clothes for washing. This implies that there was a time when she lived apart. There is a description of a shopping trip in the course of which O'Casey appropriates a piece of bacon. The topography suggests a journey from Innisfallen Parade at a time when money was short. At one point there was talk of placing O'Casey in an institution. This his mother rejected.

Once it is appreciated that the lean years for the Casey family were 1889 and those immediately following, a number of other things come into perspective and it becomes comprehensible that the little Unionist should become the young rebel. It should be noted of course that Isaac would almost certainly receive annual increments and one of five shillings is recorded. By 1891 he may well have been earning twenty-five shillings. Michael was discharged as unfit in January 1893. Beaver completed his service in February 1894. Then began long years of relative prosperity.

Hawthorn Terrace was in the next parish and O'Casey would then be expected to attend the school attached to St Barnabas, which was situated close to the important Catholic church of St Laurence O'Toole.[7] He seems to have been in no hurry however, for in 'The Protestant kid thinks of the reformation' he tells of being caught playing marbles by the Reverend T. R. S. Hunter, a conflation of T. R. S. Collins and Saul Fletcher, but essentially the latter, and severely reproved for this ungodly pastime. The minister demands that the child shall attend school. Susan quotes doctor's orders. He brushes her objections aside. O'Casey is bundled off and receives slaps on the first day. The ophthalmic surgeon, alarmed at a sudden deterioration in the condition of the boy's eyes, offers her a strongly worded note. But Mrs Casey refuses it and to her son's protestations replies, 'The doctor hasn't to keep you, and doesn't know I have to keep the minister on my hands.'

A later incident belonging to this period throws further light on the circumstances of the family. O'Casey has been called over to answer a few questions by George Middleton, an exceptionally sturdy youngster and something of a leader. It should be noted that Middleton, like O'Casey, was born in 1880, and that they would therefore be members of the same class. Why should he wish him to answer a few questions? Presumably because he was sufficiently new to excite curiosity. One of his rather younger contemporaries, Rocliffe, told Margulies that O'Casey missed classes frequently and attended with a bandage over one of his eyes. But he did not appear shabbier than the other boys. In the course of the inquiries one of the boys criticizes Mrs Casey for sending her son to school with suppurating eyes. 'Hunter makes her,' he replies. A young cynic comments that otherwise he would 'dock the parish coal', which it emerges other families receive. It is a fair inference that Mrs Casey accepted some form of relief and thereby created in her son that hatred of charity which he consistently showed.

In short, the O'Caseys suffered a sharp fall in their standard of living, and an even more hurtful blow to their pride. O'Casey's sense of the fitness of things was rudely jolted. His eyes suffered because he had not the money to defy the minister. His cultural background, and therefore his consciousness, excelled those of his schoolfellows. His circumstances both physical and financial made him less than they. In such a predicament consciousness had two resorts. One was to escape into fantasy. The other was to turn rebel. The turn of mind was early established and despite chronological uncertainties there is no reason to think the mature O'Casey misrepresented it.

The house at 25 Hawthorn Terrace is still standing today. It has only one floor. It is not a tenement nor is it situated in a slum. And there is circumstantial evidence that before 1892 the family's circumstances began to improve. Isaac had become interested in the theatre and was friendly with members of the more latterly famous Dalton family. He constructed a stage in the front room of the house, complete with footlights, and here, if tradition is to be credited, were enacted home made comedies in which, it is said, even the dog had a part. It was at this time that O'Casey made the acquaintance of Shakespeare and Boucicault, in *Richard II* and *The Shaughraun*.[8]

In the life story O'Casey describes that exciting occasion when he was to play the King in a scene from *Richard II* at a charity concert in Townsend Street. His *ipse dixit* is that he learned the part from one of three volumes of the works of Shakespeare that Isabella had won as a prize – while unable to read, one guesses. The show was cancelled owing to the death of the Duke of Clarence. This event took place on 18 January 1892. O'Casey was therefore acting at the age of eleven, and having contact with actors.

Isaac's friends were connected with the old Mechanics' Theatre, afterwards, following extensions, to become the Abbey. Working-class Dublin was as addicted to the theatre as London to the music-hall. True, at the Mechanics' serious melodrama might be interrupted by sausage-eating competitions, the winner to be measured for a new pair of moleskins. But the other theatres were to varying degrees popular as well. After each new production the malaprops were in town, last night's show being subjected to discussion and quotation, the high-flown language of the stage linking with the metaphorical idiom of the Gaelic which for many in those days had been the speech of their parents.[9] The Dubliners liked a 'good word'.

From the small size of the house it is clear that the home theatre must also have served as a bedroom. The return of Michael Casey and later of Nicholas Beaver must have put an end to the stage if not to the acting. Moreover Isabella's first three children were born at Hawthorn Terrace. But the theatre was becoming a passion with Isaac and for many years Sean imbibed it from his brother.

How far did this early acquaintance with the drama influence O'Casey's political development? To an Irishman who knew his country's past, Richard II would represent a pre-incarnation of the curse of Cromwell. The would-be absolute monarch, after suppressing the peasant revolt by treachery, led two expeditions to Ireland where he was badly mauled by Art MacMurrough, isolating himself, bankrupting himself and ultimately losing his throne. Shakespeare uses him to promote the outlook of English nationalism, independence from continental powers, hegemony within the British Isles, and for this purpose, in defiance of geography, England is transformed into an island. Now Shaw recognized Shakespeare's chauvinism. O'Casey did not. In dealing with the culture of his own country he permits himself appreciable levity. With Shakespeare, never. The difference between the two dramatists was one of class position. Men in Shaw's class knew something of Irish history. At St Barnabas school it is doubtful if any Irish history whatever came into the curriculum. Years afterwards O'Casey confessed that he knew more English than Irish history. Since he then knew plenty of Irish history, his schooling cannot have been quite so ineffective as he pretended.

Boucicault was another matter. Here was an Irish Protestant who wrote for the English stage. *The Shaughraun* was first produced at Drury Lane in 1875. But the scene is laid in Ireland. The centre of the plot is the escape from penal servitude of Robert Ffolliot, a Fenian. One highly hissable villain is Harvey Duff, the informer. But the English army officer is an innocent, poor fellow anxious to do the right thing in an incomprehensible country. The priest is the proper combination of patriotism and piety. The general effect of the play is not separatist. But it is Irish. One wonders what would be the reaction of a modern London audience to a play about the escape from prison of a member of the 'provisional' IRA. The *Shaughraun*,[10] who is instrumental in rescuing and protecting Ffolliot, is more than a stage Irishman. He is a rollicking, rumbustious symbol of the irrepressibility of the lower orders, a proletarian aristocrat.

During the period of rehearsal for the dramatic performance Irish politics moved in the shadow of the death of Parnell which took place on 7 October 1891. O'Casey tells of the arrival of the news at Hawthorn Terrace.[11] Paper-sellers cry 'Stop Press' in the small hours of a wet morning. This must have been on the 7th for Parnell died just after midnight. The little of 1891 that survives the half century's delay in the telling, is that O'Casey felt Isaac's praise for Parnell was not sincere, and that both of them blamed the priests and the 'conceited Catholic curs' of the Irish Parliamentary Party, for his downfall. Unionists have seldom remained antagonistic to dead nationalists, and many an Orangeman has been known to boast of the protestantism of Tone and Emmet, which is supposed in some mysterious way to refute republicanism, while hustling their would-be imitators hot-foot into

Crumlin Road jail. Isaac's reverent framing of Michael's drawing of Parnell, for which his father had tipped him a shilling,[12] and setting it in the window, far from being an act of national mourning, was probably one of Protestant sectarianism.

Since O'Casey so far allowed his pen to run away with him as to describe his own country as a 'land of scuts and schemers', it would be as well to recall what actually happened. It requires no imagination to appreciate that when an issue split nationalist Ireland down the middle, there must have been something to be said on both sides. The events of 1890–91 were in a sense a pre-enactment of those of 1921–22, with Gladstone, though less shamefully, in the role of Lloyd George.

In December 1889 when Captain O'Shea's writ was served on him, Parnell was at the height of his career. The allegations published in the conservative *Times*, that he had encouraged agrarian 'crime', had been proved forgeries, and the forger, Pigott, had committed suicide. The Conservatives were in office, but Gladstone, with whom Parnell was on fair terms, was committed to Home Rule as soon as the Liberals should be returned, and seemingly nothing could prevent it, provided it was possible to preserve the alliance between them and the Irish party.

Captain O'Shea obtained his decree *nisi* on 17 November 1890 and the Tory papers, *The Times* in the van, had their revenge. Nevertheless on Tuesday 18 November, at a meeting of the Irish National League, the organization that promoted the Parliamentary party, there was a unanimous decision to stand by Parnell. The demand that Parnell should retire came from three sources, the *Methodist Times*, the *Pall Mall Gazette* and the *Labour World*, in which Michael Davitt took an ultra-left position. But on 24 November Gladstone intervened. He threatened to resign the Liberal leadership if Parnell did not retire. It was being argued that the Liberals might lose the next election if he remained. The members of the Irish party were in a dilemma, and either way Gladstone had freed himself of his dependence on them. As for the priests, a few years previously Parnell had insisted on bringing them into the organization as a counterpoise against Fenianism, though now he must appeal to the Fenians against them. The tragedy was that the Irish were prepared to fight among themselves when an English politician threw them a bone of contention. But let those who profess contempt try being a colonial people themselves.

There is no evidence that O'Casey in 1891 reacted to the death of Parnell in any manner distinct from that of the Protestants he lived among. His eight-page orgiastic dance of words conveys nothing of the sense of irremediable disaster that is in James Joyce's account of the split.[13] There is song and dance, but very little said.

Only one more incident of this period need be mentioned. It is told in

I Knock at the Door, in the chapter 'Crime and Punishment'. If the life
story is to be believed, after O'Casey had received a severe caning from
the disciplinarian Hogan, he was taken away from school and his
formal education came to an end. Margulies could trace no surviving
tradition that O'Casey retaliated on the teacher. Indeed the incident so
much resembles one recorded by Joyce that one writer transforms
Hogan's cane into a pandy bat. Geography confirms that the school
was that of St Barnabas. The journey home is just as O'Casey describes
it, including the crossing of the railway. But how much schooling was he
deprived of? If he is correct in saying that George Middleton was
shortly to leave school and that the teacher threatened to refuse him a
reference unless he assisted in the assault on O'Casey, then the incident
belongs to O'Casey's last year at school. For he and Middleton were of
the same age.

The Casey family were to live in the same neighbourhood for thirty
years. What kind of a neighbourhood was it? Hawthorn Terrace and
Abercorn Road, to which the family removed later, were in a district
known broadly as the East Wall, which was bounded on the sea side by
the berths of ocean-going vessels. To the south lay the Liffey and
Dublin's most important quay, the North Wall, where cross-channel
steamers tied up, bringing in coal, timber and manufactures, and
taking away vast herds of cattle which poured down the streets on their
way to providing old England with its roast beef. To the north ran the
multiple tracks of the Great Northern Railway's main line to Belfast.
There were only two openings, one at East Wall, the other at Ossory
Road. The area was bounded on the west by the Royal Canal alongside
which ran a network of railway lines connecting the dock terminal with
Amiens Street, Broadstone, Kingsbridge, Westland Row and the rest of
Ireland. To the East Wall one might reasonably attach the district
known as the North Wall, on the far side of the canal and marshalling
yards. It was enclosed within the sweep of the GNR line to Amiens
Street.

These areas, in all directions cut off from the rest of the city,
comprised the main part of the port of Dublin. They were peripheral
and were undergoing development in response to technical changes.
For example, in 1880 there were twice as many sailing as steam ships
registered in Ireland. In 1900 the proportions were reversed. The decline
in the population of Ireland was due to the departure of farmers. The
resultant check to development was at a minimum in the ports. Two of
these, Dundalk and Dun Laoire, were the only towns outside Ulster to
show an increase in population at every decennial census. Even Dublin
suffered a decline in the intercensal period 1861–71. Population fell
from 314,811 to 312,941 within the 1936 boundaries.

But it is necessary to distinguish the old city, bounded by the circular roads but expanding towards the canals as they ran to the west, from the suburban areas now incorporated in it. These were Drumcondra, Kilmainham, and above all Rathmines and Pembroke. Here the successful bourgeoisie, lawyers and civil servants, established their handsome terraces and detached mansions, supported by plentiful servants and surrounded by exotic cordylines and flowering shrubs. As fast as these fortunate people vacated the central area their places were snapped up by incomers from the country, many of them evicted from their homes, and the character of the property changed. After 1871 the population of all areas arose simultaneously. The suburbs bloomed and the centre grew more overcrowded.

The East Wall was the only working-class or industrial suburb. It was a developing area. In Murray's *Handbook for Travellers in Ireland* published in 1896, there is a map which shows by hatching the built up areas of Dublin. The region between Sheriff Street and the sea is shown as open country intersected by only five named roads. One of these is Hawthorn Terrace. It was an extensive, comparatively sparsely populated district, with typical port industries, occupied by a riverside aristocracy of labour, stevedores, ships' engineers, railway workers of various grades, not excluding the more settled class of seamen who preferred to live decently separated from the whore-houses of Montgomery Street.

Alongside the native Dublinmen were Orangemen brought by the railway and Englishmen brought by the ferries. There was also a sprinkling of countrymen. The 1901 census returns show quite a few Gaelic speakers. Miscegenation through time produced its own synthetic uniformity and the place was as Dublin as the Coombe. While the houses were overcrowded by modern standards, there was much open space, waste land for the most part, such as carries ragwort and poppies and a stray hawthorn, and where a botanist would root about for some casual visitor that had jumped ship after a journey from the antipodes. On the flat alluvion the young people, over the years, established a patchwork of unofficial playing fields. It was not an oppressive district, but an extremely stimulating one, as O'Casey was prepared to concede when he did not have to go to school.

The accommodation of the Casey family was registered as of the second class. It in no way resembled that of the many thousands who lived in the slums. The word 'tenement' should frighten nobody. Change the name and it is your flat, apartment or bed-sitter. That is if you have it to yourself. The special evil in Dublin was the facility with which tenements could be sublet. The misery in the rural areas and the constant influx arose from an agrarian system decreed by the ruling class of England. The taxation, admitted by the inquiry of 1896 to have been excessive for the previous century, was levied by Whitehall. The laws were enacted at Westminster. Irish nationalism was never a romantic whim. It was a movement aimed at enabling the Irish people to solve their social problems for themselves. Of these the problem of housing was above all insoluble under the rule of imperialism.

Overcrowding, having its roots in Ireland's colonial position, went back long before the Union, and was the subject of many inquiries. In 1836 the Poor Law Commission estimated that there were not fewer than 30,000 to 35,000 'destitute poor requiring the interference of the legislature to provide them with the means of subsistence'. A witness deposed that he had seen '18 or 20 persons in a room about 13 or 14 feet square. I have heard of as many as 30 persons being in one room'. The principal tenant would pay about 1s 10d a week and let the corners for 5d a week to four families, presumably keeping the centre for himself.

Colonial relations were only slowly modified after 1921, and it is remarkable to find that a century after the Poor Law Commission reported, a similar system should still prevail in Dublin. According to the census taken on 26 April 1936, there were then in the city of Dublin 80,997 persons living in single rooms, and among them were 1,066 families of eight or more members in such rooms. It is a matter of living memory that at this period there were single rooms occupied by several families whose respective floor spaces were demarcated by curtains of newspapers suspended from diagonal clothes lines. These conditions were removed by the agency of the Fianna Fail party under a capitalist system. They were a legacy of imperialism and it was not a socialist task to abolish them.

It is only necessary to imagine the conditions in the slum tenements and the concomitant deprivation in matters of food, clothing and hygiene, to appreciate that O'Casey's experience was quite different. At the base of Dublin society there existed a degree of almost animal poverty which excluded all possibility of intellectual development. Above this pit of hopelessness were higher gradations from which young people might hope to escape by enlistment or entering domestic service. As some left the slums others entered. Higher again in the social scale were those who lived in what would now be called 'blocks of flats', one family to a flat. These, standing on firm ground, feared above all to be thrust into the whirlpool.

But the enormous improvements which have taken place over the past fifty years should not blind us to the fact that in his day O'Casey was among the comparatively fortunate. That is what the facts show.

NOTES

1. For those who hesitate to accept this against opposing evidence the following points may be of value. First, it is at least as old as any other. Second, the contrary evidence is conflicting and contradicted by documents. O'Casey told Lady Gregory that he was sixteen before he learned to read (*Journals*, p. 72); he told Beatrice Coogan (McCann, *World of Sean O'Casey*) 'well over sixteen'. Asked to account for school and Sunday School certificates dating from the eighties, to say nothing of prizes, which Margulies found (op. cit., p. 23) he told Krause (*Sean O'Casey and his World*, p. 9) that he could remember what was read to him so accurately that when he recited it from memory inspectors thought he was reading from the page before him. Margulies, a cautious lawyer, permits himself a doubt. Not so Krause. *Credit quia absurdum*. Is it suggested that he *wrote* from memory too? But on p. 96 of *Pictures in the Hallway* (Liberty Book Club Edition, New York) he records his writing an application for employment when just over fourteen years of age, and on p. 7 he shows himself reading at the age of ten.

2. According to 'Hill of Healing' in the life story, he was registered as an orphan on his first visit. But in the next chapter he writes that 'all this time' his father was sick. The 'Castle Ball' described in *I Knock at the Door* was probably the levée on the occasion of the visit of the Prince of Wales, on 8 April 1885. This would explain the presence in town of the other members of the family. The Parnellite party had called on its supporters to ignore the event and it was incumbent on all good Unionists to turn out, including those with 'not a flitter on them'.

3. *In Search of Community*, p. 11.

4. American writers have chosen to believe that there existed some designated category of 'common labourer' like a 'common carrier'. But the phrase required to carry this meaning is 'general labourer'. 'Common' carries a distinction of social position like its Latin equivalent '*vulgaris*'.

5. The conversation about Parnell is of course sheer anachronism. The funeral took place on 9 September 1886. Captain O'Shea filed his petition in divorce on 28 December 1889. One is reminded of another vignette in which Mrs Casey takes her son John to hospital where he dies before he can receive treatment. Returning in a cab she is delayed by a procession. Parnell is holding a meeting at the Rotunda. Assuming that the child in question was the second of the two named John, then his death took place on 3 December 1876. Parnell was not yet elected leader. Nor was he yet leader in the following August when at least he spoke at the Rotunda.

6. B. Benstock, *Paycocks and Others*, p. 198.

7. The durability of O'Casey's resentment is shown in the names he gave to these churches, St Burnupus (Burn us up) and St Damnaman (Damn a man).

8. 'Shakespeare Taps at the Window', *Pictures in the Hallway*, p. 22.

9. As late as in 1970 I remember calling on an aged Citizen Army man in Ballybough. His daughter took occasion to say to me 'Yon man's the gassest character under the canopy of heaven.' The tradition had lasted that long.

10. *Seachran*, wandering, illusory, a puzzle, out of work. There is no English word because there is no English type. A 'crank' offends by bizarre opinions. An 'eccentric' is old and slightly genteel. The word 'outlaw' presumes a recognized law. But the popular, impoverished devil-may-care is historically from the lowest rank of the tenantry and politically a figure of national resistance.

11. *Pictures in the Hallway*, chap. 1.
12. In 'We All Go the Same Way Home', *I Knock at the Door*, p. 74, Isabella, Michael and Isaac oppose Parnell, while Thomas takes his part. I suspect that the mature O'Casey's respect for Parnell has seeped into his account of former days.
13. James Joyce, *A Portrait of the Artist as a Young Man*.

[3]

TRANSITION TO NATIONALISM

Oh, my America! My new-found land!
John Donne

Soon after his fourteenth birthday[1] Sean O'Casey started work for the wholesale chandlers Hampton Leedom of Henry Street, satirized as Hymndim-Leadem, on account of their principals' pietistic leanings.

O'Casey devotes seven chapters of the autobiography to the subject of his first employment and paints an unforgettable picture of the pettifogging sycophancy of an unorganized working class divided into under-privileged and unprivileged by religious discrimination. O'Casey was a Protestant. Therefore he was on the staff. His pay was but 3s 6d a week. But he could expect annual increments. Around him, dung-eaters of various ages displayed the medical and moral effects of their diet. The vanmen were not on the staff. They were Catholics and time-workers, and afraid to cross a member of the staff because of the possibility of arbitrary dismissal. The staff were of one flesh with their employer. When he married they presented him with a clock as naturally as those of the right dimensions accepted his cast-off suits. Lickspittle competed with lickspittle unashamedly, spying on each other and on everybody else. And spying on them all was O'Reilly the door-keeper, his loyalty reserved to his master alone because he was a Catholic and untouchable.

At first the youngster seems to have been determined to work hard and get on. From the start he was entrusted with substantial sums of money. In the life story he records three increases in salary during a minimum period of two-and-a-half years. On this showing he remained with Hampton Leedom until at least November 1896, and probably a year longer. He was then earning 7s 6d a week. By the end of the first year his sense of gratitude to his employer had evaporated. According to his own account he began to supplement his wages by pilfering and one infers from what he says that the practice was not unusual. As a despatch clerk he was responsible for arranging deliveries within a certain area of the city and a vanman was assigned to assist him. All that was needed was mutual understanding and this was forthcoming. To facilitate his operations his mother sewed special pockets into his clothes. So, at least, the life story says. But it is strange that O'Casey who so indignantly rejects charity confesses so readily to theft.

These three years not only marked the end of his self-identification with authority, they saw the first awakening of his intellectual interests. No more avid grasping for 'The Boys of London' and 'Alley Sloper'. There was a kingdom of whose existence he knew, but which now he intended to invade. He began to spend his pocket-money on books and gradually re-stocked his father's depleted shelf. He had no guide; he followed where his curiosity led him. Until modern motor traffic engulfed them and the trade was monopolized by a handful of great shops, the quays of Dublin were lined with stalls protected by oil cloth from the weather and second hand classics could be had for a few coppers.

That O'Casey at this stage records only English titles should cause no surprise. Irish literature was still the province of the well-educated and the enthusiast. The great popularization associated with Yeats and his colleagues was only beginning. It required the impetus of revolution to make it thoroughly effective. The timid, willing boy became the young fellow 'with a chip on his shoulder' as he delved into science,[2] geography, history, poetry and novels, a breath of radicalism stirring from Mignet and Carlyle on the French Revolution, and from the works of Ruskin which strongly attracted him. Old Merle d'Aubigny's *History of the Reformation* was brought down from its place.

As he read, contempt for his surroundings mounted. He grew unable to suppress or conceal it. Nor was he above making a display of his knowledge. Inevitably he lost favour. It became only a matter of time before there arose some issue that would lead to his leaving Hampton Leedom for good. It was his refusal to be fined for some trifling act of insubordination.

Isaac's theatrical activities had meanwhile expanded. He had formed a dramatic society which gave performances in converted stables in Hill Street. O'Casey continued to act scenes from Shakespeare and in due course, when Isaac had transferred his energies to the Mechanics' Theatre, had the opportunity of playing Father Doolan in Boucicault's *Shaughraun*. Though it was many years before he attempted dramatic composition, and many more before he acquired a mature technique, in his early youth he learned the feel of an audience and knew what it would respond to. Early experience is of vital importance in all spheres of achievement. There would have been no Mozart if his father had been tone deaf. O'Casey moreover had further opportunities for learning when Isaac became property master at the Theatre Royal.

According to Margulies, it was in 1897 that Mrs Casey moved for the last time and took up residence at 18 Abercorn Road, in a house that is still standing. Margulies says the family occupied two rooms on the first floor. O'Casey[3] on the other hand claims the ground floor. In 'The Sword of Light' in *Pictures in the Hallway*, he describes the minister's flashing past the window which must obviously have been on street level. The reason he gives for the move is that the new house was nearer to Thomas's place of work on the railway. But it would save scarcely two minutes, even if Thomas had been employed on the railway. It seems more likely that the deciding factor was the growth of the Beaver family, for these moved to Rutland Place. Mrs Casey and her four sons occupied the house in Abercorn Road. Once more they were overcrowded by modern standards but immeasurably better off than the denizens of the slums, for if the house contained bugs and looked cheerless, at least it yielded to the ministrations of Mrs Casey, who cleaned it and made a home of it.

At the age of eighteen O'Casey began an intellectual development that carried him far from his original soil. Two new influences seem to have struck him simultaneously, one national, the other religious. The national influence was that of the tram conductor to whom O'Casey gives the name of Eamon O'Farrell. If he is a composite character, his development is traced with extraordinary perception. He is the embodiment of the best type of republicanism. Having with the sharp eye of a Fenian spotted the unusually independent youth at the Hill Street drama sessions, he was delighted to find a Protestant who was receptive to his ideas. One day he pushed into O'Casey's hand O'Growney's grammar of the Irish language, a series of simple lessons for students. O'Casey showed considerable linguistic ability and was soon able to speak simple sentences, reassuring himself that a man who spoke Irish could be as loyal to Queen and country as one who spoke English.

The other influence was the new curate, believed to be the son of J. Saul Fletcher, who came to help out when his father was sick. He was a young man of high church inclination, and described as a 'ritualist'. The ritualist controversy had originated in England. Shortly after Catholic emancipation, when the process of assimilating the Catholic gentry into the ruling class was under way, John Henry Newman, son of a London banker, founded the so-called 'Tractarian' movement. At Oriel College he had been a Calvinist. But from 1833 he conducted weekly services at 7 a.m. employing altar lights, the 'mixed chalice' of wine and water, but not, at this time, the 'eastward position'.

The movement was taken up enthusiastically in fashionable parishes in London. Here the 'eastward position' was adopted, together with candlesticks on the altar, a crucifix above or below it, and even a screen with gates before the chancel. Newman himself was received into the

Catholic church in 1845, ordained in 1847 and appointed rector of the Catholic University of Dublin in 1854. In 1865 he published his 'Dream of Gerontius' which was immortalized by Sir Edward Elgar in that woebegone oratorio which surely stands as the epitome of the reactionary in musical art.

His famous 'apologia' was a reply to an attack on him by the 'Christian socialist', Charles Kingsley. Those of his following in England who remained within the established church found themselves assailed by the Church Association which brought against them a series of legal actions. The 'ritualists' refused to accept the jurisdiction of the judicial committee of the privy council in religious matters, and some of them were imprisoned for contempt of court. In 1888 the Bishop of Lincoln was arraigned before Archbishop Benson and five episcopal assessors, and as a result it was decided that the 'mixed chalice' and the 'eastward position' were legal, but that certain other practices were not.

Historians of the Oxford Movement, of which 'ritualism' was an offshoot, have no doubt correctly connected it with the growing cultural and aesthetic awareness of the English squirearchy, and advancing knowledge of the liturgy of the early church which was not so bare and whitewashed as puritans believed. These considerations would of course weigh little in the rural parishes of Ireland, where everybody knew everybody else and the minimum change was required, if the ascendancy were to remain ascendant. In the North on the other hand, ceremonial was anathematized as the mark of the beast. Here the Protestant community was paid its commission from the proceeds of colonialism, in return for splitting the nation. Assimilation to Roman practice would endanger this agreeable system.

But in Dublin, predominantly but not overwhelmingly Catholic, with an old-established school of divinity at Trinity College whose earnest young students scanned the copious literature that crossed the channel for new inspiration and new attitudes, and with its variety of social distinctions, somebody was bound to start the hare. The ritualist controversy was present throughout the nineties. In 1892 the court of the general synod was called upon to rule that a crucifix, which the rector of St Bartholomew's had placed behind the altar, must be brought in front of it. From time to time there were storms in other tea cups. When the Reverend Harry Fletcher, who had not long left Trinity College, despite having served in several western parishes, introduced into St Barnabas not only crucifix and altar cloth, but 'intonation' and the 'eastward position', the orangemen were aghast. Windows were smashed and the organist knocked unconscious. It was alleged that members of the orange-oriented Protestant Defence Association had adopted the practice of sending 'emissaries' to stir up riots against the 'ritualists'.[4] In the East Wall district their assistance would probably be superfluous.

It has been suggested that Fletcher brought back O'Casey to his devotions. But there is no evidence that he had ever neglected them. He was indeed intensely religious for many years to come. He underwent the rite of confirmation at his eighteenth birthday. It should be remembered that early confirmation was a product of the twentieth century. Soon afterwards, on Fletcher's recommendation, he went to work at Eason's the wholesale newsagents. On his way there on the first day, he wondered what his pastor would think if he knew he had O'Growney in his pocket.

O'Casey's account raises many chronological problems and one is tempted to think that he is ante-dating his interest in Irish by several years. But he told Cowasjee, in a letter dated October 1958,[5] that while he was interested in the language in the late nineties, he did not join the Gaelic League until about 1903, and there are no firm facts that conflict with this explanation.

His confirmation took place in the spring of 1898. It is therefore difficult to account for the description of frost and deep snow through which he trudged on behalf of Easons. There is a reference to the Fashoda incident which occurred in October 1898. One would certainly not expect frost and snow in the early autumn. It can therefore be guessed that the snow, and possibly the incidents connected with it, were transposed from the Hampton Leedom period and from the winter of 1895, which I remember people speaking of in my young days. There was no comparable period at any time of the year for a number of years, as can be seen from the records.

In the life story O'Casey describes his meeting Sean Connolly who, eighteen years later, lost his life in the assault on Dublin Castle. He was then a despatch clerk at Easons. O'Casey proclaims himself a Gael and uses the words *is Sinn Fein*, which he had acquired from O'Farrell. The 'Sinn Fein' party was founded in 1905 by Arthur Griffith. But the words were used before that time to denote the policy of constitutional resistance, as Griffith put it, necessitated by Ireland's inability to defeat England on the battlefield. The phrase is literally translated 'we ourselves'. But as a laconism it is capable of idiomatic use within wide limits. It can express a sense of unity among those present, for example in avoiding a dispute. Or it can convey 'we mind our own business' and, by implication, you would do well to mind yours. Padraig Colum[6] suggests that its first use to indicate Griffith's policy may have been in William Rooney's letter to Griffith, who was then in South Africa, and that he may have taken it from a poem by Douglas Hyde published in Alice Milligan's *Shan Van Vocht* in March 1898. But the phrase there is

Sinn Fein amhain, ourselves alone, which is of respectable antiquity.

It is unlikely that the phrase in its shortened and improved form[7] would so quickly have reached a tram conductor who did not know Irish. But Sean Connolly was in touch with Griffith's circle. Nobody has so far identified the tram conductor. Is it possible that Sean Connolly was the begetter of O'Casey's Gaelic interests, which he temporarily dropped after he left Easons? O'Casey might be indisposed to admit the paternity, in view of his subsequent dispute with the Citizen Army of which Sean Connolly was a prominent member.

It is clear that at this period O'Casey must have been a prey to a conflict of loyalties. He claims to have demanded of Sean Connolly, 'Do you believe that Ireland ought to be free and that the English are our enemies?' This is some distance from loyalty to queen and country, unless, on the principle of the Jacobite toast, O'Casey 'couldna quite render' which queen and what country.

That he began to make the transition to nationalism around this time is supported by another anecdote in the life story. He referred to it again in a letter to Canon Fletcher dated 1 December 1941 and published in Dr Krause's collection.[8] Whether his claim to have remained at Easons only a week is correct or not, certainly he cannot have remained there long. One evening when he was reading Ruskin, Eamon O'Farrell called, bringing the evergreen *Speeches from the Dock* and Tone's autobiography. Their conversation was interrupted by the arrival of Fletcher who explained that as a result of the discontent that had been aroused by his 'ritualist' innovations, his bishop had advised him to find another parish. O'Casey had not had the courage to tell him he had left Easons. Now he had come to say goodbye.

O'Casey's ability to capture, or perhaps reconstruct significant conversation, enables us to visualize the positions of the two visitors and O'Casey's uneasy wavering between them. O'Farrell is singing Fenian songs, softly so as not to awake Mrs Casey in the adjoining room. O'Casey yields to the magic of John Kells Ingram's fine song and, to relieve the tension, O'Farrell asks what he is reading. It is Ruskin's *A Crown of Wild Olives*.[9] O'Farrell is scornful. What has Bradford Exchange to do with them? Or an English gentleman with an Irish? O'Casey attempts a defence, but Ruskin gets the worst of it.

But at this point Fletcher arrives. They discuss Christian doctrine, the 'ritualist' commenting on what Anglican and Roman Catholics have in common. For no apparent reason O'Casey decides to air his Irish. Fletcher scarcely shows enough interest to waft it away. The Irish gentleman seems completely anglicized. Indeed he continued his ministry in Westbourne Park, London, to return to Ireland only after many years.

After his departure, O'Farrell, who has been hiding in the shadows behind the sofa, emerges to continue his conversation. He declares his political faith. He regards the Irish Parliamentary Party as the agent of imperialism. He has no confidence in Connolly's socialists. He is a physical force Fenian. When he leaves, O'Casey is thinking seriously about life and politics, but is obviously not entirely converted to republicanism.

He seems to have continued in this undecided state for some time. In October 1899 the Boer War broke out. Thomas was recalled to the colours. According to the life story he was at this time a temporary postman earning 12s a week. But it must be remembered that Michael and Isaac were still at home. O'Casey might be short of money; the household was not. He accompanied Thomas to the boat, carrying his rifle for him. But his 'world was divided against itself'. When weeks went by and nothing was heard of Thomas, O'Casey feared that he had been killed[10] and reflected bitterly on Irish manhood wastefully expended in England's wars.

Dublin was alive with controversy. Last time England had been involved in a major war, Ireland had been broken and dispirited by famine and emigration. Now matters stood differently. The land was in process of being restored to the people, the tenants being advanced state mortgages out of the profits of empire. The landlords were being transformed into rentiers. With the loss of their economic power their political importance declined. The local Government Act of 1898 established democratically elected authorities which nationalist, republican and Labour were rapidly making their own. Though Home Rule was in temporary abeyance, there was much talk of devolution. If there was no uprising to assert the principle that England's difficulty is Ireland's opportunity, and some regretted that there was not, it was to some extent because a peaceful constitutional path to freedom seemed open. It was when it was seen to be closed that the people turned to revolution. Meanwhile patriotic Irish people applauded the Boers and the Irish who were fighting on their side, and those less patriotic remembered the imperial forces.

It is remarkable that O'Casey in his life story selects but one day in a period which must have affected him strongly. This was the famous occasion when Connolly, Maud Gonne and Arthur Griffith defied the authorities by holding a proclaimed meeting in Beresford Place, while Joseph Chamberlain, as the nationalist papers put it, slunk furtively into Trinity College to receive his honorary degree. O'Casey, who was in the company of Eamon O'Farrell, was involved in the baton charge and claims to have unseated one mounted policeman and won a free whiskey and a fair lady.

Perhaps because his loyalties were divided, O'Casey seems to have taken no part in the work of the Transvaal Committee. These same divided loyalties may explain why his interest in national affairs developed first in relation to the language movement. He was of course only twenty, yet if he had entered that door, he would have found then and there what he had to seek through years of frustration. The committee met in the rooms of the Celtic Literary Society at 32 Lower Abbey Street. Here was one of the most stimulating circles in Ireland. Brought together by William Rooney in 1893 as a more radical break-away from an older organization, the members of this society strove to repeat at the close of the century what had been attempted by the Young Irelanders in the forties. Murtagh Lyng was an early member. Connolly attended from his earliest months in Dublin. There was also Fred Ryan who later edited Scawen Blunt's anti-imperialist periodical *Egypt*, Peadar Maicin, Frank Cahill and Thomas Cuffe. The society worked closely with the Young Ireland Society and the Eureka Literary Club headed by W. B. Yeats and Maud Gonne. More loosely connected were Hubert Oldham, Stephen McKenna, Dr George Sigerson, Douglas Hyde, Arthur Griffith and John O'Leary.[11]

One assumes that while O'Casey was prepared, partly out of curiosity, to attend a public demonstration, he was not yet sufficiently committed to take political action. He does not mention the visit of Queen Victoria the following April, when, as in 1885, the pauper children were brought out to line the streets. In that month Isaac, who had abandoned his stage career and was working in the distribution department of a publishing company in which he secured part-time work for his brother, married Josephine Fairtlough and left the family home.[12] Until Thomas's return in the autumn Michael Casey was presumably the main breadwinner.

The decisive factor in holding back O'Casey from involvement in the political movement on whose fringe he stood, was the appointment in 1899 of Rev. Morgan Griffin as rector of St Barnabas. He was the first man of wide culture O'Casey had met since the death of his father, to whom he had had access only at second hand, through the recollections of his mother and the remnants of his library. Griffin had been educated at Trinity College, and had served in Tipperary and Wicklow. From 1897 to 1899 he had been deputy secretary of the Hibernian Bible Society. He was as humane as he was scholarly and O'Casey fell very much under his influence.

It would seem therefore that for the next few years O'Casey was immersed in parish affairs. He became secretary of the Society for Foreign Missions. He taught children in the Sunday school and sang in the choir. He was a regular attender at prayer meetings and acquired the art of extemporizing in imaginative language and at 'brave length'. Visitors would discover him poring over the Bible, large parts of which he knew by heart.

One imagines that it was through the good offices of Morgan Griffin that George Middleton was persuaded to find O'Casey work as a labourer on the Great Northern Railway of Ireland. In this employment which lasted for ten years, the slim pallid youth filled out and became bronzed and muscular. The workers he mingled with now were not the debilitated cringers and fiddlers of family commerce, but the rough tough adepts of industry, men who could use a sledge with the precision of a scalpel, and could down a pint of porter before you could say *prosit*, a low lot thought the gentlemanly O'Casey when he first met them, and before he identified himself with their interests.

The Orangemen who had ousted Harry Fletcher seem to have over-reached themselves during the incumbency of his successor. From Margulies and the account in the life story one gathers that their attempt to use the church for an Orange festival, possibly on the twelfth of July, was resisted by Griffin. They dominated the vestry and either they or the minister would have to go. O'Casey undertook a campaign of canvassing throughout the parish, with the result that at the next election all the Orangemen lost their seats, much to the disgust of George Middleton.

By the time he had reached his early twenties, therefore, O'Casey had travelled a long way. He had ceased to be a Unionist, and was on the threshold of the Irish Ireland and republican movements. For understanding how he finally committed himself, we lack one vital piece of information, the name of the man who sounded him and swore him into the Irish Republican Brotherhood. Perhaps it will emerge some time. In religion, though he remained almost fanatically evangelical, he interpreted Protestantism in a broad non-exclusive manner. If he was not yet conscious of his new class status as a manual worker, still he was open to working-class influence at the point where it was bound to be strongest, at the place of work. In the next chapter we will follow his evolution as an Irish nationalist.

NOTES

1. So says the life story, April 1894; 'Comin' of Age' in *Pictures in the Hallway*, p. 94. As usual there are chronological difficulties. O'Casey tells of calling on Isabella who was living in Summerhill, so that she can draft a letter of application. But from entries in the register of births it is clear that her son James Thomas was born at Hawthorn Terrace in October 1895. She subsequently moved to Rutland Place, N., which is near Summerhill, and was there on census night 1901.

2. He mentions *The Story of the Heavens* by Robert Ball, then Astronomer Royal of Ireland. This was one of the most widely read books on the subject of astronomy throughout these islands. He also mentions Darwin's *Origin of Species*. He found both of these works beyond him at the time.

3. 'Death on the Doorstep', *Pictures in the Hallway*, pp. 220, 291, and 297. See also Ayling, *Sean O'Casey, Modern Judgements*, p. 214, where Hubert Nicholson takes as autobiographical references to staircases in 'Dream Review', *I Knock on the Door*, p. 232.

4. See R. B. McDowell, *The Church of Ireland 1869–1969*, chap. VI, 'The First Fifty Years of Disestablishment'.

5. See Cowasjee, *Sean O'Casey, the Man Behind the Plays*, p. 9.

6. Padraig Colum, *Arthur Griffith*, p. 32.

7. One thinks of the Gotha Programme which originated the leftist dogma that the emancipation of the working class is the task of the workers *alone*. The statutes of the First International had the word *themselves* in its place. The distinction is valid for the Irish national liberation movement also.

8. D. Krause, *Letters of Sean O'Casey*, vol. I, p. 911.

9. Lest Ruskin be too lightly dismissed, I record that when in the summer of 1934, I asked the veteran Tom Mann what was the main literary influence on his radical youth, he replied: 'Ruskin'.

10. According to Margulies neither Michael nor Thomas ever left the United Kingdom. But Michael was at Gibraltar on his way to India when he received his discharge. While the personal records of soldiers who served in the South African war were destroyed during the Second World War, the list of those awarded medals survives in the Public Record Office, London. It contains the name of Thomas Casey, Dublin Fusiliers, discharged on completing his period of service on 14 November 1900, and awarded the Orange Free State, Transvaal, Taylor Heights, Relief of Ladysmith and Laings Nek medals. The date of discharge agrees with that given by Margulies and falls twelve years and some months after his initial enlistment. Family tradition also has it that he saw service in South Africa and the whole substantiates O'Casey's riposte to W. B. Yeats that he had mixed with soldiers all his life.

11. These names are in Colum's list (*Arthur Griffith*, p. 29), but do not appear in the society's minutes which have survived for the years 1893 to 1896. Colum writes of other meetings at Maud Gonne's rooms in Nassau Street.

12. O'Casey deals harshly with Isaac to whom he owed a very considerable debt. According to Margulies, Isaac, who was working in Liverpool at the end of the war, was prevented by war-time security provisions from returning to Dublin for his mother's funeral. O'Casey never communicated with him again. In this he showed the bitter implacable streak in his character. Isaac became a Catholic and began to use the name Joseph. He became a full-time official of the Irish Transport and General Workers' Union and was close to Larkin in 1913, though this is never mentioned by O'Casey. He figures in the dispute with O'Brien in 1924 from having on Larkin's instructions signed a false statement of accounts. In the General Strike of 1926 he would walk seven miles to work rather than take a blackleg tram.

[4]

IRISH IRELANDER

Land without tongue, land without heart.

Gaelic proverb

In 'Purple Dust in their Eyes'[1] published in 1963, O'Casey declares: 'I abandoned the romantic cult of Nationalism sixty years ago.' Whatever meaning we are intended to give this sentence, chronology proves its inaccuracy. For it was around 1902 and 1903 that O'Casey's nationalism, romantic cult or otherwise, fully developed. For the early years of this century we have the advantage of two important new sources which enable us to see O'Casey as others saw him. These must of course be collated with the life story.

The first is Ernest Blythe's *Across the Boyne*[2] and the second is Desmond Ryan's *Remembering Sion*.

Blythe first met O'Casey at the hurling in Phoenix Park and, since he was then about seventeen-and-a-half, the year must have been 1905. By this time O'Casey was a member of the Gaelic Athletic Association and a member of the Irish Republican Brotherhood. It was not long before O'Casey sounded Blythe, assured him that the IRB was preparing an armed insurrection and did not believe in assassination, and finally had him sworn in to the organization. From the confident style Blythe ascribes to O'Casey, one gathers that he had probably been a member for some time.

At the same time Blythe makes clear that O'Casey continued to be engrossed in parish affairs. There was no trace of his later agnosticism. The young Antrim man was of the 'low church'. But O'Casey had become something of an 'Anglican Catholic'. He wished to introduce into the rite of Canterbury not only confession but fasting, a curious taste in an impecunious slum-dweller who might be judged to have had enough of it. He even provided himself with rosary beads. He is said to have remarked of the Catholic religion that in the Virgin Mary it possessed what the Protestant lacked, a mother-figure.

In 'Gaelstroem'[3] he corroborates parts of Blythe's evidence. He tells of a debate on the subject of the Irish language arranged by his rector, E. M. Griffin, who presented him with an Irish testament as a memento of the occasion. It bore the date 1905.

At this time many of the cross-currents affecting the Irish-Ireland movement were noted in the columns of *The Irish Peasant*, a local paper published at Navan in Co. Meath. Its founder, James McCann, was a wealthy nationalist. Under the benign influence of the Rev. Father Farrell, who had brought back radical opinions from France, he undertood industrial projects and established his weekly in the hope of inducing others to follow suit. He was indeed anxious to establish a national newspaper and at the time of his death was contemplating a large additional investment.[4]

The first editor, P. D. Kenny, was an economics graduate who had worked in England but returned home a classical bourgeois Sinn Feiner. In his *Economics for Irishmen*, written in 1906, he urged the extension of capitalism in Irish agriculture. He was an acute observer who would tramp the country in the belief that social conditions were best observed on foot. He attributed what he considered the general idleness of western small farmers to 'survivals of communism', which he defined as 'taking according to your needs, and producing according to your capacity, with the taking and producing in common'. Its language was all he wished to preserve of Gaelic society. He wanted people to work hard and make money and in this reacted to the new opportunities provided by the land reforms and the Local Government Act. He proposed reducing the numbers and increasing the acreages of agricultural holdings, the displaced men to be employed as labourers on the enlarged farms. 'Once a man has begun to pay for work, it immediately assumes a more serious interest for him; he cannot allow his employees to "do as they please".'

The *Irish Peasant* campaigned for increased tillage and more effective use of land and fertilizers. Kenny himself favoured outright nationalization of the land, possibly under the scheme proposed by Michael Davitt. He thought the state would compel the farmer to work harder and not sit drinking what he got from the publican to whom he let his grazing.

But there were many quite content to 'do as they pleased', and others whose interests predisposed them against new brooms scouring the countryside. Peasant proprietorship and local government franchise were comparative novelties. Until they became commonplace there were bound to be exaggerated hopes and fears. The *Irish Peasant* was constantly involved in controversy; its circulation rose as it repeatedly courted clerical displeasure.

In 1904 there had been a split among the Orangemen, and Lindsay Crawford's Independent Orange Order adopted a stand favourable to both Labour and nationalism. On 13 July 1905 the Order issued a manifesto which was published in the *Irish Protestant* of which Crawford was editor. It was read by Canon Hannay, Rector of Westport, a Gaelic enthusiast who is best known for his playful and satirical novels written under the pseudonym George A. Birmingham. Hannay wrote to Lindsay Crawford suggesting that a copy should be sent to P. D. Kenny. It appeared in the *Irish Peasant* on 8 August.[5]

The manifesto urged Irish Protestants to 'consider their position as Irish citizens and their attitude towards their Roman Catholic fellow-countrymen, and that the latter should choose once and for all between nationality and sectarianism.' The manifesto described Unionism as a dead creed, called for further land reform, the rectification of the grievances of the town tenants, and the conversion of Trinity College into a non-denominational university by transferring the divinity school to the Church of Ireland.

Kenny was only responding to events. But the Catholic bishops were anxious that if events could not be persuaded to refrain from happening, they should receive no unnecessary stimulus until the government had given their lordships the assurances they were seeking in the field of university education. McCann received complaints of Kenny's editorship and a change was mutually agreed, to take effect at the end of 1905.

Perhaps encouraged by this and other rifts in the nationalist camp, in September 1905 the government announced the withdrawal of the Treasury grant for the teaching of Irish. A great protest meeting was held at the Rotunda. On 11 November the president of the Gaelic League, Dr Douglas Hyde, set out for the USA where he proposed to raise funds for the defence of the language. His arrival at Broadstone from his home in Co. Roscommon was made the occasion of a demonstration. Members of Gaelic Athletic clubs marched in formation, accompanying him to Kingsbridge where he boarded the train for Cobh. O'Casey's club provided the bodyguard. In the life story O'Casey casts himself in the role of innocent admirer while his companion, playing devil's advocate, reaches the ungrammatical conclusion that 'Hyde will always prefer having a shot at a snipe than having a shot at a Saxon.'

This procession O'Casey conflates with a previous one which took place during Irish language week in March 1905. Tableaux representing events in Irish history and the progress of Irish manufactures, were towed through the streets of Dublin. The editor of *The Leader*, D. P. Moran, had been urging the discontinuation of the Gaelic League's journal *An Claidheamh Soluis*, whose editor was Patrick Pearse, and hinting at financial irregularities. He was unceremoniously ejected from the procession together with the two members of the corporation who had given him the hospitality of their carriage.

O'Casey's treatment of the language procession seems aloof and supercilious. The life story cannot possibly reflect his feelings at the time. The old man smuggles his disillusionment into the enthusiasm of his youth. Like the members of the mad tea party he has 'quarrelled with time', but instead of its remaining always five o'clock, it is jigging backwards and forwards in a most unpredictable manner. Yet the records of the Gaelic League show that in 1906 he was the secretary of the Drumcondra branch.

The new editor of the *Irish Peasant* was W. P. Ryan, a native of Co. Tipperary. He was a gifted Gaelic scholar who had been the president of the London Gaelic League since 1902, and a writer of distinction in two languages. He took up his duties in December 1905, his son Desmond, then a boy of twelve, joining him at Navan the following spring. The paper continued to excite controversy. Local authorities had been given the power to establish public libraries and T. W. Lyster of the National Library was energetically pressing them to do so. In the towns there was no problem. Cardinal Logue himself officiated at the opening of the library in Drogheda. But what of the country? Lenten pastorals warned of the danger to the rural population if literature dangerous to their faith and morals were to be imported from England. By the end of the year the bishops were on record against public libraries in rural areas and the *Irish Peasant* was in dispute with them. Undoubtedly O'Casey formed his impressions of the influence of the Catholic clergy in these early days.

In July Lindsay Crawford, speaking at Knock, protested against the 'de-nationalization of Ireland'. W. P. Ryan enthusiastically reported him. But in October Canon Macken of Claremorris made an attack on Canon Hannay and succeeded in excluding him from the Co. Mayo committee of the Gaelic League. The *Irish Peasant* thereupon published articles critical of Canon Macken's sectarian behaviour. The Canon had fancied he detected a note of ridicule in Canon Hannay's treatment of some of the Catholic characters in one of his novels.

All this would have counted for little if the *Irish Peasant* had not chosen to attack the church in one of its entrenched positions. Over a period of months a correspondence was published calling in question the clerical control of schools. And to make matters worse McCann died, leaving his well-intentioned but politically inexperienced wife to undergo the pains of episcopal disapproval. Finally, in December 1906 the Cardinal announced that if publication of the paper did not cease, he would denounce it from the altar. Mrs McCann capitulated. W. P. Ryan moved to Dublin – with the paper, which he kept alive with a much reduced circulation.

The paper was renamed *The Peasant and Irish Ireland*. It gave hospitality to O'Casey's first known publication, an article entitled 'Sound the Loud Trumpet' which appeared on 25 May 1907. It was a bitterly satirical attack on the educational policy of the British government in Ireland, which concluded with a denunciation of British rule, disguised as thanks for benefits received. It is too sophisticated for a first literary effort. It is direct and well-sustained, containing mostly biblical allusions and is free from the distracting verbosity that mars so much of O'Casey's later work. The writer has not yet achieved unity of style and the sentences sometimes hang together somewhat loosely, but the sentiment is all of a piece, hot unbridled nationalism.

In 'Windfalls' O'Casey tells of his elation at seeing the article in print. He gives a copy to a pastor with whom he was friendly, presumably E. M. Griffin. Instead of receiving praise he is told that he is a traitor and ought to be in jail. There have been speculations on why O'Casey drifted away from St Barnabas. It would seem unnecessary to seek beyond this incident for the beginning of the process. Indeed St Barnabas continued to be a centre of Orangism. As late as 1910 members of its congregation were prosecuted for causing disturbances in Sandymount church, after the *Irish Protestant* had recommended the methods of Jennie Geddes for the prevention of the singing of the Lord's prayer. O'Casey's militant nationalism was incompatible with the prevailing Unionism. To keep the peace at home Mrs Casey placed a ban on the discussion of politics at the dinner table. O'Casey began to seek recreation at the St Laurence O'Toole's Catholic social club in Seville Place, while together with Blythe, George Irvine and Seamus Deakin he spoke at Church of Ireland debating clubs in one parish after another.

This effort to interest Protestants in the language was one of O'Casey's most constructive activities. Not that he was willing to compromise for the cause. He displayed his high church leanings in the midst of delicate negotiations with low church pastors. Nevertheless he met with a degree of success. Irish-speaking clergymen were brought to preach in Dublin and parts of the *Book of Common Prayer* were translated into Irish.

But O'Casey wanted to do more than promote the use of the language. He wanted to 'put the objects of the Irish-Ireland movement plainly before the Protestant people'. The League executive objected and their objections cannot be airily dismissed as the qualms of fat bellies and thin guts. Canon Hannay had aroused suspicions, not only in Catholic quarters, when he celebrated communion in Irish at St Patrick's Cathedral on 17 March 1906. Nor did it earn him the indulgence of Canon Macken. The proselytizing record of Protestant language movements was well remembered. Nevertheless, something of O'Casey's plan was put into effect in 1910 when the Irish Guild of the Church was founded. It was a broader organization than the Gaelic

League, except in being confined to Protestants. It attracted many clergymen who were qualified to conduct services in Irish. Among members of the Gaelic League who joined it were O'Casey's friend George Irvine, Nelly O'Brien and Lil nic Donnchadha.[6]

Desmond Ryan provides a picture of O'Casey at this period. They met when Ryan, then about fifteen years old and, already displaying an interest in socialism, visited the Drumcondra branch of Sinn Fein. This could not have been before 1908, for IRB members were not encouraged to support Sinn Fein functions until the end of 1907. Ryan recalls O'Casey's 'violent republican oration . . . stark and forceful, biblical in diction with gorgeous tints of rhetoric and bursts of anti-English nationalism of the most uncompromising style'. Members of the Socialist Party of Ireland are present. He derides their materialism. They interrupt with references to the poverty of the Dublin slums. Yes, says O'Casey, there is that, but there is something else, and dropping his voice to a passionate whisper, he utters the one word, 'joy!'

Now one learns quite young that the spirit of delight comes but rarely. Where had O'Casey made its acquaintance? Did he refer to religious ecstasy? I suspect that he may have had in mind the sense of self-realization he was then enjoying, that comes from identification with a people and a cause. In Irish nationalism the changeling believed he had found himself. Enthusiasm overbore all material clogs. The bitterness came later when he found he had not.

Ryan completes the story. One of the leading members of the SPI, Walter Carpenter, gets up to press his point. O'Casey 'rises in a fury and growls in Irish that he wishes no Englishman to teach him'. He walks out of the meeting, fists clenched. Ryan recognized in the young O'Casey a distinct 'force and character', even if he had a touch of the crank or the fanatic. His attitude to the socialists was one of suspicion and hostility. Perhaps Ryan provides an explanation for this in his account of his visit to the socialist headquarters. William O'Brien welcomed the young man, but there was a generally patronizing attitude to nationalists, despite the fact that the dominant influence in the room was that of their exiled leader James Connolly.

O'Casey's relations with his fellow Gaels were subject to sudden strains for, as Ryan put it, 'his mind had room for only one idea at a time'. He was among the defenders of Synge when, during the last week of January 1907 there were spirited protests from the audience at a performance of his *Playboy of the Western World*. Today it seems surprising that this slight comedy of rebellious youth should arouse strong emotions. O'Casey implies in his autobiography that the protests within the theatre and the demonstrations outside were due to the use of the word 'shift' in the last act, when Christy Mahon says 'what'd I care if you brought me a drift of chosen females, standing in their shifts itself?' But there had been uneasy mutterings from the start. The audience reacted against the notion of a young man who believed he had killed his father and then went bragging about it. It has been argued that in one instance the local people hid a man who had accidentally killed his father until he got away safe to America. But he hid. He did not brag. The extravagant improbabilities of the plot, the contrived belletristic dialogue and the general pointlessness of the whole show, led the Dublin audience to believe that they were being laughed at. Synge had populated the whole country with stage Irishmen.

Satire is acceptable against the background of generally accepted moral principle. The *Playboy* is completely non-moral and lacks such a reference point. Today, when both the accepted moral principle and the satire have disappeared, it is an amusing night's entertainment. Corkery[7] was surely right to acquit Synge of the slightest desire to guy the Connacht people who had given him his inspiration. But he suggests that as a Protestant he could never understand in his bones the sensitivities engendered by centuries of oppression.

This was probably true of O'Casey too, though he felt he was waging generous war in defence of the artist against obscurantism. *Vox populi* is not *vox dei*. But the masses can only be moved, in the last analysis, by real things. To take the historical measure even of such absurdities as the nazi demonstrations against Klemperer's 'Wagner in modern dress', one must remember Versailles, the inflation and the international humiliation of the German nation.

During this period O'Casey's family life was darkened by the misfortunes of Isabella. Beaver, up to then an exemplary husband who worked hard all week, amused himself with his pigeons at the weekend, and sent his children to the central model schools,[8] began to show signs of mental disease. In 1901 he had held the position of clerk. By 1904 he had been demoted to porter. In 1905 he was removed to Richmond hospital where he died of the general paralysis of the insane in November 1907. Unable to pay the rent of her apartment in Fitzgibbon Street – a poor, shabby tenement according to Margulies – and after suffering the humiliation of physical eviction, she moved temporarily to Abercorn Road with her five children. O'Casey records his resentment at being at last dragged down into tenement conditions, even temporarily. He records no protest from the patient Michael. After a few months she found accommodation in Brady's Lane, later in Church Street. She was little over forty, but made no effort to resume her career as a teacher. It is stated that she scrubbed floors for Mrs Irvine, the neighbour who gave its present name to Brady's Lane. But how far and how long this was a necessity is not clear. Her eldest daughter had been

trained to no business. But her eldest son was fifteen in 1909. By the
time of her death[9] in 1918, her children must have been in a position to
support her in comfort. When Margulies made his inquiries she was
remembered not as a slut, but as 'Lady Beaver' of the spotless white
gloves, the embodiment of working-class respectability.

On 26 June 1909 readers of *The Nation and Irish Ireland*, as the
Irish Peasant had again been renamed, learned that the professor of
Irish at St Patrick's College, Maynooth, had been dismissed from his
post. In the life story O'Casey describes the bringing of the news to
hurlers in the dressing room. For reasons best known to themselves (one
imagines part of a 'package deal') the hierarchy had declared against
compulsory Irish in the reorganized university. Dr O'Hickey
disapproved of the decision, and when it became clear that he was
unlikely to see it altered, he sent scathing letters to the press. In these
letters he denounced the opponents of compulsory Irish as a 'worthless
faction', their policy 'dastard and foolish', a 'squalid and foolish
apostasy' liable to 'precipitate such a scandal as Irish public life has not
witnessed since one of those who sold the country . . . sought the
suffrages of the burgesses of Athlone leaning on the arms of two
bishops'. He wrote of 'an act of treachery towards Ireland' and of
'centuries of national infatuation for which Irish churchmen are more to
blame than others', and more in the same vein, directed moreover,
amongst others, against men who were his ecclesiastical superiors. His
words expressed exactly the feelings of the Irish Irelanders, and he
became their hero, and especially O'Casey's.

But what was to be done? O'Casey's generous enthusiasm was at
once engaged. He identified the villain of the piece as Cardinal Logue
whom he blamed for the onslaughts on Yeats, Synge and W. P. Ryan.
He determined, he wrote in the life story, to 'fight this sanctified
coercion, this mitred tyranny'. That he lobbied hard in Sinn Fein clubs
and republican circles one need not doubt. He had inexhaustible energy
in one-man campaigns. At one point he called for a demonstration with
drums and colours in the grounds of Maynooth to demand Dr Hickey's
reinstatement. Such action would of course have wrecked the Gaelic
League. But indignation at the professor's ill usage drove all other
considerations out of his mind. When his colleagues refused to accept
his proposal, he accused them of 'white cowardice'.

In the event, the professor of theology at Maynooth, Dr MacDonald,
a former supporter of the Land League, who had agreed to advise Dr
Hickey on technical matters, suggested recourse to Rome, and an
appeal for funds drew an immediate response from the public. Whether
this was the course of wisdom has been doubted. Whatever the rights of
the question, the parties were ill matched. Dr Hickey had neglected the

sound prudential principle that before quarrelling with those on whom he is dependent, a man must put an end to the dependence. If he can not do this, then he must pursue his object by other means. The best policy might have been to apologize for the immoderacy of his language, reserve his position and fight again at a better opportunity. As it was he spent several years kicking his heels in Rome, secured no satisfaction, returned to Ireland where he was given no employment and died in the middle of the world war.[10] O'Casey's reaction to Dr O'Hickey's imprudence reveals a political trait that has already been noticed in him, that of ultra-leftism.

Among the able young men in W. P. Ryan's entourage was Bulmer Hobson. He was labour correspondent of the *Dublin Observer*, and had written for the *Peasant* and its successors. He shared rooms with Seamus Deakin, a pharmacist with a large shop in O'Connell Street. O'Casey spent many an evening chatting there with the two men. Hobson had been brought up as a member of the Society of Friends, but had ceased to practise religion. Like W. B. Yeats, Helena Moloney and other emancipated Protestants, he had dabbled in metaphysics, occultism and theosophy. He had arrived at a position of broad-minded agnosticism which may have implanted the first germs of scepticism in O'Casey's devout mind.

Hobson was at this time endeavouring to harmonize the IRB teaching of physical force with the policy of Sinn Fein. This was based on attempting to convert local government, which was democratic, into the framework of a national state, through an assembly of local authority representatives. The traditional policy of the IRB had been that of an armed uprising. This was the policy O'Casey had explained to Ernest Blythe. But according to the 1873 constitution of the IRB which was still in force, such an uprising was only permissible if a majority of the Irish people willed it, that is to say if the republicans had a mandate. How were they to secure such a mandate?

Clearly Sinn Fein could provide a means. But what then ? Was it immediate insurrection, or the defence of the revolutionary administration? One could imagine such defence shading into guerrilla war. The subject was not entirely new. For example, in Griffith's *United Irishman* of 16 February 1901, a contributor had developed the conception of 'defensive offence' in connection with the South African resistance. Hobson applied related arguments to Ireland, and there can be little doubt that it was from these discussions that O'Casey learned the principles on which he later criticized the 1916 Rising, though one ingredient was missing in 1916, the mandated administration.

W. P. Ryan's papers were doing badly. Hobson applied without success for the post of editor of the trades council's journal. Later in

1909 he returned to his native Belfast, where he became for a brief period a member of the Socialist Party of Ireland, while remaining a member of the IRB and Sinn Fein. His ideas of national policy were published by the West Belfast Branch of Sinn Fein in a pamphlet entitled *Defensive Warfare, a handbook for Irish nationalists*.

The departure of Hobson and some others threw back O'Casey on the St Laurence O'Toole social club, where he became friendly with Frank Cahill,[11] a schoolteacher who was a member both of the Gaelic League and the IRB. The two men spent many a weekend walking and talking in the country which then began at Drumcondra, and together they conceived the project of setting up the St Laurence O'Toole pipe band. This was established in 1910, O'Casey securing Tom Clarke's services as president. During the same year W. B. Yeats was widely criticized for accepting a trifling state pension. O'Casey defended Yeats.

In December 1910 the *Irish Nation* ceased publication and its editor, W. P. Ryan, returned to London. Faced with the prospect of becoming dependent on Griffith, the IRB established their own monthly, *Irish Freedom*. Its first editor was Dr McCartan, but as soon as he returned from his brief spell in the north, the effective work was done by Hobson. The paper was published from Synnott Place, not a stone's throw from Tom Clarke's shop. O'Casey was one of the helpers, and Mrs Tom Clarke long remembered with gratitude his willingness to hump parcels on his back and perform other unpaid chores. 'There's a man who puts Ireland first', said her husband.

NOTES

1. Sean O'Casey, *Under a Coloured Cap*, p. 263.
2. Ernest Blythe, *Trasna na Boinne*.
3. Sean O'Casey, *Drums Under the Windows*, p. 219. The chronology of the earlier chapters of this book is so chaotic that it may be useful to give an estimate of the probable dates involved: (1) 'At the Sign of the Pick and Shovel', 1902; (2) 'Poor Tom's Acold', 1914 conflated with 1910; (3) 'House of the Dead', 1905; (4) 'Behold, my Family is Poor', 1908, the reference to Dr Hickey being an anachronism; (5) 'Home of the Living', 1918; (6) 'Drums Under the Windows', 1905; (7) 'Song of a Shift', 1907; (8) 'Lost Leader', 1909; (9) 'Gaelstroem', 1905–10; (10) 'Hora Novissima', 1912 or 1913; (11) 'Green Fire on the Hearth', about 1912; (12) 'Prometheus Hibernica', 1909–13; (13) 'Dark Kaleidoscope', 1913–14; (14) 'Under the Plough and Stars', 1914; (15) 'In this Tent, the Republicans', 1913; (16) 'St Vincent Provides a Bed', 1915; (17) 'Prepare, Everyone with Weapons', 1914; (18) 'The bold Fenian men', 1916.
4. This was confirmed by Mr George Gilmore whose father was McCann's accountant.

5. In the chapter 'In this Tent', *Drums Under the Windows*, Liberty Book Club Edition, New York, p. 346, O'Casey makes his solitary reference to Lindsay Crawford, in the midst of a chronological tangle impossible to unravel. O'Casey takes Tom Clarke a copy of the *Irish Protestant* in which, to his surprise, he has seen an article by Lindsay Crawford praising the insurgents of 1798. Clarke at first refuses to read it, but when he is finally persuaded he is so delighted that he orders three dozen copies. Unfortunately for the story, Crawford was dismissed from the editorship of the *Irish Protestant* in May 1907, and Clarke did not leave the USA until December of that year. For a further year Crawford edited the Liberal *Ulster Guardian*, only to be dismissed for advocating official Liberal policy on devolution and Home Rule. He was virtually hounded out of public life, emigrated to Canada in 1910, but went to the USA to support De Valera in 1919. O'Casey's reminiscence may be derived from the reprint in the *Irish Peasant*. The biography of Lindsay Crawford is crying out to be written.

6. See Blythe, *Trasna na Boinne*, pp. 127–33 and David Green in *Irish Anglicanism*, ed. Fr. Michael Hurley, SJ, pp. 115–17.

7. Daniel Corkery, *Synge and Anglo-Irish Literature*, pp. 179–204.

8. Model schools were established in the eighties of the nineteenth century as part of a plan to provide intermediate education on a secular basis. They were to prepare pupils for the newly established royal university. The plan never came to fruition, the university itself remaining little more than an examining body until early in this century. The model schools in practice, therefore, were the providers of a somewhat above average education for Protestants.

9. The death was registered not by O'Casey as he claims, but by Isabel Murphy who resided in the same house and was present at the death.

10. O'Casey is mistaken in thinking he was unhonoured and unsung. Within months of his death the *Waterford News* published a commemorative pamphlet.

11. I think it likely, but have not ascertained, that this was the Frank Cahill of the Celtic Literary Society. He was later a Cumann na nGaedheal (pro-treaty) T.D.

[5]

UNREST UPON THE RAILWAY

It has been remarked that the conditions of life of the average worker, while they predispose him to resist his employer, to combine against him and even to press for legislation affecting the conditions under which he works for him, do not lead him directly to socialism. For that the germ must be brought from outside. O'Casey worked on the Great Northern Railway for ten years. He remained an Irish Irelander, known among his mates as 'Irish Jack'.

A decade is quite a long time in human affairs. It may therefore appear strange that he should be content with comparatively menial employment when he had become well aware of his intellectual capacity. In 'All Heaven and Harmsworth too'[1] he recalls the thrill of pleasure with which he suddenly apprehends his superiority to his brother Isaac. He was the youngest child, perhaps something of a 'mother's boy'. He was in one way in no hurry to grow up. But it would be pleasant to have the best of two worlds. It was not difficult to surpass the easy-going Isaac. But he could only challenge Michael in a clandestine way. When the census was taken on 19 April 1911, O'Casey gained possession of the form and completed the section to be filled in by the householder. He described himself as Seán O Cathasaigh, *fear an tighe*, that is to say, head of the household, railway labourer. He entered his brother's name and occupation in Irish also. Michael was described as a general labourer. If O'Casey was not playing a double trick on Michael, this means that Margulies was mistaken in thinking that Michael regained his position in the Post Office. In the part of the form which is filled in by the enumerator in English the head of the household is given as Michael Casey. The census confirms that the family occupied the ground floor.

It is an essay in imaginative psychology to interpret this little act of misrepresentation. If it was a joke, then the point of the joke is that those who can write Irish are better than the heads of households. He was confronting condition with attainment. But it also revealed his desire to be the head of the household, his mother's equal, not her youngest. The autobiography repeatedly claims for him responsibilities which he did not possess, actions that he did not perform. And yet if he had held down an unskilled job for ten years, surely he could have held down a skilled one, and where would Michael be then?

But people whose minds were filled with the fervour of patriotism could afford to be indifferent to such insignificant matters as their station in life and prospects of advancement. From the life story it is clear that O'Casey was frequently disappointed when others did not share his idealism. He resembled those students who, convinced there is a revolution round the corner, neglect the studies which will alone qualify them to be of any use to it. What would have happened if O'Casey had taken to writing plays when the revolution was in the ascendant? He could not, *because* the revolution was in the ascendant.

On 18 August 1911, the British railway unions called upon their members throughout the United Kingdom to withdraw their labour. The Irish membership complied. On 21 April the Dublin timber merchants locked out 500 workers who were members of the Irish Transport and General Workers' Union. This dispute dragged on long after the railwaymen had settled. Anxious to assist the men whose difficulties had been precipitated by their own action, the Irish railwaymen asked that the railway strike should be resumed. The London office of the Associated Society of Railway Servants on 15 September declared a national strike of their Irish members, but did not bring out the English. It was a familiar pattern. The Irish must help the English but fight their own battles themselves. Largely as a result of lack of co-operation from the Amalgamated Society of Locomotive, Engineers and Firemen, the Irish railwaymen were defeated and the resultant victimization was described as 'cruel'.[2]

According to the life story, O'Casey had 'joined the union' though it is not clear whether this was the ASRS or the ITGWU. One imagines the former. On Tuesday, 28 November 1911, O'Casey was handed an extra week's wages in lieu of notice and informed that his services were no longer required. He could secure no explanation for his dismissal.

Krause suggests that he had been 'overheard attacking the working conditions . . . and praising Jim Larkin.'[3] That he was well able to have his views noticed to his detriment is not to be doubted. Another suggestion is that he fell into bad odour through objecting to a superannuation scheme. But it is doubtful if any more explanation is required than that he gave himself. After the strike, members of the union were victimized.

Correspondence passed between O'Casey and the company until 5 January 1912. Two months later O'Casey sent it to the *Irish Worker*, edited by James Larkin, as the official organ of the ITGWU. The delay seems to indicate that in January O'Casey was not yet in touch with Larkin. The correspondence was published on 12 March. O'Casey explains that he had to his credit ten years' service, missing about six 'quarters' during that time, was a total abstainer, was sick for only a fortnight, nine days of it owing to an accident, and was dismissed because he 'refused to be a slave to an Irish cur or an English importation'. O'Casy had come under the influence of Larkin. He may have been introduced to him by Micheal O Maolain an ITGWU member of the Gaelic League.

He contributed a series of six articles to the *Irish Worker* describing the conditions of work on the GNR. Their chronology is curious. The first appeared on 8 June 1912 and criticizes what might loosely be called the foremen's 'truck system'. The others, which appeared from January to March 1913, allege incompetence and corruption among the mostly English managerial staff and compare the opulence of these with the 'starvation wages' of the men and boys. The attack is directed simultaneously against the employer and against the English. There is not a trace of socialist consciousness. But what is important is that O'Casey attained trade union consciousness during the years of the 'great unrest'. In his first letter he declares: 'there is no hope outside iron-hearted union'.

There is little to show how O'Casey spent the year 1912. That he was still writing about the railway in early 1913 seems to suggest that nothing had happened to take his mind off it. He was possibly unemployed and therefore dependent on Michael's earnings and his mother's old age pension. At the same time it is possible that his brother Thomas, now tolerably prosperous, may have helped out. Is it permissible to read something of this possibility into the altercation between O'Casey and Thomas's widow in 'Poor Tom's Acold'?[4] Thomas's family did not agree with O'Casey's statement that the two brothers seldom met and that 'only gossip told us where he was living.'[5]

Immediately after his marriage, Thomas Casey went to live in Richmond Terrace which I take to be part of the cul-de-sac off Summerhill. When they moved, however, it was to 6 Oxford Terrace, not a hundred yards from Abercorn Road. It may well be that immediately after Thomas's marriage to a Catholic in 1903, there was some cool feeling. The children, however, testify to hilarious family gatherings at Oxford Terrace, one in particular being that at which O'Casey tortured the neighbourhood with his bagpipes until they fell mysteriously silent thanks to a puncture contrived by Michael.[6]

According to his nephew, O'Casey worked for a few months for 'a builder he knew'. From his account in the life story of what is presumably this episode, it may be guessed that his main qualification was his lack of qualification. His duties were those of an inspector or clerk of works, but he was informed that he need not inspect too diligently. Unfortunately this advice was lost on him. He was too honest. He displayed a quixotic concern for the interests of his employer's clients. The employer tried to oil the wheels with five sovereigns. When he declined them, the contractor (named Deelish, which possibly stands for Sweetman), handed him through the gate.

He continued his work for Irish Ireland, and in the winter of 1913 was engaged in polemics with A. P. Wilson an actor and playwright who wrote a column in the *Irish Worker* under the nom de plume 'Euchan'.[7] The Scotsman had accused the Irish of living in the past. It is the old cry of the offender that by-gones should be by-gones. The imperialist is always surprised when peoples wish to recover what has been taken from them. Burke argued that people who never look backward to their ancestors will not look forward to prosperity. Euchan did not think too much retrospect good for the Irish. 'Ireland,' he wrote, 'can never be again the glorious nation she was.' 'Attacks on our cherished ideals,' replied O'Casey, 'will do no good to the labour movement.' The use of the word 'our' shows that O'Casey still regarded himself primarily as a republican. 'Ireland's past is past' insisted Euchan, oblivious of its ubiquitous presence so to speak congealed in existing relations.

Euchan's case had a specious logic. First, the present era was a commercial age. Second, Home Rule (then expected) would 'bring Ireland into commercial line with its neighbours'. By this he may have meant that it would favour capitalist development. Third, the future would then rest between capital and labour. Finally, the workers should prepare for the consequent battle.

Using vague expressions like 'commercial', 'line', 'future' and 'battle', Euchan had given voice to a typical cross-channel liberal's approach to the Irish question, completely unaware of its implicit chauvinism. For the English government 'granted' the degree of 'Home Rule' they thought was good for the Irish to have, and Irish affairs developed in accordance with its provisions, whether the Irish wanted to come into 'commercial line' or not.

O'Casey not only saw this weakness. It enraged him. His reply was adorned with rare rhetoric. For he swore 'by the blood-dripping wounds of Wolfe Tone', that 'we will enter into our heritage, or we will fall one by one.' Euchan regarded the man who could write thus as a 'dreamer' and reiterated his assertion that 'the fight of the future in Ireland is between capital and labour.' No more demands on England! He regarded what the English government was prepared to grant as final. But O'Casey did not.

In reply O'Casey offered to refute Euchan's four propositions in public debate. But Euchan turned to personal abuse and thereby admitted he was worsted. While it was true that the struggle between capital and labour must play an increasing part in Irish life, as was to be shown in a most spectacular fashion, Euchan could not envisage the special framework imposed on this struggle by Ireland's colonial position.

O'Casey's final reply is interesting because it contains his first extant reference to Connolly. And it is *favourable*. Insisting that it is not possible to separate economic from political history, he adds 'James Connolly could give you some valuable information on this question.' He is obviously referring to Connolly's *Labour in Irish History* which was published in book form in 1911. This work was described by Connolly as part of the literature of Irish Ireland. And that O'Casey should use Connolly in defence of the nationalist position shows that he did not at this time regard Connolly as the pure socialist whose disappearance he subsequently regretted. The picture of Connolly renegating in favour of nationalism was invented by O'Casey after his own views had changed. O'Casey never fell under the spell of Connolly the socialist. But like all other Irish Irelanders, he singled him out for special favour as a socialist who understood the national question. O'Casey entered the labour movement as a republican, through the gateway of trade unionism.

In the midst of the *Irish Worker* controversy O'Casey intervened in another that was proceeding in *Irish Freedom*. Some members of the IRB, notably P. S. O'Hegarty and Ernest Blythe, were seeking socialist models for the reconstruction of Ireland after the expulsion of the English. 'Ireland's freedom,' O'Casey writes, 'will be a task glorious to any generation of Gaels.' But then he adds a warning; 'Woe unto us if we hand over our ideals to be squared and shaped and glossed by those who would write in our skies that socialism is Ireland's hope, and hang round our necks the green ribbons of Cumannacht na h'Eireann.' He goes further, 'Our social progress, present and future, must be garnered from the inspiration, the purity, the fullness of Ireland's past, not from the swelling hearts of England's suckled socialists.' The 'swelling heart' was probably Walter Carpenter's. He was an Englishman with a reputation for lachrymosity who had sacrificed his business for the sake of the movement. O'Casey concludes by quoting the most radical republican voices of the nineteenth century. These were good enough for him.

At the age of thirty-three, therefore, O'Casey was critical of the Socialist Party of Ireland. But his distance from the socialists is shown by another thing. Cumannacht na h'Eireann had a year previously abandoned its separate organization and merged with other groups to form the Independent Labour Party of Ireland.

When O'Casey speaks of the labour movement at this period he means, not the socialists, but the trade union movement. In the summer of 1913 he attempted to bring about co-operation between the IRB and Larkin. His experience started a process of disillusionment with republicanism before he had acquired the political experience and theoretical knowledge to estimate the possibilities of social classes. Politically he was a neophyte and it is essential to grasp that fact.

In the life story O'Casey tells of his success in inducing the IRB to set up a committee to discuss relations with Larkin.[8] It meets in Seamus O'Connor's house. O'Casey and Sean MacDiarmada are deputed to ask Larkin for coverage of republican activities in the *Irish Worker*, which claimed a circulation of nearly 100,000 copies a week. Larkin agrees but asks in return for coverage of labour events in *Irish Freedom*. Nobody turns up to the meeting called to hear the report of the delegation, not even MacDiarmada. One member of the committee was Bulmer Hobson and it is possible that it was at this time that O'Casey began to dislike him. A pattern was being repeated. When O'Casey's interest was drifting from religion to Gaelic, he tried to bring his co-religionists with him, and was surprised that what had struck him with such force, had not struck them. Now that he was turning towards labour, he expected the IRB to turn with him.

According to the life story, O'Casey was at this time the press officer of the Wolfe Tone Memorial Committee. He claims to have arranged the making of a film of the annual commemoration at Bodenstown. Krause suggests, on the strength of an announcement in the *Irish Worker* in July 1913, that he may have been secretary to the committee. But he is not so described, and the fact that he invites delegates who have not received notice of a meeting to forward their *addresses*, suggests that he may have been standing in on account of some emergency. The names of the committee were published from time to time in *Irish Freedom*. The name Seán O'Cathasaigh does not appear. But there is a P. O'Cathasaigh. This may possibly be O'Casey, for his pamphlet *The History of the Irish Citizen Army* was erroneously accredited to P. O'Cathasaigh, and *Irish Freedom* may have originated the confusion.

O'Casey was an admirer of Patrick Pearse and quoted with approval his pamphlet on education, *The Murder Machine*. He assisted with the publicity for the fête which Pearse organized at Jones Road in aid of his Irish-Ireland school, St Enda's College. The story is told in the autobiography[9] where there is a hilarious account of the woeful events of the last day (14 June 1913) when the oil that was to have kindled the camp fires, being sprinkled too generously, was ignited by a carelessly dropped match and nearly burned down the marquee. It is interesting to contrast the eager optimism of O'Casey's contemporary publicity with the song of experience in the autobiography, where one finds unqualified sympathy for Pearse, and admiration for his advanced views on education, but tolerant amusement at what he had come to regard as his incurable romanticism.

According to Krause,[10] his fellow IRB man, Sean T. O'Kelly, found O'Casey temporary employment as a builder's labourer. He publishes a postcard dated 20 June 1913, which he understands to be O'Casey's reminder to O'Kelly of his promise to do this. The appointment was made through the 'improvements committee' of the Dublin corporation, but it does not follow that O'Casey now became a public employee. It was presumably this employment which he held when he was asked by his foreman to sign a document undertaking not to become or remain a member of the Irish Transport and General Workers' Union. He refused and was locked out.

The account given above is not what would be inferred from the life story. It must be remembered however that whatever the period he deals with, O'Casey's autobiography is a *late* source. He was moreover unusually weak on dates. For example in a letter to Horace Reynolds written in 1938 he misplaces the date of his mother's death by a year. To be uncertain with dates is to be unsure of the succession of events. To be unsure of the succession of events is the most certain way to lose their significance. And if their objective significance is lost, a subjective one can take its place.

In the life story the treatment of Connolly is not the kindest imaginable and this might seem strange in a 'working class rebel who put socialism first'. O'Casey was a communist when he wrote *Drums under the Windows*. But he was not yet even a socialist during the period he was writing about. He was antagonistic to the socialists in 1913, but not from his ultimate *left* position. On the contrary he stood to their right. In *Drums under the Windows* two currents of criticism are confused, the actual and the ultimate.

His favourable mention of Connolly in distinction to the other socialists in 1913 has been mentioned. In the life story, he presents Connolly first in the course of a reverie at work. He is thus freed from the inconveniences of time and space. Since the *Irish Peasant* is in his mind we may suppose the reverie takes place after 1905. But he then imagines himself at an open-air meeting of the Irish Socialist Republican Party in Foster Place. Connolly is speaking and supporters are selling his *Socialism Made Easy*.[11] Now Connolly undoubtedly addressed meetings in Foster Place, but not after 1903 when the ISRP disintegrated and he emigrated to the USA. And to confuse matters further, *Socialism Made Easy* is a collection of his American writings published in 1909. Now possibly O'Casey had heard Connolly in Foster Place before he left the country, and possibly his supporters were selling the British Social Democratic Federation pamphlet *Socialism Made Plain*. But from what we know of O'Casey's development it would not be surprising if he was unimpressed. He was at his most religious phase.

There are other references to Connolly. In 'Hora Novissima'[12] the subject matter of which can be assigned for the most part to 1911, O'Casey speaks of Connolly's 'ever assuring himself that his Irish Socialist Republican ten commandments beginning with the nationalization of the railways . . . would be observed by the common people'. Connolly had of course no such belief or desire. He was anxious for their enforcement by a native Irish government. But it is true that the ISRP programme contained ten points and that the first was the nationalization of the railways. But the ISRP had been defunct for eight years by 1911. Connolly had returned from the USA in 1910, but after spending a year as national organizer of Cumannacht na hEireann, he left for Belfast and did not return to Dublin except for short visits until October 1914. The Socialist Party of Ireland, to give Cumannacht na hEireann its English title, was founded while Connolly was in the USA. He was, therefore, not responsible for its programme which was not founded on that of the ISRP.

Was O'Casey relying on hazy recollections of Connolly's propaganda as it appeared to a young republican antagonistic to socialism? That he is unlikely to have reconstructed it from literary sources is shown by a significant detail. In 1945 the only extant life of Connolly was that by Desmond Ryan. O'Casey's copy of the work was misbound and lacked pages 17 to 33 which deal with the ISRP. It is difficult therefore to escape a simple conclusion. In the period preceding the great transport lock-out of 1913, O'Casey knew nothing about socialism and little about Connolly, and though he may have learned something of socialism afterwards, he did not repair the omission in the case of Connolly.

NOTES

1. Sean O'Casey, *Pictures in the Hallway*, p. 326.
2. Emmet Larkin, *James Larkin*, pp. 90–2.
3. D. Krause, *Letters*, p. 10.
4. O'Casey, *Drums under the Windows*, p. 61.
5. ibid., p. 33. It is extraordinary that O'Casey writes of his brother's working on the railway. Margulies makes it quite clear, and his children confirm it, that he worked in the Post Office, and the only connection with the railway would be that he was appointed chief sorter on the Belfast train. By the same token, the account of Thomas's pilferings on the railway must be the product of O'Casey's imagination.

6. Sean McCann (ed.), *The World of Sean O'Casey*, p. 165. Recollections of Christopher Casey, nephew of Sean O'Casey, and son of Thomas. On the whole Christopher Casey is critical of his uncle with whom he did not agree well. But there is no reason to dismiss his evidence. When I interviewed him he struck me as a reliable witness with a clear memory of past events.

7. D. Krause, *Letters*, pp. 13 *et seq.*

8. O'Casey, 'Hora Novissima', *Drums under the Windows*, p. 241.

9. O'Casey, 'In this Tent, the Republicans', *Drums Under the Windows*, p. 352. Pearse was not yet a member of the IRB, O'Casey had not left it. It may be that O'Casey was helping Pearse on the instructions of the IRB. The pun 'rebubblicans' may be a retrospective thrust at Bulmer Hobson, whom his critics sometimes referred to as 'Bubbler' Hobson.

10. D. Krause. *Letters*, p. 29.

11. O'Casey, 'At the Sign of the Pick and Shovel', *Drums under the Windows*, p. 16.

12. op. cit., p. 235.

[6]

WAR AND REVOLUTION

*Only the Irish working class remain as the incorruptible inheritors of the fight
for freedom in Ireland.*

James Connolly, *Labour in Irish History*

The lock-out began on 18 August 1913, when the *Irish Independent*
paid off forty despatch clerks who refused to sign an undertaking
renouncing the transport union. On the following day the dispute spread
to Easons when workers refused to handle the *Independent*. On
Thursday 21st, William Martin Murphy, who owned the tramway
company as well as the newspaper, suspended the parcels service and
dismissed the staff. A letter was then sent to all employees demanding a
pledge to continue working if the union should call a strike. The strike
began at 10 a.m. on Tuesday, 26 August when many drivers and
conductors abandoned their trams where they stood and went home or
to Liberty Hall.

It is established that William Martin Murphy took the offensive, and
thereby plunged Dublin into a labour war that involved 404 of the
largest employers and a majority of the working class. To take such a
risk a man must be strongly motivated. The employers' apologist,
Arnold Wright,[1] paints a picture of unhappy capitalists groaning under
the extortions of thirty strikes in the first seven months of 1913. Their
champion was Martin Murphy who buckled on his shining armour and
set forth to slay the blatant beast. From the labour side it was not
difficult to demonstrate the poverty and overcrowding that resulted
from the low-wage policy of the employers, against which the workers
were revolting.

But why go the length of provoking a clash instead of being ready for
it when it came? The answer lies in the complex and dangerous political
situation. The third Home Rule Bill had been introduced by Henry
Asquith in 1912. The Prime Minister was more interested in alcohol
than in Ireland, but he was dependent on the votes of the Irish members
for his majority. He was enthusiastically supported by his radical wing,
while his Tory opponents concentrated their efforts on the old Vendée
in east Ulster. With the aid of the Orange Order, landlords and an
important section of the capitalists tried to restore the sectarian
ascendancy that had been emolliated, if not overthrown, by

Drummond. Provocative parades led to sectarian pogroms. In 1912 2,000 Catholics were driven from their employment, together with 400 Protestants who had the temerity to object. The Orangemen then laid claim to state authority by setting up a 'provisional government' to usurp power in the event of the passing of the Bill. This 'government' then proceeded to enrol volunteers so as to have an armed force at its disposal. The counter-revolution was prepared while the Lords were delaying the bill, and the result was to divide the British ruling class more sharply than at any time since 1832.

Had the London government dealt firmly with all breaches of the law, all might have been well. Once Home Rule was established, the base of Unionism among the working class would have been destroyed. Labour would come to the fore. But the rebels had influence in financial and military circles. A policy of temporizing was adopted by the government. Once the notion of compromise was floated, they became totally intransigent and couched their statements in language which would have hanged many a nationalist in the past.

Under such conditions one could have been forgiven for thinking the Home Rule party would strive to secure all possible allies and would respond to the conciliation proposals which Larkin was making from April onward. The difficulty with allies is, however, that though they strengthen those who have them, they also gain strength themselves. Either labour must be conciliated in the interests of Home Rule, or every effort must be made to crush Larkin before the Irish legislature was established and while the British authorities were available to lend a hand. Murphy chose the latter course, and was prepared to compel others to follow him. He did not appreciate that the bargaining power of his own party would thereby be reduced, or that he had given hostages to a government which, though posing as an honest broker, was as suspicious of the Irish party as he was of the working class. He did not see that the Redmondites would be forced from one shameful retreat to another. If one is asked 'Why did the Home Rule party die in a whimper of compromise?' there is only one reply: they feared the workers. Thucydides says of the Spartans that 'most of their measures have always been adopted with a view to guarding against the helots'. The Irish capitalists were not yet the ruling class. But Murphy thought they would be wise to see the workers in helotry before they assumed that responsibility.

Since, in the view of the socialists, the defeat of Home Rule whatever its insufficiencies, or the acceptance of some disastrous compromise such as partition, would have delayed the settlement of the national question, and the consequent switching of the energies of the nation to social questions, Connolly continued to hope for a national alliance for limited objectives, while determined to protect the interests of the working class to the utmost. Such an adjustment of strategy and tactics was of course incomprehensible to O'Casey, pitched as he was into the maelstrom of class war with the scantiest political education.

The notorious baton charge, when Larkin appeared at the window of the Imperial Hotel to address the proclaimed public meeting, took place on 30 August. In the life story O'Casey describes the curious crowds, wondering idly whether a meeting would be held or not, the sudden appearance of Larkin, the instantaneous reaction of the police, and their clubbing the unarmed people with cries of 'drive the rats home to their holes'.

If, as we suppose, O'Casey was employed in the building trade, he would not receive the employers' ultimatum until 15 September. Murphy had to exert some pressure before the builders agreed to lock out their men. If O'Casey remembered aright his foreman's grim jest 'This means that Mr Martin Murphy knows what's good for you better than yourself,' then there was a sardonic *double entendre* in his words. The employer was in the same boat. O'Casey refused to sign the undertaking and was sent off the site.

As his articles show, after the 1911 railway strike O'Casey was impressed by the unfairness and mismanagement of one particular undertaking. The experience of 1913 taught him the full meaning of the word class. It was the true beginning of his leftward development. Moreover he now saw the slums at close quarters. Under the impact of this discovery he wrote: 'Twenty thousand families are wriggling together like worms in a putrid mass in horror-filled one room tenements.' He could never have written this if he had lived in such places all his life. Why had he not expressed this opinion long ago? Because the experience was new. The pretence by some of his admirers that he himself was a slum-dweller not only makes such comments incomprehensible, but belittles O'Casey.

He threw himself into the workers' struggle with typically whole-hearted enthusiasm. He became joint secretary with Patrick Lennon of the Relief Fund Committee and, according to Krause and some reports that have been preserved, the two men toured Dublin in a van, collecting funds. But he remained an Irish Irelander. In a letter to the *Irish Worker*, published on 27 September, he challenges his colleagues not without asperity. They wish labour well, but what do they do? He published the answer on 18 October. The Gaelic Athletic Association has 'nobly taken its stand with the workers'. He appeals for subscriptions from others.

In 'Dark Kaleidoscope'[2] he makes it clear that while working from Liberty Hall during the day, he continued his national activities in the evenings. It is when returning at daybreak from an all-night dance, that he begins to feel the effects of excessive activity on limited diet. It is of course quite possible that Michael was also unemployed as a result of the general disruption. After the dance O'Casey develops a weakness of the lower limbs which he cannot account for. That he is still a member of the IRB is indicated by the visit of the pharmacist Seamus Deakin who provides a doctor and helps him financially. The prescription is 'porridge', that is to say food, of which porridge is the cheapest.

The tramway company was able to keep a skeleton service running thanks to the use of blacklegs. These were deeply resented and there were frequent attacks on them which developed into battles with the police. The brutality of the police raised the question of workers' defence. O'Casey seems to have felt that the IRB should provide it. He may have been aware that groups of young IRB men were drilling under Fianna[3] officers. The Fianna were already supporting the workers. The reason the IRB did not oblige directly was that their eyes, like those of most Irish people at the time, were on the Ulster Volunteers.[4] But O'Casey believed that they should be prepared to jeopardize their long-term plans for the sake of the struggle in which he happened to be engaged. When they made it clear that they did not propose to do so, he blamed Hobson.[5]

It was Connolly who solved the problem of workers' defence in a simple logical way. The workers should defend themselves. He announced the formation of the Irish Citizen Army on 13 November. The first forty recruits mustered at Croydon Park, the recreation ground belonging to the ITGWU, on 24 November. They were under the command of Captain Jack White whose father had made history at Ladysmith.

Krause writes that a month later 'a rival group formed the nationalistic Irish Volunteers'.[6] This is to give a completely wrong impression. On 1 November, Eoin MacNeill, a leading Gaelic scholar, published a letter in *An Claidheamh Soluis* entitled 'The North began'. He made the proposal that since the Orangemen had armed against Home Rule, its supporters should arm for it. The IRB immediately saw the possibilities in the proposal and set about making it a reality. MacNeill was a supporter of Redmond's party and the opportunity was too good to be missed. Preparations were set on foot at once and the Irish Volunteers were established at a meeting in the Rotunda rink, the largest hall in Dublin, capable of holding 7,000 people. The Citizen Army had arisen from Captain White's proposal that the Union should introduce a drilling scheme to keep the strikers occupied. It was a workers' defence force, pure and simple, and it is ridiculous to ascribe to the Volunteers a desire to 'rival' it. Seven thousand do not assemble to rival forty. And in any event the rival 'group' had within nine months

100,000 members and formed the biggest Irish organization since the Land League.

If the IRB had launched the Volunteers themselves they would have been able to exclude those whom they disliked. More still would have excluded themselves from suspicion of the revolutionary organization. It was for this reason that Hobson was given the instructions, which he disobeyed, not to accept the secretaryship. Having accepted MacNeill's proposal they were compelled, whether willingly or unwillingly, to accept all those who favoured Home Rule, including supporters of MacNeill within the United Irish League. The leadership on the other hand looked on the Volunteers with suspicion. It is a lucky horse that can choose its stable companions.

The IRB thought they had included representatives of labour. But they knew too little about labour tradition to appreciate that labour would not consider itself included except by elected delegates. And the provisional committee showed incredible insensitivity when, in the midst of the greatest industrial upheaval Dublin had ever known, they chose to read the inaugural manifesto the son of a Co. Dublin farmer who had saved his harvest by using blackleg labour. A few hundred union men attended and interrupted this unfortunate young man so vociferously that he could not make himself heard. The hubbub only died down when Captain White, who had been invited, took his seat on the platform.

One can be sure that no interruptions were too vigorous for O'Casey. Indeed he became bitterly hostile to the Volunteers. This was of course a sign of his political immaturity. He still could hold no more than one idea in his head at a time. He had identified himself with the trade union movement, but he had no conception of the complexity of the issues it was concerned with. Connolly's calm estimation of the significance of events was beyond him. He was in the midst of one struggle and those in the midst of others must abandon them. Everybody who has had practical experience of politics has seen this phenomenon.

To Connolly with his profound historicism the matter might not be simple, but it was clear. English imperialism had conquered Ireland and through the course of time had implanted in the country capitalist institutions which divided the Irish people along class lines. The class which was thereby deprived of its heritage, the working class, must simultaneously resist the effect and the cause. It must fight to diminish its deprivation. But it should enter into whatever combinations might tend towards driving out imperialism, thus facilitating the uprooting of the capitalist institutions it had implanted. It was not possible to go back to the old communism. Therefore Ireland should go forward to the new socialism as soon as it was free to do so.

He saw no reason for discouraging Irish capitalists from acts against

imperialism which they might fail to think likely to bring them into
future danger from the workers. Not all thought as Martin Murphy, and
fewer would do so if the workers won the struggle. At the same time
Connolly, like Tone, thought merchants made bad revolutionaries. It is
important to remember that Connolly had been an avowed Marxist
since 1889. O'Casey was still a quarter of a century from it. To attempt
to 'correct' Connolly with O'Casey is a ludicrous exercise. As well
'correct' complex numbers by means of the rule of three. O'Casey did
not understand Connolly. And he could not have been expected to. In
comparison with Connolly's his political experience was infinitesimal.

O'Casey's frontal attack on the Volunteers appeared on 24 January
1914. The *Irish Worker* published a letter in which he attempted to
dissuade workers from joining them. His objection was that they did not
exist to serve the interests of the working class. He advises the workers:
'use all your mental and physical energies towards the advancement of
your class'. And he does not waste time reflecting that there may also be
'joy'. Yet in the controversy that followed he stood forth not as a
socialist but as a republican, a follower of Tone, Mitchel and Lalor. The
writing is imprecise, but one gains the impression that one of his main
objections to the Volunteers is the membership of followers of
Redmond. These of course included some of the employers with which
the ITGWU was in dispute. It is however worth noting that the
Socialist Party of Ireland also accepted the membership of people who
belonged to the UIL, one example being Francis Sheehy-Skeffington.

Thomas Casey died on 6 February. It would seem necessary to reject
almost totally the account of this event in the life story. It is highly
suspect. The preceding chapter relates to events that took place in 1901
and 1906. The following two relate to 1908 and 1909. He tells of
Thomas's visit to Abercorn Road after a period of sickness. O'Casey is
wearing his kilt and has left the pipe band for a few minutes while he
returns home for a letter. Thomas suffers an attack of weakness and
persuades Sean to help him home. Sean then returns to the pipes
'thinking only of Ireland'. But Thomas's son appears, to summon him
back. In 1914 the boy would be twelve years old. Sean picks up a copy
of *Sinn Fein* to take to him, something highly improbable in February
1914 in view of its editor's support for the employers. When he reaches
Thomas's house he finds him dying. He brings the Rector to comfort
him. When he dies O'Casey arranges the funeral.

These events must have fallen in February 1914 during the darkest
days of the lock-out, when there was penury in the houses and treachery
in the air. Yet O'Casey says 'his mind held only thoughts of the concert
that was to raise funds to help Dr O'Hickey in his fight in Rome'. But
that was in 1909. Again he tells of helping Thomas from Abercorn Road

to Oxford Terrace. This would be no more than a hundred yards down Church Street. But what of O'Casey's legs? And as for arranging the funeral, the death was registered by Kathleen Dowd who lived at the same address, and Christopher Casey claimed to possess a receipt showing that the arrangements were not made by O'Casey. Certainly the funeral was advertised in the Irish Times, something O'Casey would surely not be responsible for at that time, and tradition has it that the Post Office band was in attendance. One guesses the arrangements were made by Thomas's Post Office Union.

It is hard to escape the conclusion that O'Casey ransacked past time for events with which to surround his brother's death. But why? Is it possible that in the midst of the struggle, in which the workers were harassed, battered and facing defeat, O'Casey was too occupied, worn-out or impoverished to do what he felt he should have done about his brother's sickness, and therefore lifted it out bodily from 1914 and planted it back in 1909? If so, it was *fear an tighe* again – the need to re-mould reality when it was too distasteful to dwell upon. This is of course sheer speculation. It serves merely to record the historian's 'hunch' that one story covers another.

Seamus MacGowan replied to O'Casey on 7 February. O'Casey's further response appeared on 21 February. In it he attacks *Irish Freedom* for exalting the memory of the Volunteers of 1782. This is to lead men to 'perpetuate the things they ought to destroy'. It is clear that he is for a workers' army or no army at all. He goes on: 'Not in the shouts of the deluded wage-slave Volunteer, but in the hunger-cry of the nation's poor is heard the voice of Ireland.' Of course there could be no arguing with a man who can within a few sentences contrast things and identify them. Seamus MacGowan replied again on 28 February and O'Casey on 7 March. Throughout the controversy not a word was mentioned of the specific historical conditions that had called the Volunteers into being, namely the counter-revolution in the north-east. One thought the workers should concentrate on their own interests. The other wished for a union of all classes to fight imperialism. Neither could see a sense in which both were possible. But what is most striking is that O'Casey had forgotten all about the wounds of Wolfe Tone, and could now write of 'ranting extreme nationalists'. On the surface it appeared that his position had been reversed in the space of a year.

The controversy did not please the IRB. His criticism of *Irish Freedom* was one thing; his attack on Pearse for allegedly using the blackleg trams was another. Deakin who, one imagines, must have been the centre of his circle, called to warn him. After one of these visits he realized there would be no more porridge.[7] O'Casey does not say when he finally broke with the IRB, but the best guess would be in the winter of 1914, perhaps when he began to associate himself with the Citizen Army.

The industrial war was drawing to a close. The English trade unions wound up their support fund on 10 February. Only the socialists now backed Dublin. Gradually section after section drifted back to work, signing what they had to sign, but many of them retained their membership secretly. O'Casey signed[8] and presumably got back his employment, though this is not the impression he gives in his letter to Horace Reynolds.[9] In that letter, written in 1938, he describes his breach with the IRB at a general meeting where he made criticisms and was howled down, Bulmer Hobson pulling a gun. This is not at all impossible. There are many instances on record where guns were pulled during meetings. But it was more likely to happen in 1914 than at any earlier period.

It was at this time, when the function of the Irish Citizen Army as a workers' defence form was exhausted, that O'Casey became especially identified with them. He seems to have been doing some secretarial work for them in February or March,[10] during which period open air meetings in support of the ICA were addressed by James Connolly and Micheál O Maolain.

It seems quite possible that O'Casey saw the reorganization of the Citizen Army as providing a competitor for the Volunteers. At a meeting held on 22 March he was elected secretary. Captain White became chairman. At this point the Citizen Army ceased to be a workers' defence force and became a national volunteer force distinguished from the Volunteers by a working-class membership and more advanced objectives. Connolly promoted the change. For one thing he suspected MacNeill and his associates. For another he wanted something to take Larkin's mind off the lockout, for the general secretary was close to a breakdown. The renewed efforts to recruit to the ICA were accompanied by much hostility to the Volunteers. Tom Clarke commented on O'Casey in a letter to John Devoy.[11] dated 14 May, and described him as a 'disgrunted fellow'.

The new constitution of the Citizen Army ran as follows:

1. That the first and last principle of the Irish Citizen Army is the avowal that the ownership of Ireland moral and material is vested in the people of Ireland.
2. That the Irish Citizen Army shall stand for the absolute unity of Irish nationhood, and shall support the rights and liberties of the democracies of all nations.
3. That one of its objects shall be to sink all differences of birth, property and creed under the common name of the Irish people.
4. That the Citizen Army shall be open to all who accept the principle of equal rights and opportunities for the Irish people.

According to R. M. Fox,[12] whose work was commissioned by the Citizen Army (old comrades) Association, these four clauses were drafted at a preliminary meeting and a fifth was added on the motion of Countess Markiewicz, namely that

5. Before being enrolled, every applicant must, if eligible, be a member of his trade union, such union to be recognized by the Irish Trade Union Congress.

O'Casey[13] states that the additional clause was inserted at the suggestion of Larkin, who invited somebody to propose it from the floor. It would seem difficult to decide between the two versions. O'Casey disliked the Countess and R. M. Fox was a writer somewhat lacking in scepticism.

According to the life story, O'Casey 'got a room, drafted a few sentences and made out a few rules'.[14] One of these is that appertaining to union membership. But clause three is absent. Did O'Casey forget it or suppress it? Clause three rules out the principle of an army devoted exclusively to proletarian objectives. And there is no reason to doubt that at the time O'Casey was a party to it.

One fact is inescapable. The preliminary meeting, which was attended by James Connolly, William Partridge, P. T. Daly and Captain White, proposed for the ICA a strictly *democratic* programme. If O'Casey is correct it was Larkin who at the public meeting introduced the working-class demand, which though broad enough in its way, was an implicit defiance of Martin Murphy.

The first four points all seem to bear Connolly's imprint. He was the most influential person present at the preliminary meeting, and would scarcely refrain from pressing his opinion in a matter so important as the constitution of a military force. The first and fourth foreshadow the proclamation of 1916 in the drafting of which Connolly was concerned. The second in its first part rejects the partition of Ireland against which Connolly was warning week by week. In its second it shows a usage of the words 'the democracy' which Connolly had inherited from his days in the Social Democratic Federation and remained characteristic of him. There was a touch of conscious erudition in Connolly, who always pronounced the word 'capitalist' with its accent on the second syllable. The third point insofar as it pledged the ICA to sink differences of *property*, was in complete contradiction with O'Casey's sentiments of 24 January. Had O'Casey now repudiated them? Most likely two sets of conceptions cohabited in the recesses of his brain and circumstances decided which came out to meet a given situation.

At the meeting on 22 March an Army council was elected. As well as O'Casey and Captain White, those elected included the Countess Markiewicz and Richard Brannigan. He was a Belfast man whose real name was Braithwaite. He was not an ordinary Orangeman as O'Casey implies, but had been a follower of Lindsay Crawford. These two became joint treasurers. Other members of the council were Larkin, P. T. Daly and the 'pacifist' Francis Sheehy-Skeffington who became vice-chairman. Larkin's interest ensured that no impetus was lost. There were regular parades at Croydon Park. Recruiting meetings were held in several places in Co. Dublin. The Dublin trades council gave official support. But there was little response from labour organizations in the provinces. Uniforms were ordered, and at the demonstration against the partition proposals, which were to be inserted in the Home Rule bill, the Citizen Army marched behind its own flag, the famous Plough and Stars, designed by Mr Megahy of the city art gallery.

Its design consisted of a stylized plough in dark red on a peacock blue field on which were superimposed the seven brightest stars of *Ursa major*, the Plough, Merak and Dubhe marking the coulter and Benetnasch the handle. The significance of the design has never been ascertained. One suggestion is that it symbolizes Lalor's famous demand 'Ireland her own from the sod to the sky'. If so it corresponds to the first clause of the Citizen Army constitution.

In the life story O'Casey claims that he objected on principle to the purchase of uniforms, preferring a force in civilian attire which could melt into its surroundings. This was in essence Hobson's defensive warfare. But the contemporary records do not confirm this. In his *History of the Irish Citizen Army* O'Casey refers favourably to the provision of uniforms. Reports survive advising the expediting of their supply and these reports bear O'Casey's name.[15] Frank Robbins moreover claims that he heard O'Casey speak in favour of uniforms at a public meeting. They were ordered from Arnott's. Their design is usually attributed to Boer influence, but a specimen in the National Museum was made (after 1916) from a uniform worn by an Australian soldier.[16]

Relations between the Citizen Army and the Volunteers reflected the complexities of the political situation. The Parliamentary Party represented medium to large native capital and the upper professional classes, with some landlord links. The biggest capitalists were of course unionists. It was still immeasurably the strongest national force. But it began to compromise itself rapidly once it began to nibble at the bait of partition. Each retreat it made aroused indignation among the genuinely nationalist elements who formed the overwhelming majority of the Volunteers. These in turn emphasized what was common to the Volunteers and the Citizen Army. The two organizations moved under the influence of forces which drove them together and forces which drove them apart.

O'Casey emphasized the repulsion. He wanted to debate with him when MacNeill pledged the Volunteers' allegiance to the expected Home Rule government. Countess Markiewicz and Captain White sought accommodation. The Captain indeed offered MacNeill affiliation provided the ICA was allowed to retain its separate identity. In his reply MacNeill is said to have referred to the ICA's recent confrontations with the police. White then wanted to denounce him. But his colleagues were not prepared to accept the implication that they desired affiliation. The Captain resigned and Larkin became chairman. This was in early May 1914. O'Casey claims that the membership rose to around 1,500. This seems a high figure, but it is possible.

In his heavily censored *History of the Irish Citizen Army*, published in 1919, O'Casey records the events of the summer of 1914 which led to his resignation from the ICA. He gives no dates, but the implicit chronology, like that of the life story, bristles with contradictions. O'Casey's claim to fame rests on his drama; it is fortunate that he was not compelled to rest it on his history. Thus in Chapter Five he describes how the ICA participated in the 1914 Bodenstown commemoration. This took place on 21 June. The memorial committee regard the workers as roughnecks and are hesitant about inviting them. They are swayed by Tom Clarke who has been a trade unionist himself. Larkin attends. O'Casey comments with evident nostalgia: 'It seemed that the fraternal association of Citizen Army soldiers and Volunteers around the grave at Bodenstown had started in the breasts of both organizations a desire for close communion in thought, principle and action.'

In Chapter Seven he remarks that the 'incidents that took place during the celebrated episode of the Howth gun-running had engendered a fellow feeling between the rank and file of both movements, that was very near akin to comradeship'. So there was sweetness and light on 26 July also. But in Chapter Eight comes the painful denouement: 'By their action in surrendering to the demand of the Parliamentary party for the inclusion of a large number of their nominees upon their provisional executive, the Volunteers made the cleavage of principle between themselves and the Citizen Army deeper than ever.' He adds that the 'new situation which had so unexpectedly been created caused a division in the council of the Citizen Army itself.' A special meeting of the Army council was called. O'Casey proposed a resolution demanding that Countess Markiewicz should discontinue her association with Cumann na mBan, the women's auxiliary of the Volunteers. The rejection of this resolution led to his resignation. He was too pure to mingle in such company.

But unfortunately for O'Casey's explanation the acceptance of

Redmond's nominees had taken place on 16 June, five days before the reconciliation at Bodenstown and over a month before the Howth gun-running. The circumstances were as follows: By 1 May the Volunteers had 75,000 members. The Parliamentarians were not reassured when MacNeill offered the fealty of an organization in which key positions were held by members of the IRB. They thought it wise to try to muzzle the tiger before going for a ride on it. They enmeshed MacNeill and Casement in a web of intrigue, then issued an ultimatum. They must be allowed to nominate sufficient additional members to the executive to give them a majority. Fearful of the consequences of internecine war with the Parliamentarians, mindful of a cargo of arms that was promised, and confident of the superior discipline of his organisation, Hobson persuaded his colleagues to agree to Redmond's request. Thereupon the wealthy classes, including bewhiskered brigadiers and portly lords, poured into the organization with their retinues.

One need not dispute that O'Casey resigned as a result of the defeat of his resolution critical of the Countess. The question is when. The assertion of a date in mid-June is destroyed by the reconciliation at Bodenstown. In the life story there is a very puzzling account of the Howth affair.[17] He explains that he has 'left the council of the Citizen Army', but on learning of the landing he hastens to Croydon Park, which is on the way to Howth, and finds that the Volunteers have been involved in a mêlée with the security forces. Some have taken refuge in Croydon Park with their rifles, while others have scattered the rifles. He superintends the collection of the discarded guns. It seems unlikely that he would have been accorded such authority if he had resigned from the council two months previously. And previous accounts agree that O'Casey did not merely resign from the council but severed his connection with the ICA.

On the evening of the gun-running, Scottish Borderers opened fire on an unarmed crowd at Bachelors' Walk in the centre of Dublin. There was intense public indignation and Volunteers and Citizen Army men joined together to form the guard of honour at the funeral of the victims. The reconciliation of the two organizations may not have been to O'Casey's liking, for his actions at Croydon Park were marked by a distinct hostility to the Volunteers.

Indeed, one suspects he may have been the man Colonel Maurice Moore, who visited Croydon Park in an attempt to recover guns the Citizen Army had taken, called 'my rude friend'.

War broke out on 4 August. There were immediate manoeuvres designed to convert the Volunteers into Territorials under the War Office. On 20 September Redmond offered them for service abroad. Five days later the original committee seized the premises, the Citizen

Army standing by to assist if necessary, and Redmond's supporters were expelled. O'Casey's demand had been met. For MacNeill was no longer one of them. And O'Casey says nothing about this.

The evidence seems to point to a date in September. There seems to have been no logical reason why he should then launch his attack on the Countess. It has been suggested that he took umbrage in a matter of utter triviality.[18] And in order to give his action the appearance of a political justification, he transplanted it back three months. It was *fear an tighe* once more. The desire to remould the past nearer to the heart's desire was a mark of the man and became a mark of the playwright.

O'Casey was never again at the centre of any political organization that was not itself peripheral and he seems to have done little public work for several years. The war went its well known course. The economic development of the country was hastened but according to a distorted pattern. Farmers waxed fat on the high food prices. Families which had not known a square meal in years lived royally on 'separation allowances'. At the same time employers deliberately dismissed workers in the hope of driving them to enlist. The Trade Union Congress, which since 1912 had included the Labour Party, denounced the war as an imperialist scramble for markets, colonies and spheres of influence. Implicit in this denunciation was the recognition of the decision of the International Socialist Congresses at Stuttgart, Copenhagen, and Basle to 'utilize the economic and political crisis created by the war to rouse the masses and thereby hasten the downfall of capitalist class rule'. In a dependent country like Ireland the first step could only be an attempt to overthrow English authority, for otherwise the Irish were condemned to move only when the English decided. There was no distinctly Irish initiative possible that did not begin with an effort for independence.

Connolly fully appreciated the international significance of his policy. 'Starting thus,' he wrote, soon after the outbreak of war, 'Ireland may yet set the torch to a European conflagration that will not burn out until the last throne and the last capitalist bond and debenture will be shrivelled on the funeral pyre of the last war lord.'

Larkin left for the USA at the end of October. Connolly became acting general secretary of the union. In his *History of the Irish Citizen Army* O'Casey writes that after the change of leadership the 'attitude of passive sympathy of the ICA to the Volunteers gradually gave place to active unity'. He admits that Connolly had never associated himself with any of the attacks that had been made on them. O'Casey explains this not by Connolly's interpretation of the decisions of the International, but by a 'revolutionary change' in Connolly's nature. He had 'stepped from the narrow by-way of Irish socialism on to the broad and crowded highway of Irish nationalism'. Indeed 'the high creed of Irish nationalism became his daily rosary, while the higher creed of international humanity that had long bubbled from his eloquent lips was silent for ever, and Irish Labour lost a leader'.[19]

In the life story he goes further. He writes: 'Connolly had left his union to give all he had to the Citizen Army.' He repeats the absurd canard, originated in the earlier work, that Connolly believed that capitalists would not destroy capitalist property – as if Connolly could possibly have believed it in the midst of the greatest war in history when millions of pounds worth of property was going up in smoke every week.

In the *History* he emphasizes Connolly's romanticism, expressing itself in bad patriotic verse and a sentimental play. And 'contrary to his life-long teaching of socialism, was the fixing on the frontage of Liberty Hall (of) a scroll on which was written "we serve neither king nor kaiser but Ireland."'[20] Perhaps the epigram which most succinctly expresses O'Casey's final grudging, half-admiring incomprehension of the men of 1916 is that in the autobiography.[21]

They had, he says 'a vanity that none could challenge, for it came from a group that was willing to sprinkle itself into oblivion that a change might come in the long-settled thought of the people. . . . Here was the purple heart of Ireland.' Amphetomine sulphate! The pep-pill, giver of false confidence in the performance of folly. An ugly metaphor and a bitter pun.

It was five years before Desmond Ryan's short biography of Connolly was published. It was not a satisfactory book. It had been the intention of W. P. Ryan to write the life of Connolly, but he gave the material he had so far collected to his son, when the strain of the civil war period had brought the young man to the verge of a nervous breakdown. And O'Casey had had a considerable start.

It remains, however, a historical fact that Connolly did not leave his union. Nor did he neglect it. His herculean labours in restoring its solvency after Larkin had gone to the USA deserves more than a little credit. During the winter of 1914–15 he was constantly engaged in wage campaigns. He negotiated increases for the dockers, dock labourers and stevedores, led a strike of labourers in railway goods yards, and carried through the delicate negotiations with the Registrar of Friendly Societies who had wished to remove the union from its list. He extended the organization of the union in the provinces. And he remained its acting general secretary to the day of his death.

The banner bearing the legend 'We serve neither king nor kaiser but Ireland' was raised at the time when the Irish Neutrality League was being promoted. There was quite a period during the Second World War when the United States acted on the principle that her services would be at the disposal of neither king nor fuhrer. If one of these had compelled her to fight against her will, perhaps her citizens might have had to be content with banners. But how this action contradicted Connolly's life-long teaching of socialism is beyond conjecture, unless what is meant by socialism is talking about socialism, while the practical tasks of the movement slide. Connolly's teaching, which anybody who doubts it can read for himself, is that the struggle for national independence and the struggle for socialism in Ireland *cannot be dissevered.*

Perhaps for Connolly's efforts at versification there is less to be said. Nobody has yet hit on the notion of comparing him with O'Casey as a playwright, though if anything can be thought of, somebody will usually be found foolish enough to do it. At the same time O'Casey was far more prolific in indifferent patriotic verse than Connolly, and was glad to have Connolly publish it in the *Workers' Republic.*

But there is not a scrap of evidence that O'Casey held these harsh views of Connolly while he was alive. The *Irish Worker* was suppressed at the end of 1914 and Connolly established his own press in the basement of Liberty Hall. That O'Casey contributed to the *Workers Republic* poems like 'The grand oul' dame Britannia' shows that he cannot have been far out of sympathy with Connolly at this time.

He explained to Horace Reynolds in the letter already mentioned that after 1913 he found it difficult to get regular employment. As a result his health deteriorated and he suffered a period of sickness. He underwent an operation for the removal of what he described as tubercular glands. In the letter he credits the ITGWU with securing him a bed in the hospital. In the life story he attributes it to Larkin. The time of the operation was August 1915. Larkin had been away for nine months. In several accounts of O'Casey's life at this period the tubercular glands are offered as the reason why he took no part in the Rising. It is certainly stated that the wound had not healed though nine months had gone by. But perhaps this explanation is not required.

First O'Casey was no longer a member of the IRB or the Irish Citizen Army. He was under no obligation to take part in the Rising. But even if he felt that he had a moral obligation, after all the sun-burstery of the past fifteen years, then a new difficulty presented itself. Michael returned to the colours in April 1915. While Isabella helped with some of the household chores, O'Casey was alone with his mother, who was in her late seventies. Again several times in the life story he indicates first that he was 'no hero' and second that he had a sense that he was capable of great achievements. He may have realised that while he was no pacifist, still he was a man of peace. If so, he was fortunate. A man should never try his courage further than he knows it will go.

He wandered the city during Easter week and saw what was

happening. The nearest the fighting came to him was a bullet in his
bedroom wall, an unpleasant night rounded up with others in St
Barnabas Church and being unceremoniously tipped into a grain store.

And yet, illogical as it might seem, not being out in 1916 affected him
far more deeply than being out in 1913. In *Inishfallen, Fare Thee
Well*[22] he says 'the Easter Rising had pulled down a dark curtain of
eternal separation between him and his best friends'. From the time he
left the Citizen Army his social life centred in the Laurence O'Toole's
club. He steadily moved toward literary pursuits.

NOTES

1. Arnold Wright, *Disturbed Dublin*.
2. Sean O'Casey, *Drums Under the Windows*, p. 305.
3. Na Fianna Eireann, republican 'boy scouts.'
4. See Martin and Byrne, *Eoin MacNeill, the Scholar Revolutionary*. F. X. Martin
   refers to the drilling of Orangemen in Dublin, and drilling against them in the
   Midlands. Whether he is justified in saying that the IRB was at this time preparing
   an armed revolt is less certain. Their policy still seems to have been founded on the
   probability of Home Rule which was threatened by the Orangemen.
5. Apart perhaps from Stephens, no man in Irish history attracted more unjust blame
   than Hobson. This was because of a gentlemanly *amour propre* which held him
   from defending himself in public. He told me that as chairman of the Dublin
   Centres Board he had the duty of informing O'Casey of the decision of the
   organization. He complained that O'Casey suppressed part of the policy decision,
   namely that individual members of the IRB were at liberty to assist the workers in
   any way open to them, as O'Casey himself was doing and as IRB men in the Fianna
   were doing. He emphasized, moreover, that his sympathies were entirely with the
   workers, so much so that Connolly invited him to join the staff of the union in
   Belfast. There is corroboration in the fact that during the Christmas recess he
   shared a Young Republican platform in Belfast with Ernest Blythe and Nora
   Connolly.
6. D. Krause, *Sean O'Casey, the Man and his Work*, p. 22.
7. O'Casey, 'In this Tent, the Republicans', *Drums under the Windows*, p. 347.
8. O'Casey told me 'I signed.'
9. D. Krause, *Letters*, p. 696.
10. In his letter to the *Irish Worker* of 7 March, O'Casey complains of having received
    no reply to requests for the use of Volunteer Halls for ICA drills. Either he was doing
    work for the ICA before 24 January, or he had appealed to the Volunteers for co-
    operation after launching a bitter attack on them, the conclusion from which was
    that the workers should stand alone. The latter would be in perfect accord with
    'ultra-left' psychology. I have seen it happen a hundred times.
11. In the letter which is printed in *John Devoy's Postbag*, Desmond Ryan (ed.), vol. II,
    p. 445 (omitted from index), Clarke refers to 'O'Casey'. Unless the anglicization
    was Ryan's, this must have been one of the earliest instances of the use of the form
    of his name under which O'Casey became famous. At this period he always

subscribed himself Seán O Cathasaigh. There is a possibility, however, that he was known to Tom Clarke and his colleagues as Casey, and that Ryan decided to affix the O for the sake of identification.

12. R. M. Fox, *History of the Irish Citizen Army*, p. 64.

13. O'Casey, *History of the Irish Citizen Army*, in Hogan, *Feathers from the Green Crow*, p. 193.

14. O'Casey, 'Under the Plough and the Stars', *Drums Under the Windows*, pp. 334–5.

15. Report of visit to Kingstown (Dun Laoire) 16 July 1914, signed Lt. J. Byrne and Seán O Cathasaigh, but written in Byrne's hand, among the O'Brien papers, National Library of Ireland. This letter disposes of any suggestion that O'Casey resigned his position on account of the crisis following the Volunteers' accepting Redmond's nominees.

16. I am obliged to Mr Padraig O Snodaigh for this information and for showing me the uniform in the National Museum. Whereas Arnotts' accounts have been preserved, the specifications do not seem to have survived. The uniforms to which the accounts refer were ordered in July 1914, and the accounts were presented in September.

17. O'Casey, 'Prepare, Everyone with Weapons', *Drums under the Windows*, p. 391.

18. O'Casey's sensitive and emotional nature resented every slight, real or imaginary, especially when he suspected a class bias. Many years ago Mrs Tom Johnson told me that the Countess borrowed the Citizen Army room in Liberty Hall for a rehearsal, and left a piano in it. O'Casey resented the implication that he should remove it, and left the premises in high dudgeon. She believed that this trifling incident provoked his dispute with the Countess.

19. Hogan, op. cit., p. 226.

20. ibid., p. 229.

21. O'Casey, 'The Bold Fenian Men', *Drums Under the Windows*, p. 401.

22. O'Casey, *Inishfallen, Fare Thee Well*, New York, 1949, p. 392.

[7]

AND NOW WHICH WAY?

The Irish revolution was supported by the majority of the people because it seemed to offer the only available protection from the counter-revolution launched in the north-east by the Unionists who were opposed to Liberal reforms. The first popular reaction was the establishment of the Irish Volunteers to protect the 'rights and liberties' of the people. Their progressive significance was grievously underestimated by O'Casey. The second was the Easter Rising, the narrower base of which has been attributed to faulty timing; it was anticipated that the war was likely to end soon and England's difficulty would cease. The third was the establishment of the new Sinn Fein, an amalgam of patriotic groups, and the victory of that party in the general election of 1918. The fourth was the Declaration of Independence and the effort of the revolutionary Dail Eireann to govern Ireland. The attempt to suppress this native government led to two-and-a-half years of urban and rural guerrilla warfare. The struggle was fought to a standstill in July 1921. The ceasefire was followed by an agreement in accordance with which each side continued to hold what it could. The consistent republicans who were unwilling to accept the resultant compromise, were defeated in a costly civil war. The revolution was thrust back from its high-water mark, but not to full ebb. It moved in a curve which mounted rapidly from April 1916 to March 1919, more slowly from then to May 1920, fell gradually until July 1921 and catastrophically from then to April 1923.

Its political content was the national liberation of a colonial people, but whilst this issue necessarily took precedence, the balance of class forces within the revolutionary camp, and in particular the strength and influence of the working class, decisively influenced events at every critical point.[1] The revolution provided O'Casey with subject matter for three plays, a satirical sketch and an allegory. It will therefore be necessary to ascertain, as far as possible, O'Casey's attitude to the events of its successive stages, while they were taking place, and then at the time he was writing about them. Finally the plays themselves can be discussed in the light of the results.

That the Irish people were not ready for the Rising, and did not understand it until after the executions, imprisonments and deportations, is generally known. To say this is in no sense to endorse the strictures of those who wish to represent it as a 'terrible mistake'.

War has been defined as a history of mistakes. Everybody who understands Irish history knows that the Rising was an inevitable battle in an inevitable war. If its purpose was, as O'Casey put it, to change the long-settled thought of the people, then it must be credited with outstanding success. But the purpose of those who led it was not to 'sprinkle themselves into oblivion' for this purpose. It was to make an attempt to drive the English out of Ireland while they were engaged elsewhere and, failing this, to register Ireland's belligerency on her own behalf at a time when death and destruction could not be avoided. The first might possibly have been achieved but for the countermand by MacNeill, which led to the postponement of the Rising by a day, and paralysed the Volunteers in the rural areas and in such important centres as Cork City. At the time of the Rising the British Cabinet were discussing a negotiated peace and there is no reason to exclude an Irish settlement from the possible results. The Rising could have stopped the war and saved millions of lives, just as a year later the Russian Revolution did in fact stop the war, despite all efforts to continue it. This was the conception Connolly had; it was in accordance with the decisions of the International.

Naturally when all this was at stake there was wild hysteria in England. Nevertheless the Prime Minister was forced to admit that the insurgents 'fought bravely and did not resort to outrage'. On that very day the *Daily News*, the journalists' paper, published a letter from George Bernard Shaw. In it he warned the English ruling class that 'the shot Irishmen will take their places beside Emmet and the Manchester Martyrs . . . and nothing in heaven or earth can prevent it.' He concluded with the fine words, 'I remain an Irishman and I am bound to contradict any implication that I can regard as a traitor any Irishman taken in a fight for Irish independence against the British government, which was a fair fight in everything except the enormous odds my countrymen had to face.'

Shaw had known none of the leading rebels personally. O'Casey knew most of them. His feelings must have been sharper if more complex. We can of course dismiss the absurd picture of the future dramatist standing coldly aloof on his socialist principles, disdaining to notice a middle-class rebellion. This is an invention of the literary critics. They cannot understand that O'Casey remained an Irishman too. Dr Krause publishes his two kindly letters to James Shields, a member of the Citizen Army and the O'Toole's club, who was interned in Fron Goch concentration camp in Merioneth.[2] These were sent in June and July 1916. They refer to the departed men in the most cordial terms and mention collections being made for their dependents. To know that fifteen men he had known and worked with had been summarily shot, without the preliminary of a proper trial, must have been shattering to O'Casey.

At this time there appears a new note in O'Casey's writing, a note of fatigue and disillusionment. For the first time the observer and the commentator predominate over the enthusiast and man of action. 'Ah! Fill the cup, what boots it to repeat how time is slipping underneath our feet.'[3] In this quotation from Fitzgerald comes the first implication of agnosticism. The letter which contains it is signed 'poor old Seán O Cathasaigh'.[4]

O'Casey says very little about his reactions to the Rising and its immediate aftermath. It was always assumed in republican circles that his subsequent political attitudes were strongly determined by his failure to participate. This was the frost that attacked the flower. There was uncertainty for two or three years more, and then came the evidence of the gradual building up of a new position, as would happen if injured self-esteem slowly healed.

Something of this appears in his treatment of the prisoners who on their return to Ireland were given a triumph Caesar would have envied. O'Casey long remembered his own non-combatant status. '"Was he out in Easter Week?" became the touchstone of Irish life.' When the youngest 1916 men expressed an opinion, veterans of former wars must remain silent. This would not suit O'Casey. As he approached forty and fresh youngsters gained laurels, the old rebel found himself increasingly out-rebelled and no longer a political mentor. The result was to drive him to his true métier. He wrote sketches, poems and ballads, and began to act again. Literature became his craft and gradually his main occupation. But its subject matter remained for the most part politics into which he still made periodical incursions.

The Rising had momentous political consequences, though not entirely those foreseen by its leaders. No man who dies for his beliefs can be sure that others will live for them. The Irish TUC met at Sligo in August 1916. If it had endorsed Connolly's stand, doubtless Labour could have stood at the head of nationalist Ireland. But were its leaders adapted to such a role? And what if the English trade unions and those based for the most part in the anti-nationalist north-east were to secede? This fear dominated the thinking of Tom Johnson and his colleagues who had brought some kind of organisation into being from the ruins of Liberty Hall. In effect the movement decided to preserve its unity by confining itself to economic matters. The result was to reap to the full the harvest of trade union members whose numbers shot up dramatically in the next two years. But where were these to look for their politics? The Redmondite party was discredited and in the absence of a united anti-imperialist alternative, they flocked into the only political organization whose name they knew. The British propagandists had called the Rising the Sinn Fein rebellion. Thousands joined Griffith's organization though it had taken no part in the Rising. Between the Plunkett convention of April 1917 and the Unity convention of October of the same year, a new organization was brought into being, though it adopted the old title Sinn Fein.[5]

O'Casey from time to time felt he had something to say on current affairs and a letter from his pen was published in the Dublin *Saturday Post* on 22 September 1917.[6] In it he recognizes the fact that workers participate in organizations outside the labour movement. He refers specifically to Sinn Fein and the Orange Order. He explains this not by the existence of a national liberation movement to which it was necessary to have an attitude, but by the fact that humanity has many interests and many pleasures 'besides a loaf of bread and a few fish'. His suggestion is that 'if the workers must or will attach themselves to organizations other than Labour, then let their activities in these movements be such as to make them recognize and submit to the claims and aspirations of the working class'. By means of lectures and pamphlets, 'we must teach the workers that they are the prop of all things'. Later he makes it clear that if this propaganda embarrasses Sinn Fein, so much the worse for Sinn Fein.

He thus shows himself strongly affected by the economism of the Sligo TUC. Elsewhere in the same letter he echoes the thinking of the 1917 TUC held at Derry. Faced with the obvious political progress of Sinn Fein, the leaders, still expecting Home Rule from England, decided that Labour had no political role until after national independence was won, and that then the class war would rage furiously. O'Casey made this theory his own and often returned to it. But while advising workers in national organisations to conduct working-class propaganda which would possibly influence the leaders, he does not support official participation in national organizations, and criticizes William O'Brien and his colleagues for taking part in the work of the Plunkett convention, when they had been delegated to 'explain the hopes and ideals of Labour and then retire'.

O'Casey was thus as far as ever from understanding the relation between proletarian and democratic issues. He had accepted without reflection that the workers functioned as workers solely in the economic sphere. He did not understand Connolly's position that national independence is an essential demand of the labour movement. Consequently when he was shocked into taking up the cudgels on behalf of the nation, he reacted like the most naive Sinn Feiner.

Three days after the letter was published in the *Saturday Post*, Thomas Ashe died on hunger strike after forcible feeding. Ashe, whom

O'Casey knew as a piper, hurler, Gaelic Leaguer and republican, had like most IRB men, supported the workers in 1913. He had also led the only wholly successful operation in the Rising of 1916. He was at the time of his death the head-centre of the organization and thus regarded as the president of the Republic. Whether O'Casey knew this or would now have been influenced by it cannot be said. What is certain is that he was grieved and shocked beyond measure. He wrote two similar pamphlets in memory of Ashe, and these were published by Fergus O'Connor, formerly an internee at Fron Goch. The tone of the pamphlets is hotly and demonstratively nationalist. It is as if the clock had been turned back five years.

The Sacrifice of Thomas Ashe contains O'Casey's earliest comment on the Rising. Granted the emotion under which it must have been written, it is as fair a sample of sunburstery as was ever penned. Of the Rising he says 'men fought and fell with the glow of burning buildings on their faces, and the glow of enthusiasm lighting their hearts in the effort to establish an Irish Republic'. Ashe was sentenced to two years' imprisonment, as O'Casey apostrophises him 'because your have a free soul, and your soul is Irish'. He concludes: 'Labour has lost a champion, Irish Ireland has lost a son; militant Ireland has lost a soldier; but all have gained a mighty and enduring inspiration.' So much for the Plough and the Stars.

On 25 November there was a concert at the Olympia Theatre in aid òf necessitous school children, in which O'Casey functioned in multiple capacities. It was held under the auspices of the St Laurence O'Toole club and was no doubt organized with a view to Christmas. O'Casey made the arrangements. He sang his satirical ballad against the followers of Redmond, 'The constitutional movement must go on'. And he played the part of a romantic English tourist desirous of finding some Irish rebels, who had some found for him.[7] It has been remarked that though he practised the English accent hard, he proved unsuited to the part. His voice proclaimed his birthplace unmistakably. From the advertisements in the printed programme, which includes one for O'Casey's memorial to Ashe as well as from the items performed, the strong Sinn Fein tendency of the gathering is obvious.[8]

On New Year's Day 1918, Isabella died of influenza. In the life story O'Casey records the crushing effect of this event upon his mother.[9] In a letter to Fergus O'Connor he explains that now that Isabella is not able to look after her, much of his time is occupied with household chores. One inclines to the speculation that 1918 was the period in which O'Casey, compelled to rely on Susan's old age pension, indignantly refused employment that was found for him. It is inconceivable that at a time of relatively plentiful employment an able man would reject work and live in poverty, unless there was some compelling reason. During this period he fed O'Connor with songs and prose matter, for which he received modest but very acceptable payment. Moreover he was becoming a businessman, able to bargain for his price, and the prospect of making a living from literature was beginning to attract him.[10]

In January 1918 at O'Connor's request, O'Casey wrote an electioneering song in favour of Sinn Fein, presumably for the municipal elections. It was entitled 'Hurrah for Ireland and Sinn Fein'. It begins 'Ireland's hour is striking now, Sinn Fein's hand is at the plough'. It is 'romantic nationalism'.

Gradually O'Casey grew more ambitious. He persuaded O'Connor to issue a collection of his ballads under the title *Songs of the Wren*, that is to say rebel songs. He suggested the republication of the poems of John Boyle O'Reilly, at the same time suggesting that his future publications should appear under the name of Shaun O'Casey instead of Seán O Cathasaigh. In March he wrote to O'Connor about the songs of James Connolly. The Socialist Party of Ireland had republished the ballads of their dead leader and O'Casey wished O'Connor to distribute them. At this time O'Casey made no disparagement of Connolly's verse.

In the early part of 1918 O'Casey seems to have recollected his juncture with Labour and it is possible that he may have attended a meeting of the Socialist Party of Ireland.[11] He contributed articles to *Irish Opinion* which had been taken over by the Irish TUC in December 1917, and was now being published under the editorship of A. E. Malone and the general direction of Thomas Johnson. In January 1918 he contributed a love song. In March he addressed himself to the restoration of the Irish language. His proposal had a markedly Sinn Fein tinge. It was to 'elect an all-Ireland executive, representative of the Gaelic League, Labour, the teachers, with men of science, art and literature, to resolve upon all educational problems, and frankly to make the continuance of the "National Board" impossible.' Finally in June he welcomed the spread of Labour ideas in the teaching profession.[12]

It seems likely that it was during this period when O'Casey was taking an interest in educational questions that he began to try his hand at serious drama. The result was *The Frost in the Flower*, submitted to the Abbey the following year.

The text has not been preserved but the subject matter is known. A young teacher applies for a higher appointment which to his surprise he is offered. Lacking confidence in his own abilities he declines it. The central figure is based upon Frank Cahill, with whom O'Casey regularly took an evening walk and at whose house he frequently dined.[13]

Coston[14] suggests that this play was first written between 1910 and

1912. This is very doubtful. It is one of the judgements that have arisen because of the absence of an O'Casey chronology. It is generally accepted that Cahill was deeply upset and, out of consideration for him, the club decided not to produce it. It seems wiser to assign the play to the period when O'Casey was beginning to have differences with Cahill and to draw away from the O'Tooles, that is to say to 1918–1919.

Michael Casey was again discharged from the army and returned home in September 1918. Two months later Susan died. This was a devastating blow. O'Casey was the only one of her children who was with her all the time. According to Margulies he sat up all night weeping uncontrollably. But there is much exaggeration and misstatement in the autobiography. For one thing he was not alone. And it was Michael who registered the death. That the undertaker's driver should take it upon himself to refuse to move the corpse before the funeral expenses had been placed in his hands is improbable. There may of course have been some other unpleasantness. In *The Star Turns Red*, written in 1937–39, one of the more unpleasant characters is an undertaker's debt collector. Undertakers were accustomed to giving credit to poor clients. But it so happens that Michael arranged the funeral. The brother was spirited away in the interests of drama.

And the story of the cheque for £15 that nobody would cash while the hearse waited, is probably borrowed from another occasion, if it is not sheer invention. It is described as payment for the *History of the Irish Citizen Army*, due on the day the book was published. But the work did not see the light of day until July 1919. One dare even doubt the story of the breaking of 'sprigs' of musk, fuchsia and geranium, to place on the coffin as symbols of gold, frankincense and myrrh. These plants do not usually flower in November, even indoors. It is doubtful whether the fuchsia would have leaves on it. And for some reason which botanists have been able only to speculate upon, musk lost its distinctive perfume simultaneously throughout the world around the year 1880, and would hardly be cultivated as a house-plant in 1918.

The 'khaki' election took place on 14 December. O'Casey once more wrote election ballads for Sinn Fein. In this election Labour offered no candidates. They had been told that Sinn Fein would oppose every candidate who did not sign a comprehensive undertaking to the effect that under no circumstances would he take his seat in the Westminster Parliament. But this was the last time O'Casey helped Sinn Fein. Moreover, he lived in expectation of a bitter struggle between Sinn Fein and the Labour Party, which he believed inevitable. He had to this extent come round to Euchan's position.

After the death of his mother, O'Casey's emotional life centred on the young woman he calls Nora Creena in the life story. She was Maire

Keating, daughter of a retired policeman, a member of a devoutly Catholic family living in First Avenue, off Seville Place. He had met her in 1917 when she had a part in a play performed by the O'Toole's drama club. The members of the Royal Irish Constabulary were renowned for educating their children. Maire Keating was twenty-two, a teacher and a pianist. She and O'Casey became friendly in 1918 and throughout 1919 and 1920 they used to meet six times a week, O'Casey grudging her the seventh day. To her he poured out his enthusiasms, Keats, Shelley, Milton, Dumas, Thackeray and above all Shaw. He wrote her love poems which at least had the merit of scanning.

For a time there seemed a possibility that he might change his religion. The parish priest at least thought so and tried his hand without success. The girl's parents entertained no such expectations and were completely opposed to the liaison from the start. O'Casey was never allowed in their home, and she was involved at one time in subterfuge, at another in recrimination. The religious barrier was absolute and the financial barrier helped to make it so. It may be that O'Casey's revived anti-Catholicism dates from the period of this unsuccessful courtship, the only one recorded before he met his wife.

For two years O'Casey lived alone with his brother at Abercorn Road. Their relations steadily deteriorated. Neighbours remembered hearing their quarrels. O'Casey charges his brother with 'coarseness, vulgarity and vicious meanness', the products of excessive drinking. From the life story it would appear that Michael's counter-charges were effeminacy and egotism. He professed contempt for the aspiring writer, perhaps finding it hard to acknowledge genius that did not fill the larder. There was of course courage and some ruthlessness in O'Casey's course of action. But Michael could not be expected to applaud it.

Krause prints no letters written by O'Casey in 1919. There is however a reply from Bernard Shaw to whom he had sent the manuscript of a small book called *Three Shouts on a Hill*. It consisted of essays on labour, nationalism and the Irish language. According to Krause they were based on earlier work and were possibly the product of reworking rather than rethinking. In his reply Shaw asks an incisive question, 'Why do you not come out definitely on the side of Labour and the English language?' He adds that the 'national question' is a nuisance and a bore. But he is realistic enough to appreciate that it will insist on being settled first. From Shaw's reply it is clear that O'Casey remained confused about the relations between the causes he had espoused.

He was in this unclear position when he wrote his *History of the Irish Citizen Army*. The book was issued in July 1919 and some of its references to past history have already been noticed. It is as confused as it is inaccurate. Its sole merit is that the writer is trying to find his way. Four paragraphs from the preface will serve as an example:

It is impossible yet to say whether the events of Easter 1916 will achieve a democratisation of Irish nationalism, or whether the latter influence will deflect itself towards the broader issues of the Irish Labour movement.

Present events point to the probability that Jim Connolly's earlier ideals will be covered by the ever-rising tide of a militant nationalism, though it also seems certain that the younger and more progressive elements of national thought will endeavour to associate with national advancement the upliftment of the Irish working class.

It appears certain that nationalism has gained a great deal and lost a little by its Union with Labour in the insurrection of Easter week and that Labour has lost much and achieved something by its avowal of the national aspirations of the Irish nation.

We can only hope that nationalism, in its new found strength, will not remain deaf to the claims of Irish Labour for a foremost place in the National Being, and that the sacrifice of Irish Labour through the Citizen Army may not be forgotten by those who are working towards the regeneration of our common country.

This is not the writing of a man who knows his own mind. Every concrete thing is presented as an abstraction. George Russell's pamphlet *The National Being* had been reissued in 1918, and perhaps at that time O'Casey had not the contempt for the economist, journalist and mystic that he later professed. There was much vague writing at this period, before the realities of the revolution had made themselves plain in action.

What this preface seems to show, however, is disappointment with Dail Eireann. The 'Democratic Programme' of Dail Eireann had made promises. The needs of the workers had been ignored. A wave of intense Labour agitation swept the country, sometimes in pursuit of economic objectives, at other times, as in the case of the 'Limerick Soviet' for purposes connected with the national struggle. Cathal Brugha first and De Valera after him failed to see how this mass activity could be harnessed to the purposes of national liberation. As with the Redmondites and Larkin, so with the Griffith supporters and Irish Labour. The only escape from this position was that Labour should be at the head of the national movement. But Labour, for whatever reasons – good, bad or indifferent, according to the point of view from which they are examined – had declined the leadership when it was available, not in April 1916 but in August.

In the postscript O'Casey writes, 'In Sheehy-Skeffington and not in Connolly fell the first martyr to Irish socialism, for he linked Ireland not only with the little nations struggling for self-expression, but with the world's humanity struggling for a higher life.' What had happened was that Sheehy-Skeffington, it is believed with a view to bringing about a cease-fire, presented himself as an easy prisoner to an officer, Bowen-Colthurst, who murdered him in a fit of anti-Irish hysteria. So what is the meaning of O'Casey's obscure statement? It is that Sheehy-Skeffington was a better 'socialist' for attempting to halt the fighting and being murdered for it, than Connolly, who led the fighting and was murdered for that. Whether such a proposition could be true or not depends on what the fighting was about. The fighting was about national independence. Connolly could be regarded as a martyr for socialism only in the indirect sense that national independence is necessary for the achievement of socialism. Sheehy-Skeffington could only be a martyr to socialism if the correct way to achieve socialism was to halt the struggle for national independence. It would be more sensible to leave socialism out of it. It did not enter into the case.

O'Casey considered Sheehy-Skeffington the 'living antithesis of the Easter Insurrection', which he had clearly decided to repudiate. He was the 'purified soul of revolt against not only one nation's injustice to another, but he was also the soul of revolt against man's humanity to man'. Here we see the ultra-leftist unconcerned with the actual wrongs that people are trying to right, because the action taken to right them does not remove all other wrongs as well.

But was not the Easter Rising a revolt against man's inhumanity to man? What but inhumanity was ever seen in the whole of English policy in Ireland? It is possible of course that when he caught sight of a possible purple passage O'Casey's pen ran away with him. As for his prophecy that the teachings of Sheehy-Skeffington would have a greater influence than those of Connolly, time has already told. Both Connolly and Sheehy-Skeffington were the victims of imperialism and their deaths were a sad loss to the Irish people.

It should be mentioned in passing that O'Casey's attitude to the Easter Rising may have been influenced by Larkin. In 1917 he claimed to have sent Connolly a message instructing him not to commit the Citizen Army to the Rising. Both at the time and in 1918 he applauded its heroism in unequivocal terms. But his later correspondence constantly repeats the opinion that Labour has been pushed out of its rightful place by Sinn Fein. This line of thought would become known to O'Casey once Delia Larkin returned to Dublin, if it had not already been communicated by Micheal O Maolain and P. T. Daly.

It has been necessary to stress that O'Casey blamed Connolly for abandoning internationalism at a time when he was trying to put into effect the precise decisions of the International. This has not been done mainly to justify Connolly. It has been necessary in order to identify the special contradiction in O'Casey's thought, and to show how it arose from actual issues of Irish history and politics. His inability to think his way through to clarity may have a bearing on his greatness as a dramatist. Thinking is done by means of words. It aims always at precision. But parallel with science there is art. Since art is essentially the representation of things, it can express their complexity and contradictoriness with an immediacy impossible to science. If O'Casey had been able to solve the intellectual conundrum of the Irish revolution, something which only Connolly was in fact able to do, or had the mental equipment to do, O'Casey might have remained an enthusiast and man of action. He could not do so. But he was gifted with the ability to set before us pictures in which the unresolved issues are embodied and move before our eyes. He therefore contributes to a solution although he does not provide one. Nor is it his business to provide one.

NOTES

1. For a detailed analysis of this question see my *Liam Mellows and the Irish Revolution*.
2. D. Krause, *Letters*, p. 58.
3. ibid., p. 60.
4. 'High Road and Low Road', *Inishfallen, Fare Thee Well*, p. 1.
5. See Dorothy Macardle, *The Irish Republic*, Gollancz, pp. 241 et seq.
6. D. Krause, *Letters*, p. 62.
7. All such tourists were not actuated by romanticism. Davitt tells of a 'Mrs T' who invited to a champagne dinner at the Gresham Hotel practical jokers whom she believed to be preparing to 'move the adjournment of the House of Commons' *à la* Guy Fawkes. This was in 1884. In 1920 a similarly inquisitive individual was introduced not, as he expected and believed, to Mr Michael Collins and his bold bad men, but to the gentlemen of the Dublin press who drew him out and made a fool of him. So art imitates life, and life art.
8. D. Krause, *Letters*, p. 65.
9. 'House of the living', *Drums Under the Windows*, p. 114.
10. D. Krause, *Letters*, pp. 67–86. According to Gabriel Fallon, O'Casey and Frank Cahill saw Gogarty's *Blight* at the Abbey. On the way home Cahill said: 'You could write a better play than that.' *Blight* was performed in December 1917. Dr Krause, who presumably also had it from O'Casey, says the occasion was that of O'Casey's first visit to the Abbey (on the proceeds of the Ashe pamphlet?) and that he was accompanied by Mr and Mrs Kelly. He does not mention Cahill, who, incidentally, is not referrred to in the autobiography.
11. The party is given the title Irish Socialist Party in O'Casey's letter to Fergus O'Connor (D. Krause, *Letters*, p. 79.) I have a strong recollection, fortified by a note made at the time, that O'Casey told me that he was once a member of the Irish

Socialist Party. But the correct name of the party was Socialist Party of Ireland. O'Casey uses this title in 'High Road and Low Road', *Inishfallen, Fare Thee Well*, p. 8. But as usual in the autobiography the chronology is in confusion. One receives the impression that O'Casey's participation in the concert was in some way connected with his socialist activities. But it bears all the marks of a church charity with strong Sinn Fein sympathy. Senator Roderick Connolly, whose authority is not in doubt, told me that he had no recollection of O'Casey's ever having been a member. I am inclined to credit a loose association perhaps as late as 1919. But of course he may have attended meetings from time to time.

12. R. Hogan, reprints the song and the three 1918 articles mentioned in Krause (*Letters*, p. 70) in 'Feathers from the Green Crow', pp. 141, 35, 39 and 7. Krause (ibid.) mentions three other articles published in the same paper (*Irish Opinion*) in 1916 and 1917. These are not from O'Casey's pen, and one presumes that Hogan failed to print them because he felt doubtful of them. They are signed S O'C, but the writer was a Sean Conlon, a Cork man prominent in Gaelic League circles and a friend of Con O'Lyhane.

13. Margulies, *Early Life of Sean O'Casey*, p. 63.

14. R. Ayling (ed.) *Sean O'Casey, Modern Judgements*, Coston, 'Prelude to Play Writing', p. 5.

[8]

COUNTER-REVOLUTION

The character of the popular movement that developed in Ireland in response to the war and the war economy has already been described. The experienced bourgeois politicians of the Parliamentary Party were excluded from it. There were three great mass organisations, the Sinn Fein party, the Volunteers and the trade unions. In all of them new men had come to the fore. In Sinn Fein and the Volunteers the leaders were men of position if not of substance. The rank and file tended to be workers or modest farmers. The trade union movement, while electing its own leaders and retaining some experienced figures from the past, confined its daily operations to economic questions and acted politically only in consort with the national movement. In the secondary role of Labour we have already traced a source of weakness.

The revolutionary assembly which declared the independence of Ireland was not representative of all classes. The few surviving Redmondites did not attend. And while the workers were 'represented' in the formal sense, they were not represented from their own numbers. They did not represent themselves. Labour had shrunk from contesting the election, hesitant about giving a commitment to have done with Westminster for ever. And it is worth observing that during the period of dual power which followed the declaration of independence, the trade unions continued to do business with the organs of Westminster, while simultaneously supporting the Dail. In doing so they recognised an actual balance of forces, but within this they were not seen pushing forward the transfer of all power to Dail Eireann, or attempting to determine its policy. The political spokesmen for the nation were thus neither capitalists nor manual workers, but belonged to intermediate strata, barely describable as forming a class, who had no cohesive economic strength of their own, but relied on the consent of the main classes who though less numerous were strongly organised.

This small bourgeoisie which comprised the greater part of Irish society was extremely varied. There were small and medium farmers. The interests of the latter abutted on those of the ranchers and cattle-dealers, those of the former on the interests of land workers. There were shopkeepers close to the local people and merchants with more extended connections; self-employed artisans, maybe a couple of men running a forge who shod their neighbours' horses, and small manufacturers supplying a more extended market. There were school teachers and lawyers, curates and parish priests, clerks and accountants, nurses and doctors. It was as if the antagonisms and distinctions that divided the main classes held the small bourgeoisie together, as mutually repellant electrons stabilize atoms and make solid matter possible. The members of each profession strove to improve their position within the station of life to which they had been called, simultaneously depending on and competing with those around them.

But whatever the internal tensions, there was one over-riding external resistance, that against English rule, whether typified by the soldiery, the Castle bureaucrats, the taxmen, or the economic institutions that had been implanted or preserved. At the end of the war these had grown peculiarly oppressive, as the development of the south and west was deliberately sacrificed to the policy of building up a Vendée in the north-east.

From this it should be clear how pointless it is to bewail 'nationalism' as if it were some species of unholy spirit inducing pentecostal dementia. Those people had burdens on their backs and wanted them off. The landlords and some of the capitalists, especially those of the favoured north-east, were privileged and were therefore not national. But the capitalists in general suffered disadvantages which they sought to have removed through reform. When their own party lost its mass following they supported the Dail but tried to prevent its going too far. The working class constantly found its industrial interests frustrated by the machinery of the British state. They therefore supported the Dail in hope of better things. It was thus not possible to disentangle the social and national aspects of the struggle. They were distinguishable but not separable.

Given the social composition of Dail Eireann one would expect within it conflicting tendencies, not necessarily immediately expressed by a division into parties. One would also expect the bourgeois orientation to predominate. Indeed the failure of Labour to secure direct representation was at once an expression and a confirmation of that position. These were the contradictions over which O'Casey racked his brains. The situation can be seen with crystal clarity half a century later when all the historical material has been sifted and assessed. But events when they are happening are quite a different thing from events under the historian's scalpel.

The consequences of Labour's exclusion were shown during the first month. The great Belfast engineering strike was allowed to pass without a word of support from the revolutionary assembly. It may not be too much to say that the unity of Ireland was lost in those fateful days. But it would not even enter the head of the small manufacturer, Cathal

Brugha, who headed the Dail, that a strike could possibly be more than an annoying interruption of the normal course of business, like a gas leak or a thunderstorm. The golden opportunity to unite the common people was let slip. The Dail preferred to rely on forces outside Ireland. For a few months hopes were rested on the peace conference. Then President De Valera left for the United States to solicit the good offices of England's principal imperialist rival. The strongest potential ally, the working class of Britain, received comparatively little attention, for the same reason that the Belfast strike was ignored – an underestimation of the power of the working class.

The dominant tendency in its extremest form was personified in Arthur Griffith. He had been for many years an advocate of the restoration by consent of the co-ordinate monarchy of 1782. Many of his colleagues were republicans and members of the IRB, though not De Valera and Brugha, who had left it. The IRB was anxious for something better than Grattan's Parliament, but for the time being Dail Eireann had no connection with England. Time enough to object when a connection was suggested. Some of them toyed with the idea of a second insurrection that would transfer all power to the Dail. But it was Arthur Griffith's Sinn Fein policy that found favour. It was not, however, adequate to the needs of defence against the British state. It was speedily supplemented by a form of what Hobson had called 'defensive warfare'. This began spontaneously but was later recognized by the Dail. O'Casey took no part in it despite his retrospective recommendations in the life story. In short, the Dail attempted to administer the country and to treat the British state as an interloper. Departments of trade, finance, local government and defence were established. To finance operations republican bonds, redeemable after the international recognition of the Republic, were issued. And where these operations tangled with the British state, trouble began.

The English authorities were slow to move. They watched uneasily while an immense wave of labour unrest swept the country. The workers would have followed any responsible revolutionary lead. In Limerick, following the rescue of an arrested Volunteer, the military tried to impose a system of permits to control entrance and egress. In the general strike that followed, the workers seized the city and administered it, issuing their own currency. It was not until September that the English government moved. Then Dail Eireann was proclaimed. Newspapers which advertised republican bonds were suppressed. Troops poured in as one county after another was placed under martial law. But the Dail committees met in secret. Official bodies steadily transferred their allegiance and the sporadic raids for arms gradually assumed the proportions of a guerrilla war, which intensified alongside the repression that had provoked it.[1]

The Government of Ireland Bill providing for the establishment of two parallel subordinate administrations in Ireland, one of six, the other of twenty-six counties was introduced in Parliament on 22 December 1919. Preparations for partition were begun at once. But the prospect seemed so unthinkable that warning was not speedily taken. Arrests, suppression of newspapers, raids for republican bonds occupied everyday attention. Justices of the Peace resigned in increasing numbers. The Royal Irish Constabulary became disaffected, some of them undertaking intelligence work for Dail Eireann. The Castle authorities introduced military permits for motor vehicles. The Drivers' and Mechanics' Union maintained a strike for three months. After a sweeping victory for Sinn Fein in the municipal elections of January 1920, the English authorities began arresting and deporting 'persons suspected of complicity in outrage'.

When it became known that the result was merely to drive more people into the camp of Sinn Fein, there was a new departure. The 'black-and-tans', a piebald riff-raff from the scum of English society, were brought in as special constables. They were assisted by better educated storm-troopers known as auxiliaries. The brutalities and atrocities of these creatures live in memory today. Like the Drogheda massacre, the pitch-capping in 1798, and the so-called famine, their crimes will never be forgotten. Their appearance was a declaration of war against the common people. The Volunteers resisted. Wanted men were sheltered. Shop-keepers provided credit. The whole of nationalist Ireland was held together by bonds of common danger.

But social questions pushed their way forward. In the spring of 1920 a movement for agrarian revolution swept the west of Ireland. The postwar boom was ending. If men could not get land they must emigrate. They began to seize and break up the farms of landlords and ranchers. These in their turn flocked to Dublin, not to the British authorities whose writ could no longer be enforced, but to Dail Eireann. They begged the revolutionary assembly to halt the revolution. Dail Eireann complied. A system of arbitration courts was instituted. There were occasions when Volunteers arrested and imprisoned their own neighbours. Dail Eireann was taking over some of the less savoury functions of the British state and becoming that much more acceptable to the propertied classes. To Arthur Griffith this was statesmanship. But the west opted out of the revolution.

Then the north was dragooned out of it. Incited by the old jury-packer, Edward Carson, Orange hoodlums drove out of the Belfast shipyards, not only the Catholics, but everybody who objected to the savagery of their onslaught. It must not be imagined that this was a movement of the whole Protestant community. The hoodlums held red-hot rivets before men's eyes, and to save their sight they were compelled

to curse the Pope. After the expulsions from the shipyard a general
terror was unleashed on the Catholics of the north. In the first four days
nineteen were killed and four injured. The British government took no
action. This prepared the way for partition.

The situation in August 1920 was described by Thomas Farren in his
presidential address to the Irish Trade Union Congress:

The country has been turned into an armed camp. The soldiers of a foreign
power are billeted all over the country with all the paraphernalia of war. The
country is being governed by naked force, and in the attempt to carry on this
system of government, England's army of occupation has truly lived up to the
reputation it has made for its brutal treatment of the people they are trying to
keep in subjection. During the past four years our people have suffered
martyrdom at the hands of the greatest tyrant in history, a tyrant whose empire
was built on the murder and spoliation of every unfortunate people who
possessed anything worth stealing and were not in a position to defend
themselves. During that period the acts of aggression committed against the
Irish nation are appalling, 75 people were murdered, 2,412 were deported.
There were 653 armed assaults on unarmed civilians, 26,000 raids on private
houses, 7,504 arrests, 2,194 sentences, 413 proclamations and suppressions,
53 newspapers suppressed, 532 court-martials, and in addition several towns
were sacked and property worth hundreds of thousands of pounds destroyed.
And all this suffering at the hands of one of the defenders of small nations, of
whom Connolly said: 'In the name of liberty it hangs and imprisons patriots,
and while calling high heaven to witness its horror of militarism it sends the
shadow of its sword between countless millions and their hope of freedom.'
And why have our people had to endure all this agony? In a word, because the
people refuse to submit to a foreign domination.

What was O'Casey's political attitude at this time? There is no
reason to doubt that it was identical with that of Thomas Farren. His
main effort of course went into his writing. He had sent two plays to the
Abbey, the second called *The Harvest Festival*. At this time he was
modelling himself upon Shaw and attempting the theatre of ideas.
Nobody writes plays about a revolution when it is in progress.

What is probably most eloquent is that in the life story O'Casey takes
for granted his hatred of the black-and-tans. And the quotation from
Farren should dispose of any suggestion that there were Labour men
'putting socialism first' or holding aloof from their 'excessively
nationalist countrymen'. In *Inishfallen, Fare Thee Well*[2] O'Casey tells
of how, after tension had been mounting between himself and Michael,
he decided to take himself off. This was towards the end of 1920 and a
curfew between midnight and 5 a.m. had been in force since February.
The decision to go is a sudden one. O'Casey finds himself with a sack of
books on his back while Volunteers press forward for an ambush. In his

haste he has forgotten the curfew. He hears shots and grenades. The republicans are attacking the tans. What was O'Casey's reaction as remembered many years afterwards? It was: 'God make their eyes keen and their hands steady.' One can be quite sure that he remembered well.

O'Casey went to live for a while with Micheal O Maoláin (usually surnamed *as Arainn* from his being a native speaking Aran islander) a prominent Gaelic teacher and arranger of childrens' excursions to the Gaeltacht. O Maolain was a 'difficult' man. He was deeply involved in the trade union controversies which surrounded the person of P. T. Daly. He was bitterly opposed to Daly's main opponent William O'Brien. The dissident group included Delia Larkin who had returned to Dublin in 1918. At this time she was pressing for action in support of her brother James Larkin who had been arrested in the United States. He had been involved in an attempt to set up a Communist Party, and in May 1919 was arrested during the Palmer raids and charged with criminal anarchy. Palmer himself was shortly afterwards involved in a bootlegging scandal. But that was not criminal anarchy. In May 1920 Larkin was sentenced to from five to ten years in prison, and lodged in Dannemora jail. Republican groups prepared a plan of escape, but he seems to have felt too old for jumping over prison walls. The English Government showed characteristic charity in refusing passports to Thomas Foran and his son who wished to visit him. Delia had established a social centre at a hall in Langrishe Place, five minutes walk from Mountjoy Square where O'Casey was now living. Here she organized concerts and plays and campaigned for her brother's release. O'Casey was appointed doorman and general factotum at thirty shillings a week.[3] He subsequently became secretary of the release committee. While members of the Socialist Party of Ireland attended the centre, which was maintained financially by the playing of 'house', it was a centre of Larkinism rather than of socialism.

The first half of 1921 was the period of bitterest fighting, despite the peace feelers and indirect negotiations that had begun. De Valera had failed to rally support in the USA except from the Irish. It was not until after the Second World War that the USA felt strong enough to challenge England's position in the world and shatter her hegemony. And the pretext for that was not Ireland but the USSR. In 1921 the two powers were edging cautiously towards the accord of the Washington naval treaty. The secret contacts seem to have begun after Griffith assured London financiers that their investments would be safe in an Irish Republic, and was publicly rebuked for it by Labour. Not only the landlords' land but the capitalists' profit was being guaranteed. The struggle between right and left within the national movement was moreover subtly transformed. This has happened repeatedly in Ireland when popular movements have neglected their social base. The test should have been made 'people versus privilege'. It became war or peace. Thus when the draconic Restoration of Order in Ireland Act introduced a degree of repression beyond any previously known, the issue was between those who wanted more and more spectacular guerrilla actions, and those who wanted a settlement.

The raid made by the military on Mountjoy Square, described by O'Casey in the life story, took place on Good Friday, 25 March 1921. It centred on no. 10 but the whole area was cordoned off and subjected to searches for twelve hours. Arms and 'seditious literature' were captured. Cellars were dug up and five arrests made, one of them of Schweppe, whose daughter is said to have been the model for Minnie in the *Shadow of a Gunman*. She was a quiet studious girl determined to make the best of herself though beginning in limited circumstances. No mischance befell her. O'Casey's house, no. 35, was raided, but O Maoláin in later years declined to corroborate the particulars which were introduced into the life story.

The partitioning of Ireland was at this time in full swing. The plan was by the duplication of posts to create two parallel administrations, and at the appropriate time fasten on each its own regional parliament. The Government of Ireland Act permitted the utmost flexibility. More than the customary bludgeoning and trickery was required. There must be opportunity to execute the treason. Meanwhile raids, searches, arrests, reprisals on innocent parties, murder and torture performed their traditional functions in upholding the rule of law.

The season was pointed when the national alliance was faced with the necessity of deciding between the two main classes that had up to now been on the one side in the conflict. The year 1921 opened with 100,000 unemployed, and the English authorities were hopeful that emigration would soon resume, preferably on a massive scale. For those who had work, the employers proposed a general round of wage reductions. The workers, led by the Dublin dockers, determined to resist. The well-motivated efforts of the Dail department of labour to mediate in the cause of national unity, were impatiently swept aside. In 1919 the political situation was such that the employers decided to make concessions. Now they wanted to take them back.

It was at this point that organized Labour at last found its political voice. At Easter the Irish TUC issued its manifesto 'The Country in Danger'. It proposed moratoria on rents and land annuities, a maximum rate of profit to be determined by independent experts and the repatriation of Irish assets held in London. This was no socialist programme. It was expressly stated that it was derived from the Democratic Programme of Dail Eireann, which had been quietly dropped in deference to Griffith's theories.

If this programme had been adopted by Dail Eireann there was still a chance that the revolution might have been saved. But as Johnson ruefully commented, the sole response from the employers was a reiteration of the demand for wage reductions. The bourgeoisie unhesitatingly put class before national considerations. They added one more to the list of betrayals Connolly had catalogued in *Labour in Irish History*. Dail Eireann made no response. The petty bourgeoisie stood unsupported, uncertain, vacillating and ready for political disintegration. The workers resisted the employers' offensive with reasonable success. The bourgeoisie grew more impatient. They sighed for a strong government whose writ ran, as it had run before the divine rights of property had been profanely brought into question. The English fought the Irish nation as a whole, making little distinction of class. Dail Eireann would not fight the capitalists when they exposed their national apostasy. This meant they would have to stop fighting the English. Such was the ultimate result of Labour's decision not to lead the nation.

It was under these conditions, when the base of Dail Eireann was so disastrously narrowing, that the English government made indirect overtures to De Valera, President of the Republic. Parallel elections were held. On 7 June the Viceroy opened a six county Parliament. Sinn Fein held every seat in the twenty-six counties save those of Trinity College. But partition was a *fait accompli* One third of its population had been withdrawn from the Republic. Talks about talks led to talks themselves and hostilities ceased on 11 July 1921.

During the summer O'Casey wrote a play called *The Crimson in the Tricolour*, which, perhaps understandably in view of political events, he used to develop his theory that after the conclusion of the national struggle Sinn Fein and Labour must clash. It was seriously considered for production and in October 1921 Lady Gregory wrote to Lennox Robinson expressing interest but at the same time showing her political acumen.[4] 'We could not put it on while the revolution is still unaccomplished – it might hasten the Labour attack on Sinn Fein, which ought to be kept back till the fight with England is over, and the new government has had time to show what it can do.' There seems to have been further consideration of the play. Yeats had it in June 1922. It was not finally rejected till September of that year. The situation by then had undergone a total transformation. It seems therefore that the events of mid 1921 confirmed O'Casey in the belief that Labour must fight Sinn Fein. Almost certainly this was because he did not recognize them as representing intermediate strata, because the bourgeois party had disappeared. If he had recognized its true status he might possibly have seen the alternative of a progressive national government with Labour support or even participation.

Throughout the negotiations which dragged on till December 1921, the English allowed it to be believed that the new state which they had established at so much labour and expense was negotiable. Thus the Irish representatives were entoiled in further commitments as the talks proceeded. At the end of November the successful outcome of the Washington naval conference freed English diplomacy from the fear of American intervention. The Premier, Lloyd George, was enabled to present the Irish with a set of proposals which must be accepted or the alternative would be 'immediate and terrible war'. The delegates after some hesitation, capitulated, Griffith in the van. The resultant accord was called the 'treaty'.

It gave Ireland more independence than its critics allowed, but considerably less than its supporters claimed. Its worst aspect was the annexation of 5,242 square miles of Irish territory. England would only return them if Ireland re-entered the United Kingdom. Thus every advance towards independence on the part of the twenty-six counties, however strongly dictated by economic necessity, would involve a severing of ties within Ireland. Inevitably there was a split. The more bourgeois oriented sections of the national alliance collaborated in establishing the Provisional government, which first supplanted Dail Eireann and then stole its name. Into this group the disembodied soul of the old Redmondite party slid as by instantaneous metempsychosis. The bourgeoisie had a party once again. A quarter of a century later O'Casey poked fun at the efforts of publicans and shop-boys to transmogrify themselves into dignitaries and courtiers. But over a period the old soul mastered the new bodies.

The Dail supported the 'treaty' by 64 votes to 55. De Valera then tried to reach a compromise by offering a less obnoxious draft treaty known as Document no. 2. It was rejected by the 'treaty' party, and the split was confirmed. The opponents of the 'treaty' argued that England had not acceded to Ireland's demand and that therefore the war should be continued. But what was to be done if fellow-Irishmen stood in the line of fire? Repeatedly the anti-treaty party approached lines of policy which might have halted the counter-revolution by raising popular issues, which were bound to be dealt with in an unpopular sense by the 'treaty' party. They all but appealed to the landless men in May. They discussed appealing to the workers in September. But respectability gripped them even as they performed the most desperate actions.

Organized Labour, convinced that they had been betrayed and abandoned, cried with Cathal O'Shannon 'a plague on both your houses'. At a special congress held on 21 February 1922, Thomas Johnson read the executive memorandum which contained the words: 'Those whom we trusted and who were best able to weigh the forces, material and moral on either side, arrived at a certain conclusion. They decided that the terms of peace were the best that could be obtained in the circumstances.' But the difficulty was that they decided it by so narrow a majority. Conference therefore passed a resolution demanding a plebiscite on the subject of the 'treaty'. When a few days later this was refused by Griffith, the executive proceeded to select candidates for the coming general election. Labour was to defend itself as well as it could.

No doubt it was possible to read into this the discarding of outworn nationalist prejudices and the emergence of socialism, shining bright. Any who did so deluded themselves. The struggle for independence had been forced on to the defensive because Labour had been unwilling to take the lead in it. Now the same policy was being continued under new circumstances. It is of significance to note that the Labour left demanded a stand against the 'treaty'. Larkin expressed this view in the USA. So did the small Communist Party of which Roderick Connolly was the leader. This was the old Socialist Party of Ireland renamed in accordance with the terms of affiliation to the Communist International. And there is some evidence that O'Casey was with them.

This evidence takes several forms. Following the split, some of the more radical leaders of the Volunteers seized and entrenched themselves in a number of buildings in Dublin. Among them was the Orange Hall. R. M. Fox, who had just left Oxford and intended to settle in Dublin, was taken to the Orange Hall by O'Casey and they were both admitted after a security check. O'Casey afterwards explained to Fox that the check was carried out because there were war materials stored in the basement. O'Casey must have been *persona grata* to the extreme republicans.

Second, around the same period the anti-treaty Volunteers to whom it is now necessary to restrict the term 'republican', published a weekly journal called *Poblacht na hEireann* (Republic of Ireland) which was nominally edited by Liam Mellows. O'Casey wrote a satirical story called the 'Seamless Coat of Kathleen' which was published in this journal on 29 March. It was a satire on the *Ard Fheis* of Sinn Fein which was held on 21 February. The 'seamless coat' was the 'national unity' which held Ireland in a straitjacket.

This attack on 'national unity' had nothing to do with the notion that now national freedom had been achieved, the time had come for Labour to launch its offensive against Sinn Fein. That situation never arose because national freedom was not achieved. The matter was more complicated. First, it is noteworthy that after the Ard Fheis, O'Casey still offered his services to the most consistent republicans. Second, though we do not know when the article was submitted, it was not published until the end of March. It may be useful to find out what happened between the two dates.

The *Ard Fheis* itself provided material for a farce rather than an allegory. After the preliminary speeches were over it became clear that a majority of the 3,000 delegates were opposed to the 'treaty'. Perhaps it would be better to say that a majority dared not go back to their electors and admit to supporting it. At the same time they had no policy for fighting it. The pro-treaty faction proposed an adjournment. The next day's session began late. The delegates waited while delicate negotiations were conducted by the leaders of each side. Somebody started up a patriotic song. When the leaders appeared on the platform it was to propose that the *Ard Fheis* stand adjourned for three months. This was done in the interests of 'unity'. Those delegates who were squeamish about endorsing the 'treaty' were enabled to do precisely that, but to wear gloves while they were doing it.

The Communist Party warned Sinn Fein of the danger of 'three months false unity.' On 7 March, the Provisional Government started to recruit a police force who drilled with firearms. On 15 March the Dail Cabinet banned the Army Convention that had been called for 26 March. Orgies of anti-Catholic violence swept the six counties. The Army Convention was held in defiance of the ban. Four fifths of the total strength of the Volunteers were represented. The decision to continue to support the Republic was unanimous.

But where was the Republic? Griffith and Collins ran the Provisional Government and Dail Eireann in parallel. And since Dail Eireann contained a majority of supporters of the Provisional Government, the Republic was in a position to disestablish itself, or declare the Free State Parliament to be Dail Eireann. The republicans were ultimately forced to establish their own government, but for the moment much confusion and hestitation was caused by Griffith's policy.

The result of the Army Convention was that the 'treaty' party had lost its army. But it had financial resources and speedily repaired the deficiency. In the meantime, however, 'unity' had lost its sacredness and O'Casey's article was timely.

The allegory is far from perfect and the historical allusions do not always correspond. The sentiment is obviously anti-treaty. The readers of Poblacht na hEireann would recognize the references at once. 'Unity' was the device that had wrecked the Dail. 'Unity' was the cry that paralysed Sinn Fein. But 'unity' was not going to divert the army from its duty. In one paragraph O'Casey seems to be presenting the philosophy he had by then arrived at: 'The wearing of the garment is always an evil, and it only becomes a necessary one when it is worn to prevent an outside force from clothing her with a garment laced with iron, intended to crush the very heart out of her.'

The implication of this is that England was no longer the immediate enemy. This position was occupied by the 'treaty' party also, but from an opposite standpoint. The logic of the situation was therefore civil war, whence three months of efforts by the republicans to escape from it. As the spring advanced, a sense of disorientation and powerlessness gripped many Irish people. The British troops had gone. But every day seemed to increase the prospect of the Irish fighting each other. What an end to the years of struggle and fraternity! Every attempt to build bridges between the opposing sides was immediately frustrated by intervention from London. Soldiers used to take the shilling. The 'treaty' party had taken the pound, and were tied to British policy. The insults and humiliations Churchill and Lloyd George heaped upon Griffith and Collins, who knew they had not got independence, fanned their hatred of those who refused to share them. Finally when the two sides agreed to fight an election on an agreed programme, the 'treaty' party were summarily told to break their pact. Before the new Dail had time to meet, the ultimatum came from London, its pretext the assassination of Sir Henry Wilson. The buildings held by the republicans were under armed attack.

The fighting in Dublin was over in a few days. Then began a war in the country, first territorial, then guerrilla. The republicans fought without hope of military victory and half-heartedly. They followed the pattern Sinn Fein had shown to the British. They used force not to destroy their opponents, but to bring them to a better accommodation. It was a certain recipe for defeat. When defeat stared them in the face the character of the struggle changed. The Provisional Government displayed all the brutality and ruthlessness of their British predecessors. The old gamut was run through again, searches, raids, arrests, suppressions, reprisals, murder, torture and executions. It is possible now for the historian to show that the prime mover in all this was the English ruling class. But would it be incomprehensible if at the time, sincere Irish patriots should say 'if this is what Irishmen can do to each other, I am finished with nationalism for ever'? The Irish had been shut up in a box and forced to fight each other like the gladiators of old. What sentiments animated the combatants? Hatred of the Emperor? No – hatred of each other. England was forgotten, except that some on the republican side, believing they were fighting the wrong war, fought less effectively on account of it.

The devastating effect of this internal counter-revolution on the national consciousness can scarcely be imagined now. It is idle to say 'why did they not give in?' Counter-revolutions are not like that. The new state was determined to eliminate all challenge to its authority. Ultimately its opponents would have to recognize it and oppose it by other means. That could not happen while there was a wisp of hope.

Some republicans, however, refused to take part in the fighting. One such was Dan Breen, the guerrilla leader; another was the Fianna leader Eamonn Martin. Others behaved like the man who after an unsuccessful strike tears up his union card. They became embittered against the things they had supported.[5] More perhaps just sighed at the passing of a splendid vision and, while adjusting themselves to the world as it was, wrapped themselves in nostalgia for the 'four glorious years' and the fine people 'you don't meet today'.

A feature of the counter-revolution was its effort to borrow the garments of the revolution. This was of course the strongest guarantee that all memory of the purpose of the revolution would ultimately be expunged. The new state was founded on a lie, namely that Ireland had self-determination. To bolster the lie the Parliament of the Free State, established by British Act of Parliament, usurped the name Dail Eireann. Whether the constitution of the Free State was good, bad or indifferent it came into force by consent of London and the Irish had not determined it for themselves. The essential part of national independence is sovereignty. The essential part of a revolution is power. Discussion of such subjects was not encouraged.

Aspects of Irish nationality positive in the presence of sovereignty and social development were thrown like a smoke-screen to conceal the absence of the essential. The Irish language was pressed into the work of embellishment. It cost no more to overprint the British postage stamps, 'Rialtas sealadach' than 'Provisional Government', or 'Saorstat Eireann' than 'Irish Free State'. Things that had been liberating influences were made accomplices in restraint. The new government made a great show of developing the Irish language, not by spending money, but by passing laws. An atmosphere of pious catholicity was encouraged. A species of Catholic puritanism came into favour which matched the work that Calvin was put to in Belfast.

A 'Free State' view of history developed, not out of a conscious desire to misrepresent the past, but because the past is always seen in retrospect as necessarily leading to the present. That sincere and gifted historian Desmond Ryan produced a life of Connolly which discerned in him no intellectual development and made him a fit foreunner of the Free State. The process did not get fully under way until 1926 when Piaras Beaslai's *Life of Collins* became the Free State myth of origin.

The *Shadow of a Gunman*, the first of O'Casey's plays to deal with the revolution, was begun in April 1922. The draft of the first act was completed by October and the play was handed in at the Abbey on 21 November, just after the first executions had taken place. The period of composition was thus that of the civil war.

O'Casey's attitude to the civil war during its progress must be deduced from very late evidence. In the life story he pays a tribute to the uncompromising republican Cathal Brugha who came out of the Hammam hotel, blackened with smoke, a revolver in each hand, firing until he was shot dead himself. He also pays tribute to Collins who, of the Free State leaders, retained the most independence, and would surely have cheated the English government if he had had an opportunity. Griffith he does not admire. He recollects the machine-gun and rifle fire, the return of flames and explosions. But the predominant emotion is one of horror and disgust at the fratricidal strife, a horror and disgust in which the republicans appear as foolish romantics, the 'treaty' forces as the successors of the colonialists. It is the classical republican position, minus the acceptance of the need to fight. His story of the young irreconcilable cycling away frantically into the mountains pursued by men who may have sworn him to die for the republic, only to be brutally murdered by them, as he begs them to spare an old comrade, is an unforgettable picture of the times, though scarcely autobiography. O'Casey's three great Dublin plays were written in pain, anger and disillusionment. All the high hopes of the past, even things thought secure and eternal, came crashing down.

This is apparent in the *Shadow of a Gunman*. Taking Lady Gregory's advice to concentrate on characterization rather than to attempt the drama of ideas, he makes his central character a working-class poet, Davoren, something of a despiser of his own class who do not appreciate him. He is subjected to one interruption and annoyance after another as he tries to compose his Shelleyan pastiche. He foolishly allows himself to encourage an attractive young woman, Minnie, in the supposition that he is a gunman on the run, though his own final hindsight into himself is 'poet and poltroon'. He has to maintain the pretence when two neighbours call to solicit the assistance of a republican court. The tenant of the room he shares, is a pedlar, Seamus Shields, whose friend Maguire, a Volunteer, obligingly leaves what proves to be a bag of bombs in the apartment, while he goes out to take part in an ambush. Why he should leave his bombs behind is not clear; one would think them the very thing for an ambush. Davoren has to keep up his pretence before Tommy Owens, a typical public house patriot, and his undeserved reputation is bruited abroad. The sequel is a raid by the black-and-tans. Believing that Davoren is not a shadow but a real gunman, Minnie whisks away the bombs which she hides in her room. They are discovered there. She is arrested and shot dead while trying to escape.

Now O'Casey presents the events of 1921. But he informs them with the atmosphere of 1922. The dialogue consistently reveals reactions whose origin is in the year of the great disillusionment. Indeed O'Casey himself seems a little uncertain over the time of the action. We are told at the outset that the period of the play is May 1920. Raids of this kind were not proceeding at that time and we have seen that O'Casey's own experience of a full-scale raid dates from March 1921. But in the statement of the plaintiffs to the 'gentlemen of the IRA' we hear that a 'persecution' began on 10 June 1920, which is said to be eighteen months in the past. So we are brought to December 1921, the time of the truce. Now it seems that O'Casey was himself connected with litigation in a Republican Court in October 1921.[7] That his characters speak of future events in the past does not daunt O'Casey in the least. His concern must be with something else.

A few examples will illustrate. In the first act Seamus refers to the national colours as 'green, white and yellow'. The colour in the Irish flag is Orange. What has caused the difference? Partition. Shields is a former IRB man who has completely lost faith in the national struggle. This would not be likely in 1920 or 1921 when the struggle amounted essentially to self-defence. 'Upon my soul' he says, 'I'm beginning to believe that the Irish people aren't an' never will be fit for self-government.' In 1920 or 1921 they had not yet had an opportunity to demonstrate their degree of fitness. His attitude to Maguire's ambush corresponds to the feeling of sympathizers for the desperate escapades of the republicans when the civil war had been lost. In the second act Shields complains that instead of the gunmen dying for the people, the people are dying for the gunmen. This was a common attitude in 1922, but not in 1920. Kathleen ni Houlihan has become a 'raging divil now'. 'Are we ever again going to know what peace and security are?' asks Davoren. Such a sentiment is much more likely when fighting has been resumed, after peace has been enjoyed and expected to last. 'Oh. The country is hopeless and the people is hopeless,' says Shields. This is another civil war attitude unthinkable in 1920 or 1921 when England was with justification blamed for all the suffering. And finally, if by way of allegory O'Casey intended Minnie to represent the Republic, there would be many in the Abbey audience who would feel Davoren's conscience-stricken lamentation, 'We're a pair of pitable cowards to let poor Minnie suffer when we know that we and not she are to blame', to be fair comment on themselves, for they had let Childers and Mellows die, though they were completely innocent men.

The *Shadow of a Gunman* offered no solution. But it enabled its audiences to cathartize the collective sense of guilt of a generation whose splendid hopes had almost miraculously dissolved. Hence its power. 'Damn the people!' cries the poet Davoren. Every night more of them poured into the theatre. Soon crowds had to be turned away and the Abbey was saved from bankruptcy.

NOTES

1. In O'Casey's lyric, 'Call of the Tribe', preserved in Maire Keating's copy, published in McCann, *World of Sean O'Casey*, p. 36, and referred to in *Inishfallen, Fare Thee Well*, p. 4, there are references to 'England's legions' (for so I read *legends*) to deportations, a 'proscription' and to concessions designed to head off the national demand. While the expression 'world's slaughter' might indicate a date of composition during the 1914–18 war, the killing was being competently kept up, and other references could indicate a date of composition in the spring of 1920, when the new Government of Ireland Act was taking its leisurely course through Parliament. The instruction from William O'Brien to his staff to 'have nothing to do with that fellow Casside' might coincide with Larkin's imprisonment and O'Casey's involvement with Delia Larkin and O Maoláin.
2. *Inishfallen, Fare Thee Well*, p. 45.
3. There is of course a possibility that O'Casey was already employed at Langrishe Place before the move.
4. D. Krause, *Letters*, p. 95.
5. Eamonn Martin used to joke about his twelve years as a revolutionary and declare good-humouredly: 'It was all a complete waste of time.' Cahir Healy, a sincere patriot and fine poet who led a deputation from the Fermanagh County Council to beg Dail Eireann not to forsake those in Ulster who, having pledged their allegiance to the Dail were now to be thrust under the Belfast tyranny, turned to constitutional politics. In after years he used to speak contemptuously of 'sunburstery and Patrick Pearse', which he came to consider the acme of impracticability and humbug.
6. D. Krause, *Letters*, p. 105.
7. D. Krause, op. cit., p. 95.

[9]

DAYS OF CONTEMPT

At the end of April 1923 the long awaited Larkin returned to Ireland. Great hopes had centred on this event. 'There'll nothing happen till Big Jim comes back' was the constant plaint of his stalwart supporter, Barney Conway. But it was not the man but the situation that was wanting. When Larkin arrived in 1907 revolution was germinating. Events seemed in conspiracy to assist the agitator. In 1923 the revolution was over and only darkness seemed to lie ahead. Larkin's first action was to stump the country for peace, so that the political process might be resumed. His may have been the final influence persuading the republicans to 'dump arms' the following month. He then involved himself in a violent struggle for power in the Transport Union, doing in his own field precisely what he had counselled the republicans to desist from in theirs. He was defeated and lost his influence as a national leader, though not his great prestige.[1]

There were at that time over 11,000 military prisoners in Free State jails and the number was being increased daily. Detention without trial was legalized by means of a Public Safety Act passed in July against Labour opposition. A general election was held on 27 August, every conceivable obstacle being placed in the way of the republican candidates. The number of seats was increased by twenty-five. The 'treaty' party increased its representation by five, the republicans by eight. De Valera, who came out of hiding to fight Co. Clare, was whisked off the hustings into jail, and headed the poll with 17,000 votes. It remained the case throughout this period that if the republicans had taken their seats, the Cosgrave government could have been toppled with the aid of Labour votes. But since taking their seats would have involved swearing an oath of allegiance to the English Crown, they adopted a policy of abstention from parliament.

The election campaign inspired O'Casey's first 'political fantasy', a short allegorical sketch called *Kathleen Listens In*. Radio was a recent invention and 'listening in' was an expression derived from the practice of wearing headphones. Kathleen is of course Kathleen ni Houlihan, symbol of Ireland, though the symbolism is not perfectly consistent, and O'Casey remarked that nobody properly understood it except himself. When Kathleeen does not want to meet her suitors she avoids them by 'listening in'. She lives with her parents (the government) who have sold the family cow *druimfhionn donn dilis*, the sweet brown cow with the white back, another symbol of Ireland, but here seeming to represent national sovereignty) in order to buy a house, which is of course the Free State, and in particular the Free State Parliament.

Representatives of various interests press themselves upon Kathleen and the parents, and O'Casey satirizes them one by one. Two republicans leave the house because of the English symbols and decorations that are being brought in (the oath) among them poppies reminiscent of the world war. 'You'll grow shamrocks or you'll grow nothing,' says one of them. Miceawl O'Houlihan, when invited to sing the 'Soldier's Song', sings instead the popular song 'It ain't gonna rain no more' which was heard everywhere in 1923. Of course, when the republicans are out of the house they talk about getting back into it. And at the end of 1925 De Valera decided to enter Parliament even if he had to split the republican movement, and already the subject was under discussion. When they ask for Kathleeen they are told she is 'listening in'. When they ultimately obtain audience she refuses to listen to their patriotic songs and tells them she is practising foxtrots for her debut at the League of Nations (the Irish Free State was admitted as a member on 10 September 1923).

Fun is poked impartially. The Gaelic League is represented by an overbearing dotard who wants to compel people to speak Irish. This is a reference to one of the government's demonstratively nationalist measures, the introduction of compulsory Irish in schools. O'Casey was opposed to this on the ultra-left grounds that you could not teach starving men Gaelic. But of course you could not teach them mathematics either. The allusions to Irish history are numerous and ingenious. There is a reference to the government's brass band. The audience would think of Sadleir and Keogh and the 'Pope's Brass Band'. When Miceawl says of the family cow, 'Who'd have a better right to sell it than us?', they would think of the Act of Union when a man was told, 'You sold your country!' and he replied 'I did, and I was devilish glad I'd a country to sell.' Miceawl complains that when he got £19 19s 11½d for the cow, he was blamed for not getting £20. This is a reference to the difference between the 'treaty' and 'Document number two'.

Jimmy, who represents the labour movement, asks what is the good of loving Kathleen if she will not take any notice of you. This refers to the Free State's neglect of social questions and the abandonment of the national struggle by Labour. The favourite republican slogan 'An Irish Republic, one and indivisible' is ridiculed in the words 'one and invisible'. Jimmy concludes with the assertion that 'socialism is the only hope of the workers', a statement which in the circumstances amounted to saying that there was little hope for them at all.

The play was performed on 1 October and was given a most unusual reception. All the thrusts went home, but those at whom they were directed were silent, while their opponents rocked with laughter. Fallon[2] estimated that 'barely more than ten per cent of the audience laughed together'. The play did not unite the audience. There was no encouragement to rise above the limitations of faction, and for a strong reason. The British ruling class had formulated an insoluble conundrum, which they then handed to the Irish to solve. It remained unsolved, for Britain held the key. The Irish turned their anger and frustration on each other and O'Casey saw and shared their bitterness and mocked it. The satire in *Kathleen Listens In* contains nothing of the universal. It is not that of Dean Swift whose merciless exposure of man as he is arises from the nobility of his conception of what man should be; it is that of a man who has lost his bearings and cries, 'A plague on all your houses.'

There is a reference to 'going to Russia', but it tells nothing of O'Casey's political attitude. It seems most likely that his interest in and sympathy with the USSR were aroused when Larkin returned from that country in 1924.

In his next play, *Juno and the Paycock*, O'Casey dealt seriously with the issues of the civil war. Johnny Boyle has fought as a boy in 1916 and during the Anglo-Irish war has lost an arm. Now in the midst of the civil war he has turned informer and brought about the murder of his comrade and neighbour, Commandant Tancred, by the 'treaty' forces. There were of course no informers in 1916 and few between 1919 and 1922. But the civil war loosened all bonds of solidarity and O'Casey hints at personal jealousy between Tancred, the commandant, and Boyle the quartermaster. The first lines of the play report the murder. In the second act IRA men accuse Johnny of complicity. In the third act he is taken out and shot.

Such then is the skeletal structure, treachery followed by detection and revenge. Against the background of this relentless logic, of which we are constantly reminded by the terrified Johnny's brief entrances, the egregious bottle companions, Captain Boyle and Joxer Daly, fritter away a non-existent legacy; Mary Boyle's head is turned by a middle-class admirer who deceives her and decamps; Juno Boyle keeps a roof over their heads until, overcome by the execution of her son and the profligacy of her wastrel husband, she takes Mary away to seek a new life.

The play was first performed on 3 March 1924, shortly after it was completed. At this time every Irish person was appalled and revolted at the evil that had befallen the country. Of all O'Casey's plays it is the richest in memorable lines. Who has not heard, 'What can God do agen the stupidity o' men?', or 'The whole world's in a terrible state o' chassis'?[3]

The most famous passage of all, representing the whole drama in microcosm, is the cry of Juno when revenge has taken its course and the stultification and emptiness of fratricidal strife strikes her with uncontrollable force: 'Sacred heart of Jesus, take away our hearts o' stone and give us hearts o' flesh! Take away this murdhering hate an' give us Thine own eternal love!'[4]

The suggestion has been made that the tendency of the play is pacifist. But that was no part of the situation in Ireland. The reality was disgust with the particular war that had just ended. The Irish people did not know where to lay the blame and among them was O'Casey. For nowhere does he display the slightest consciousness that the British politicians who caused it were openly gloating when the Irish were killing each other.[5]

O'Casey had by now become a figure of importance. People stopped him in the street and requested his autograph. He was still working in the building trade but was preparing to give it up. Yet at this time he chose to insist on the poverty and ignorance of his youth. During the run of the *Shadow of a Gunman* he had told Lady Gregory[6] that he had 'carried the hod', and added that, though he had been among books as a child, he was sixteen before he learned to read or write. She noted in her journal that he was 'learning what he can about art' and had bought books about Whistler and Raphael. A year later, at Coole, he told her that he had decided to teach himself to read when he was fourteen.[7] But on the very next page Lady Gregory records how four days later he told Mrs Warren, a clergyman's wife, of his disappointment at finding that a Sunday school prize awarded him was a missionary and not an adventure story.

Until his plays came to be performed at the Abbey there is not the slightest complaint of poverty in anything that O'Casey wrote. It may be that the 'poor mouth' was a reaction to the new social surroundings in which he now found himself. He was an intellectually self-made man. His introduction into literary circles in Dublin brought him into contact with people who never had to struggle for knowledge. They were men and women with Rathgar accents able to dispute without expletives and wound with easy nonchalance. He on the other hand, though the possessor of the best of good manners, that is to say, natural good manners, spoke in the accents of the East Wall, and was no match for the *literati* in poise and sophistication. Perhaps he enjoyed being a new phenomenon and exaggerated his singularity; perhaps he compensated a feeling of inferiority. And once he had adopted the pose, there was nothing for it but to keep it up.

In the life-story he describes a discussion with Lennox Robinson who asked him if he had seen the plays of Andreyev, Benevente and others. O'Casey suspected a name-dropping competition and countered with

Webster, Forde and Massinger. 'Oh! My gawd!' ejaculated Robinson. People of Robinson's class had been taught about such people. O'Casey had had to explore for himself. Fallon explained to him that Robinson was merely mentioning work that O'Casey might have seen in the Irish Drama League productions at the Abbey.

Again, while O'Casey bubbled over with creative genius, he was still not quite sure of pronunciation and spelling. He had read many words which he had never heard spoken. He was not sure what was standard and what was dialect. For example, in *Juno* he spells often 'ofen' in order to ensure that the dental is dropped. One need not go to O'Casey for such uncertainties. Old dictionaries advise that the word clothes should be pronounced 'cloze'. But the spread of education resulted in the paradoxical 'correction' of the correct and modern dictionaries advise 'clothes' which thousands of people say. In *Kathleen* he writes *practice* for *practise*, and elsewhere he has *you're* for *your*.

Perhaps he saved himself embarrassment by exaggerating the humbleness of his origins and the defectiveness of his schooling. To snobbery he returned inverted snobbery. But that, though inverted, it remained the same thing, is shown by his mischievous delight when he caught Lady Gregory reading 'Peg of my Heart', and Yeats pretending he knew all about Dostoyevsky, though he had borrowed his novels from Lady Gregory only the week before. He was able to convince himself that he knew as much as the 'elegant people' of the salons. And indeed he knew far more.

It was shortly after the production of *Juno* that O'Casey paid a visit to Coole. Lady Gregory, whose seat it was, was a member of the Persse family, known as tolerably 'good landlords' in South Galway. She had known the great English anti-imperialist, Wilfrid Scawen Blunt, for many years, and partly under his influence had become a strong Irish nationalist. She participated in the 1798 centenary celebrations. It was through Blunt's good offices with his cousin, George Wyndham, that the Abbey patent was secured. She was a fine playwright, humane, popular and amusing, and as a woman of extensive culture was in touch with all that was best in Ireland.

The civil war distressed her cruelly. She was not the woman to cry, 'A plague on both your houses.' She understood perfectly well that it was England's claim to sovereignty in Ireland that was the malignant fomenter of strife. To a republican priest, Father Kelly, she said, 'One should not be more angry with Government or Republicans than with different sections of one's own mind, tilting to good or bad on one or the other side, in many questions besides this.' The remark shows the originality and profundity of her mind. She tried to persuade the Free State government to secure a modification of the oath of allegiance to

the English Crown, that would permit the republicans to enter
Parliament. This had been the object of the much maligned Document
No. 2. By the middle of 1922, however, the split had grown too wide for
bridging.

Lady Gregory is one of the few characters in the life story whom
O'Casey treats with unfailing kindness and respect. She had known
Yeats in the Irish Literary Society in London and had assisted his
career. Her enthusiasm for O'Casey was of immense help to him. At
Coole he experienced for the first time the life of cultured leisure that is
broken only by self-imposed tasks, and perhaps wished to make it his
own.

But how are we to assess the remarks that she recorded of him in her
journal? She can hardly have reproduced them very inaccurately. But
did she believe that the first book he read was d'Aubigny's *History of
the Reformation* and the second Locke's *Essay on the Human
Understanding*? Perhaps O'Casey told her that these were the first of
his father's books that he read. Why, further, did he inform her that he
had been a socialist, and give as the reason for his changed opinion, that
when he worked for a producers' co-operative society the men would
not trouble to work because there was no employer to control them?
There had been many such co-operatives during the revolutionary
period and in the case of one of them, the Arigna 'Soviet', the owners of a
coalmine that was taken over paid the workers compensation for
improvements they had made while it was in their hands. As a further
reason he adds that the undertaker who refused to move the coffin until
he had been paid was a 'Labour man'. As we have seen, the story is
suspect, and one would certainly not expect O'Casey to abandon
socialism in 1919 when he had scarcely espoused it.

One receives the impression that though he was as oppposed as ever
to the poverty, ignorance and inhumanity of capitalism, in the general
débâcle O'Casey had lost confidence that there was a way forward. In
social matters this confidence was not restored until he had spent some
years in England. In national matters it was never restored. The
disillusioned republican was a common phenomenon in the twenties
and thirties, and indeed until the disillusioned generation began to die
out.

O'Casey's next play was a one-act farce which is of little
consequence. It consists of episodes in the life of a small shopkeeper,
whose three suitors are unable to protect her from irate customers,
thieves or a gunman. She is rescued by Nannie, a game, down-and-out,
methylated spirits drinker. The central theme is not political, but the
characters hit out copiously against poverty, parsimony, hypocrisy, the
indecisiveness of parliaments, the empty braggadocio of the male sex

and the teaching of Irish in schools. According to Robert Hogan, who is usually acute in his judgements, *Nannie's Night Out* is one of the 'superb one-act plays of the modern stage'. But Gabriel Fallon begs to differ. Politically speaking, it is complaint without revendication. Two of the characters speak nostalgically of the British régime and it is the first play in which O'Casey introduces religion by making one of the characters Protestant.

Further evidence of O'Casey's nihilistic frame of mind at this time comes from Mr Bob Stewart who, one need not doubt, is the communist organizer referred to in January 1925 in a letter from O'Casey to Lady Gregory. Stewart was living at Larkin's house. The Communist Party of Ireland had fallen on evil days and Larkin had indicated an interest in reviving it. Stewart was making his experience available to him.[8] He used to complain of the pointless chatter of so many of Larkin's visitors, one of whom was O'Casey. 'He's a great conversationalist,' said Larkin. 'Aye,' said Stewart, 'But one that's got nothing to say.'[9] If O'Casey had expressed strong socialist views at this time Stewart would have been interested in view of his mission. The talk that the Scotsman found pointless was doubtless the reminiscences of defeated revolutionaries, the endless discussion of 'if only'.

It was some time before O'Casey could decide on his next play. And when his mind was made up he had some difficulty in settling down to it. According to Fallon he set a piece of cardboard on his mantelpiece, on which was written in large letters, 'Get on with the bloody play.' He succeeded in completing it in August 1925. But in this same month, before it had been read by the directors, the first rift opened between the playwright and his theatre. The cause was his outspoken criticism of an admittedly poor production of Shaw's *Man and Superman.* It is possible that there were those who were jealous of O'Casey's success. According to Lady Gregory, at the end of the year he was taking about £60 a week, by no means an inconsiderable sum in those days. The result of the quarrel was that he was barred from the theatre's green room, and lost the 'theatre workshop' that was so important for him. In the life story he gives the impression that the dispute with the Abbey players took place *after* the production of the new play, *The Plough and the Stars*, and it is pressed into service as part of the explanation of his leaving Ireland.

The government was now subsidizing the Abbey and had nominated a distinguished economist to the Board. He had to show what he was made of and raised objections on moral grounds to passages in the play. Compromises were effected and the play was put into production. O'Casey had lost his close relations with the players and paid the penalty. One objected that her part was 'not genteel'. Another refused to speak the word 'snotty'. It has been suggested that there was deliberate miscasting, but a sailor does not sink his own ship. Certainly the old spirit of cooperation was there no longer. Moreover it was possible to adjudge the play anti-republican. O'Casey had regressed still further from the national idealism which has sustained him for so many years. W. B. Yeats, a strong government supporter, was delighted with it, anticipated ructions, and felt very pleased with the prospect.[10]

The structure of the play is simple enough. Jack Clitheroe is a Citizen Army man sulking because he has not been made an officer. He rediscovers domestic bliss and makes himself very attentive to the wife. But then he finds out that in fact he had been promoted and that his wife burned the letter of appointment, in order to keep him at home. From then on the ICA takes precedence and the basis of the conflict becomes clear. It is between a man's vanity and a woman's selfishness. For the selfishness of Nora Clitheroe is attested on several occasions. The struggle between the vain and the selfish thus obscures that between personal and social imperatives. The time is November 1915.

When Clitheroe has flung out of the room, he goes to a demonstration which is to be followed by an attack on Dublin castle. A consumptive child, Mollser, asks Nora if anybody who is supporting the parade 'has a tither of sense'. In the second act, set in a bar, we see the figure and hear the words of the orator, while a series of trivial episodes inside the bar show how little events outside impress the ordinary people.

The Covey, a dogmatic socialist, torments Peter Flynn, the sentimental nationalist who belongs to the National Foresters. Mollser's mother, Mrs Gogan, tangles with the Unionist virago Bessie Burgess, Fluther Good, the carpenter, first defends and then goes home with the prostitute, Rosie Redmond.

The words of the orator are taken from Patrick Pearse and include the famous passage in which he describes bloodshed as a 'cleansing and sanctifying thing'. Now there is some rewriting of history here. The ICA mock attack on Dublin castle was undertaken in October 1915. The co-operation between the ICA and the Volunteers did not come about until 1916. Strictly speaking Connolly should have been the speaker. But O'Casey wanted to show the effect of Pearse's oratory.[11]

Clitheroe and two companions, one from the Citizen Army, the other from the Volunteers, enter the bar in a mood of exaltation. They order drinks. Then they raise the Tricolour and the Plough and the Stars. Beneath the uplifted flags they swear that Ireland is more than a wife, Ireland is more than a mother, and they are prepared to face wounds, imprisonment and death for her independence. The ordinary people get on with their ordinary business.

In the third act, set in the lowly street where the Clitheroes have their tenement, we learn that the Rising is in progress. All but the consumptive girl and the timid National Forester enter into an orgy of looting and drinking. Clitheroe is away fighting. His wife has been out all night trying to find him and bring him home. She has come back in a distressed state. But he comes, with one other, helping a wounded comrade to a place where he can receive medical attention. Nora Clitheroe has no eyes for the sick man. In hysterics she begs her husband to desert. He refuses and goes on his way.

The last act is set in an attic inhabited by Bessie Burgess, a street fruit-seller and Orangewoman with a son at the front. In previous scenes she has appeared as an unpopular virago. Now common danger has obliterated differences of faith and politics. News is brought that Clitheroe has been killed in the fighting. But his wife cannot be told. She has suffered a miscarriage and has gone out of her mind. Mollser has also died and soldiers enter to escort the coffin to the burial ground. A republican sniper has been picking off their comrades one by one. Nora, incapable of understanding the danger, goes to the window. Bessie Burgess tries to pull her away, is taken for a sniper and shot dead. All the men in the house are then rounded up and taken away, not without protest, and the soldiers then drink a cup of tea.

The conclusion to be drawn from all this is that a man brings disaster on himself, his wife and an innocent neighbour, by following his social conscience and going out to fight for Irish independence. Bernard Shaw dealt kindly with Saint Joan who was burnt at the stake for engaging in a somewhat similar enterprise. Her heart would not burn. But there is no justification of the Rising in O'Casey. Clitheroe's social conscience is depicted merely as the rationalisation of his desire for the good opinions of others and his desire to cut a fine figure. And there is no exposure of that stupendous international crime which was being committed at the same time, the imperialist world war, which O'Casey denounced in his next play. There is the greatest unanimity among literary critics that *The Plough and the Stars* presents the Rising and the motives of those who took part in it, in a poor light.

James Agate,[12] writing in 1926, says of Clitheroe that 'his patriotism and personal ambition are like a pair of horses pulling away from each other'. This is not strictly true. But ambition is recognized.

P. S. O'Hegarty[13] commented in 1927:

It is a fact that there was drunkenness and looting among some of the Dublin poor in Easter week, but it is an untrue picture which gives nothing else but that. And I think the role assigned to Mrs Clitheroe, that of holding back her man, is quite untrue.

The end of the fourth act does perfectly give you Ireland immediately after the Rising; but to the extent that the third and fourth acts do not do justice to the Rising itself, the play is an untrue, or rather, incomplete picture.

Another Irish critic, L. P. Byrne, writing under the name of A. E. Malone in 1929, summarizes the message of *The Plough*:[14]

Death, destruction, suffering, waste; all in the sacred name of patriotism. Again it is the women who suffer, the women who are great. 'Is there anybody going with a titther of sense?' asks the consumptive child.

Bonamy Dobrée[15] writing in 1939 declares:

What we are invited to consider is the things men do to each other, the appalling horror of the whole thing, the nasty mess that men in their folly and their aspirations, their heedlessness and their ideals, are making of life . . .

Jacques Barzun in 1959 described the play as 'an episode in the reckless Easter Rebellion of 1916'. In 1960 Dr Krause wrote the first full length study of O'Casey.[16] He concentrates his attention on literary values, but his ascription to O'Casey of an 'anti-heroic' vision and his stress upon the irony of the events which transform speeches about blood sacrifice into blood sacrifice itself, imply that he also agrees that O'Casey's appraisal of the Rising was a negative one.

Saros Cowasjee quotes Nora Clitheroe's words to her husband, 'Your vanity will be th' ruin of you, and me, yet'. He comments: 'But Clitheroe has no eyes for the truth, and O'Casey, doubting whether the audience have either, concludes the act by letting the consumptive child Mollser ask Nora "Is there anybody going, Mrs Clitheroe, with a titther of wit?".'[17]

John O'Donovan wrote of *The Plough* in 1966, in which year the 1916 jubilee committee discreetly requested the Abbey not to perform this play: 'O'Casey's viewpoint has not changed. It is still "you lost your best principle, me boy, when you lost your arm",' the words of Juno to Johnny when, maudlin with fear, he boasts of his patriotism.[18]

Finally we have the unreserved comments of Herbert Goldstone, written in 1972.[19] In his opinion the first act shows 'the tensions and prejudices of the Irish and some of their ridiculous feelings'. The second act shows 'the frenetic, irrational behaviour of these people as they are aroused by the passionate rhetoric of the speaker and as their own everyday frustrations and prejudices become accentuated'. The third act 'reveals the absurd and yet genuinely heroic action, as well as terrible suffering, that took place'. Goldstone is the only critic who admits the heroism. But he has no doubt that Clitheroe fights because of his vanity and the attraction of a fine uniform, and that only Mollser can see 'how foolishly the Irish act in the grip of nationalist fervour'. Now the only characters that show nationalist fervour, if we exclude Peter Flynn's empty ostentation, are those who take part in the Rising. The conclusion is obvious. The actors on the stage do not speak for themselves. They speak words O'Casey has put into their mouths. They are characters he has invented. There is an almost universal impression that the Rising was not to be commended. And, it must be remembered, this impression was first conveyed to an audience most of whom remembered it quite well, and had known some of the participants.

Reference has already been made to O'Casey's statement to Lady Gregory that the insurrection was a 'terrible mistake', and that other statement in the life story that 'the Easter Rising had pulled down a dark curtain of eternal separation between him and his best friends'. This curtain did not exist in 1917. It began to descend in 1919. It was not a separation in space/time. It was a separation of opinion. It became a complete barrier only when 'the few that had remained alive and delightful, now lay deep, with their convivial virtues, under the rubblement of the civil war'. He had already reached the conclusion that the Rising was a mistake. In *The Plough and the Stars* he suggests an unworthy motive for the mistake, though he does not carry this to its logical conclusion. And from where does he get the vanity and ambition? From later history. He cannot leave the past alone. He gives the men of 1916 the weaknesses of the 'trucileers', the men who flocked into the Volunteers between July and December 1922, men who had never fired a shot, but who strutted about giving themselves airs in neat uniforms.

It has already been suggested that the deep hidden trauma of O'Casey's political life was that he was not out in 1916. That he was under no obligation is accepted. Clitheroe's forename is Jack. Jack Clitheroe joins the Rising and brings ruin on himself and his family. Jack Casey was living alone with his seventy-five-year-old mother. His mother was 'more than Ireland' – and understandably so. Only one motive could have induced him to take part, concern with what people might say, and did say, about him. If O'Casey had got himself killed in 1916 it would have been for vanity. *The Plough* shows what might have happened if he had succumbed to it.

This, I am convinced, is the emotional fulcrum of *The Plough*. It is 1916 seen through the eyes of those who did not take part, commented upon by one who had a reason for taking part but a more compelling reason not to do so. When O'Casey was accused of presenting the insurgents as cowards, he replied indignantly, 'There is not a coward in the play.' The non-combatants suggest cowardly motives, but the actions of the fighting men show courage. The play derives its fascination for Irish audiences from posing a centuries-old dilemma of

Irish life, imposed on the country by the claim of the foreigner to its territory. Some revolt, others suffer on. One is reminded of Proust. Françoise asks the gardener whether it will be war or revolution. He replies that revolution would be preferable, as then only those who want to need fight.

The issue of socialism is not to the fore in this play, despite the Covey. He has no role comparable with that of the communists in the later plays. He is something of a 'jackeen', cocksure but with a ready caution, a talker, grossly insensitive and dogmatic.

There is a splendid array of secondary characters, used for the most part to stress the isolation of the revolutionaries from the ordinary people. This point is stressed so far as the suggestion that the people have spontaneously attacked them. I am aware of no historical justification for this, though it is true that one individual made herself unpleasant at the College of Surgeons. There is no evidence that the rebels used dum-dum bullets. The Prime Minister himself acknowledged that they did not resort to outrage.

Though it is not our primary concern, it is worth making the point that *The Plough* is the first play in which the dialogue is affected by the preciosity and pleonasm that characterized so much of O'Casey's later writing. This takes the form, for example, of alliterative adjectives very much the enemy of their noun, a trick presumably borrowed from Synge. We have 'hardy habit', 'luscious lies', 'dread dimness', 'madly mingling memories'. The longer passages can be tiresome, as for example 'let patience clip away the heaviness of the slow moving hours', or 'a kid swinging heavy words which he doesn't know the meaning of, and uppishly trying to down a man like Mr Fluter here, that's well flavoured in the knowledge of the world he's living in'. A writer will of course write to please himself, but there is a point beyond which undue decoration incurs the suspicion of artistic elitism.

The Plough and the Stars opened to a full house on Monday 8 February 1926. There was generous applause, Next night there was some hissing, most directed against the prostitute in the bar scene. On the Thursday night pandemonium was let loose. Of course there were many reasons given. Some objected to the prostitute. There were no such things in Ireland. There were of course. But the Free State government had effectively cleaned up the area around Amiens Street Station where over many years the British soldiers had found elysium, and the names of the streets were changed. Others objected to the taking of the tricolour into the bar. But the real reason was the anti-national tendency of the play. The student protesters were led by Frank Ryan. They objected to the implication that the men of the Citizen Army were actuated by vanity and ambition. At that time the Free State government was preparing to capitulate on the readjustment of the border to take account of the wishes of local inhabitants. If the rock of the Republic, declared in arms in 1916, was to be split, then there was nothing ahead but national collapse.

There is no doubt that O'Casey was grievously upset by the riot. Yeats on the other hand was smiling blandly, and had a prepared speech which he handed to the press, and then read into the uproar. In the life story O'Casey declared that 'for the first time in his life, Sean felt a hatred for Cathleen ni Houlihan sweeping over him'. Nevertheless, he agreed to debate with the rioters in the hall attached to Mills' restaurant in Merrion Row. He was opposed by Hannah Sheehy-Skeffington and defended by a young student poet, Lyle Donaghy. When he had made his defence O'Casey sat down to loud applause. The affair has suffered much misrepresentation. It was not a case of 'outraged nationalists' taking offence at O'Casey's internationalism, but of using the occasion, as Yeats used it, in the course of the struggle between the 'treaty' party and the republicans, both of which were classified as 'nationalists'.

In the life story O'Casey gives the impression that from the time when *The Plough* went into rehearsal he was thinking of going to England where he would find 'fairer comfort, greater space, and a steady quietness'. Indeed the 'land of Nelson and Clive' (of all people!) was beckoning. If he correctly remembered his motive, then the Abbey audience cannot be held guilty of provoking his departure. Elsewhere he says he left because he had 'had enough of it'.

What seems best attested is that he left in order to be present when *Juno*, then playing successfully in London, was transferred from the Royalty to the Fortune. This took place on 8 March. He remained in order to receive the Hawthornden prize which had been awarded him. The ceremony took place on 23 March. He had come from poor troubled war-torn Ireland to safe, strong, imperial England. It never struck him that this contrast was of the two sides of one coin. But why should he? Something else had happened. He had met his future wife. He made one brief visit to Dublin to wind up his affairs and thereafter, but for a brief holiday, remained a voluntary exile for the rest of his life.

NOTES

1. 'The Irish can sell you terribly,' O'Casey said to me. 'They sold Jim Larkin.' While this statement might be thought a little harsh, it illustrates O'Casey's unswerving loyalty to Larkin and his chagrin at the events of 1923.
2. Gabriel Fallon, *Sean O'Casey, the Man I Knew*, p. 14.

3. In the early years of this century the mispronunciation of chaos as 'chowce' was a standing joke in Dublin. It originated in Cork where a theatre manager taking the part of Othello had to say: 'When I love thee not chaos is come again.' For years afterwards, his appearance on the stage was likely to be greeted with 'Bravo chowce!' See J. W. Flynn, *Random recollections of an old Playgoer*, quoted in Justin McCarthy, *Irish Recollections*, p. 37. O'Casey provided the modern twist.

4. There is a more earthy *cri de cœur* which O'Casey probably knew, in the 'Party Fight and Funeral', Carleton, *Traits and Stories of the Irish Peasantry*, vol. 1, p. 227. 'Oh. My God! When will it be ended between friends and neighbours, that ought to live in love and kindness together, instead of fighting in this bloodthirsty manner.' O'Casey's is, of course, derived from Ezekiel (37: 26) and one wonders how far this immensely complex man secretly thought of himself as one sent to prophesy against the transgressions of his countrymen.

5. See the speech by Lord Birkenhead, 23 July 1923.

6. *Lady Gregory's Journals*, p. 72.

7. Op cit., p. 78.

8. Bob Stewart, *Breaking the Fetters*, p. 147 et seq.

9. ibid. In his book (p. 149) Stewart writes that Larkin was 'not speaking' to Delia, his sister, and communicated with her via their brother Peter or himself. Although I did not make a note at the time, my recollection is that Stewart told me, twenty years before he wrote his book, that Larkin's difference was with his wife, and that they usually communicated through Delia. The reason was that Larkin had advised the republicans to give up their arms. They decided instead to conceal them, and his wife allowed them to create a cache under Larkin's own floor boards. Another aspect of the situation was Larkin's willingness to conduct political activity, but dislike of formal parties. It is possible he encouraged his 'conversationalists' whenever Stewart wanted to get down to business.

10. Gabriel Fallon, op. cit., p. 86.

11. It is sometimes pointed out that just before the Rising Connolly wrote that without the shedding of blood there is no redemption. I have suggested elsewhere that he was harking back to discussions of the justification for the violence of the Paris Commune. In other words Pearse was offering his own blood. Connolly was out for somebody else's.

12. Ronald Ayling (ed.), *Sean O'Casey, Modern Judgements*, p. 79.

13. ibid., p. 64.

14. ibid., p. 74.

15. ibid., p. 98.

16. D. Krause, *Sean O'Casey, the Man and his Work*.

17. Saros Cowasjee, *Sean O'Casey, the Man behind the Plays*, p. 66.

18. Sean McCann (ed.), *The World of Sean O'Casey*, p. 192.

19. H. Goldstone, *In Search of Community*.

[10]

GOODBYE TO ALL THAT

Caelum non animam mutant qui trans mare currunt.

The distinguished immigrant who arrived at Euston was nearly forty-six, though in order to qualify for the Hawthornden prize, he had been compelled to forget his date of birth, and incidentally mortgage the chronology of his unwritten autobiography. He looked young. But he was a man of exceptionally rich and varied experience that had been lived and felt. Few had done such a variety of things. Very few had held so diverse an assortment of passionate beliefs, each leaving its secret trace on the palimpsest. He continued to vent his feelings in the language of the Bible though he now proclaimed himself an atheist. He continued to cherish the Irish language. Certainly he preserved the tenacious dogmatism typical of the physical force republicans. He remained a Labour supporter, but for the next few years said little about socialism.[1]

He went to England a disillusioned ex-Republican, a member of a generation whose landmarks had disappeared. After the 'treaty', native Irish institutions had openly assumed responsibility for preserving what was still in effect the old colonial system. In years to come this phenomenon became widespread and came to be known as 'neo-colonialism'. The imperialist government stipulated the political framework and maintained the reserve power. Its local collaborators worked the machinery and incurred the odium. O'Casey fled from the stagnant parochialism engendered by this system, but he did not understand it. He was leaving counter-revolution behind. Arriving at his destination he was immediately carried off to the drawing rooms of the class that had engineered it. He was interviewed by the BBC, besieged by reporters and photographers, elected to the Garrick Club, and taken to the opera by Lady Londonderry who had pretensions as a literary hostess. According to Gabriel Fallon, his publisher had to wait a fortnight for a luncheon appointment. There was no greater social asset than the writer whose 'blazing masterpieces', as Agate called them, were acclaimed the greatest plays since the days of the Elizabethans.

Why such a reception from such people? Partly of course because jaded palates demand exotic dishes. This Irishman was a novelty. But the political situation in England must be credited with due influence. In March 1926 the Conservative government, which had gained office as a result of what has been widely condemned as a political forgery, was preparing to do battle with the trade unions. The working class was to be put back in its place. Already the good life of 'pre-war normality' was beginning to revive. Boulestin's and the Berkeley were competing with the Savoy Grill for the custom of gourmets. An atmosphere of ease and confidence was relaxing stage and salon.

The general strike which paralysed the country for nine days came in May. O'Casey had been casting doubts on the principle of militancy. Those who knew nothing else were aware that there had been a riot at a Dublin theatre and that O'Casey had implied that those who flout authority only penalize their wives and children. The repudiation of republicanism by an Irishman is always sweet music in sophisticated London. Why could the British workers not see that their intransigence merely faced their families with starvation? That O'Casey's position derived from ultra-leftism dismayed polite society not to the slightest degree. It was a situation O'Casey could never have anticipated. It was at this point that he began his second life, which we need follow in less detail than his stormier youth. He was still capable of vast development, but there were fewer upheavals.

For the next three years he was mainly absorbed in personal affairs and writing the play which he began in September 1926. He found time to send good wishes to a Labour candidate in a Scottish by-election and he voted Labour in 1929. He expressed approval when the guerrilla leader Dan Breen decided to enter Parliament.[2]

Otherwise he engaged little in politics. He became friendly with Bernard and Charlotte Shaw. Augustus John painted his portrait. He married the gifted and beautiful actress Eileen Carey. His cultural horizons broadened immeasurably. He acquired additional poise and self-confidence. And he remained Sean O'Casey.

He completed *The Silver Tassie* at the end of 1927. But there is still some uncertainty over what he did with it. In the life story[3] he tells of the visits of Lennox Robinson and W. B. Yeats who sought assurances that the new play would be offered to the Abbey. But he then says that he had 'promised the first glimpse of the play to Sir Barry Jackson'.[4] Why? There is no doubt about what Jackson believed. He returned the manuscript and explained that he could not put it on because an English audience could not stand it. O'Casey then describes the difficulty of the producer, Raymond Massey, Augustus John's church window and gun in the second act, and C. B. Cochran's mysterious influence. That is to say he breaks chronology and wherever chronology is broken a dog is buried. He records C. B. Cochran's complaint that he should never have

given the option to another party while the play was under
consideration by a London manager.[5]

The obvious inference, though it has been challenged, is that O'Casey
offered the play first to Jackson, then to C. B. Cochran. The Abbey got
to hear of it and made their inquiries. Jackson having declined, C. B.
Cochran accepted. What is certain is that the Abbey rejected it on 20
April on the classical grounds that they knew what was good for
O'Casey better than he did himself. They wanted him to go on writing in
his old style, and thought they could treat him like a bold child.

The Silver Tassie was a new departure. During the late twenties there
was a vogue of writing about the First World War. Most of its products
were well-groomed nostalgic pieces in which officers and gentlemen
emitted the cosy sentiments of the cricket field. O'Casey had
determined to show war through the eyes of the ordinary soldier. The
title was taken from a Scottish song, but the story is 'Johnny I hardly
knew you.' Saros Cowasjee[6] has pointed out that the plot is almost
exactly copied from Wilfred Owen's poem 'Disabled'. And indeed there
are other signs of Owen's influence, epecially in the celebrated second
act. Owen came from an evangelical background not dissimilar to
O'Casey's and there may have been an instinctive fellow-feeling.

Harry Heenan, a young man with no claim to character, culture or
convictions, epitome of the 'sensual man', has scored the goal which
brings his football club the silver tassie. He is seen in the first act, full of
exhilaration and animal spirits, animated conductor of an orchestra of
admirers, club members, neighbours, parents and girl friends. But this is
the last day of his leave. He departs with others to the trenches, among
them Barney Bagnal and Teddy Foran. It is goodbye to Dublin.

The second act provides a staggering contrast. The scene is a ruined
monastery behind the trenches. A scene of jagged desolation stretches
to the horizon, but the stage is dominated by a huge damaged crucifix
(which may owe something to Owen's 'At a Calvary near the Ancre'),
the figure of the Virgin and an enormous howitzer. Fitful signs of
military activity indicate the imminence of an enemy offensive. With the
exception of Bagnal, who is tied to a gun wheel as a punishment for
stealing a chicken, all the characters of the first act have disappeared.
They are replaced by anonymous symbols. As in one of Stockhausen's
sound sequences, there is no anticipation, since there is no reason for
one thing to happen rather than another. The wounded go by on
stretchers. A staff officer reads out inoperable orders whose precision
contrasts with the general confusion. The soldiers grumble and curse
but not in normal speech. Everything is chanted. When the attack
comes they spring to action, and the act ends with a verse prayer to the
gun. This may have been inspired by Owen's sonnet 'On seeing a piece
of our artillery brought into action'.

The third act opens in a Catholic hospital in Dublin. The old characters are back again, but those who have taken part in the war are transformed. Harry Heenan, paralysed from the waist down, is awaiting an operation and cannot quite escape from 'hope's accursed bands'. Teddy Foran is blind. The hero is now Barney Bagnal who was wounded while saving what was left of Heenan's life, and to whom Heenan's girl friend has deserted. Heenan works off his bitterness against his rival in the last act, but ultimately decides to face his future as resolutely as he may.

Now undoubtedly the Abbey directors had expected a play in O'Casey's well-known manner. All three artistic directors, Yeats, Lady Gregory and Lennox Robinson recorded their disappointment, Yeats in a famous letter to O'Casey. His observations deserve respect, despite the rough handling O'Casey gave them in his reply. He enjoyed the first act. He thought the second 'an intensely interesting technical experiment', but too long for its material. After that there was 'nothing'. He missed a dominating character, a dominating action, psychological unity and unity of action. He thought the reason for O'Casey's failure, was that 'the greatness of the war' had thwarted him. 'It has refused to become mere background, and obtrudes itself upon the stage as so much dead wood that will not burn with the dramatic fire.' The dramatist should be able to reduce the whole history of the world to the status of wallpaper. He thought O'Casey had been unable so to reduce the war because he was not 'interested' in it as he was interested in the Anglo-Irish and civil wars. He never stood on its battlefields or walked its hospitals. Hence he wrote out of his opinions. It is of interest that Yeats also disliked Owen's war poetry, though there was no question that Owen stood on the battlefields.

It was easy for O'Casey to demolish Yeats's arguments, though they expressed a real objection. O'Casey had mixed with wounded soldiers during his stay in St Vincent's hospital. Anybody living in a working-class neighbourhood would have seen mutilitated and shell-shocked veterans in various degrees of physical and mental decrepitude. (Moreover in his own brother, Michael, he had an example of a soldier whose military service had brought upon him the disability which was the presumable cause of his failure to marry.) He declared that he had mixed with soldiers all his life and asked why dramatists were barred from scenes that they could only imagine. So there began a war of words. But Yeats had said that O'Casey wrote out of his opinions, which means that they were not Yeats's. It will be as well to try to ascertain them.

That O'Casey regarded the World War as a disaster is obvious. But the play contains no evidence that he wished to oppose pacifism to this evil. One would think the prayer to the gun would dispose of that, especially since O'Casey omits the curse which Owen bestows on his gun. There is no evidence in the play that he had in mind any form of opposition whatsoever. The characters whose lives are wrecked accept their fate and say 'blessed be the name of the Lord'.

But to O'Casey's knowledge, two revolutions, the Russian and the Irish had been born out of opposition to the war. The International had been explicit. The answer to war was revolution. Connolly had urged resistance to the war, beginning with a campaign against excessive exports of food. He thought this might lead to 'armed battling on the streets', bring Ireland out of the war, and end with the overthrow of capitalism in Europe. To Connolly this was what 1916 was about.

But O'Casey had rejected the Easter Rising in *The Plough and the Stars*. Consequently *The Silver Tassie* was deprived of an answer to the war, and had to end on the tinkling of a ukelele. There is not even a revolutionary opposition to the war at an English level, a hint of the fraternisation of Christmas 1914, or the great mutinies in the French army.

The complete absence of national sentiment and the atmosphere of 'aristocracy of labour' can create the impression, in some productions, that the characters could all be Protestants. (Was there ever a football club attached to St Barnabas, and did O'Casey play the 'foreign game' before he turned to hurling?) *The Silver Tassie* earned O'Casey Shaw's description of him as a 'blighter and blaster of your species' and the encomium 'titan'. But why blast the species? Because he does not know what part of it is to blame. This question can be considered further after the discussion of certain questions of form.

The Silver Tassie has remained a subject of controversy mainly on account of its technical experiment in the dramatic method known as Expressionism. The Expressionist movement began in Germany towards the end of the nineteenth century, as a revolt against prevailing conventions. One of its leading exponents in the twenties of this century was Ernst Toller, whose *Masses and Men* O'Casey had seen in the Theatre Club performance at the Abbey. There was an ultra-left streak in Toller, and O'Casey may have reacted to it and tried to imitate his style.

The prevailing dramatic method of modern times is that of realism. Everybody knows that actors do not perform in their personal capacities, but pretend to be people they are not. The principle of realism is that everything is done to encourage the audience to accept them for what they represent. They must therefore represent recognizable things and arouse no sense of incredulity. No realist producer would make Napoleon six feet high, for fear the audience would say to themselves 'that's not Napoleon'. It is obviously possible to push this principle to such finicky extremes that it can defeat its own object. This charge has been levelled at the 'naturalist' school of realism, though nobody who reads Stanislavsky's *My Life in Art* can doubt its possibilities. The method of realism is unquestionably sound. The aim of the realist theatre is to cut a temporal section through a part of life and invite the audience to react to it in accordance with their own experience. But are there other methods?

In narrative, the story-teller can break off his tale and interpolate passages of explanation. This is because he appears before his audience in person, whereas the dramatist does not. This restriction is likely to prove the more irksome when the dramatist wishes to carry his audience beyond their experience. Shaw felt it necessary to accompany his plays with long prefaces.

The interdiction of comment is by no means general throughout theatrical history. The primitive theatre knew nothing of it. Far from being an excrescence, the Greek chorus, for example, derives from the origin of Attic drama in gentile initiation ceremonies.[7] In the last act of *The Silver Tassie*, O'Casey converts some of his characters into a chorus who comment on the ebb and flow of life around them. The author's aim is doubtless universalization. On the other hand the characters cease to contribute anything but a sense that the drama is about to end. Lorenzo da Ponte did the same thing in *Don Giovanni*, at the very end converting the entire cast into a chorus to point a moral. O'Casey's moral is little more than that a man must accept his fate. Some grow, others die.

Perhaps a more effective means of commenting is the use of symbols. This is a feature of all the plays of O'Casey's English period. For those seeking their political content they introduce a fresh element of risk, especially when two languages are used simultaneously and the symbolism is carried forward simultaneously on a number of levels. The use of symbols involves the audience in a double suspension of disbelief. On the one hand an actor must be accepted as what he purports to be. But if the symbol is to stand out, then there must be something that is inconsistent with his simple role. If a soldier wastes time praying to a gun when he should be firing it, perhaps one thinks war has become a ritual, or that the church is joined with the state in a vast conspiracy of destruction. The scene becomes an enacted parable, Aesop on the stage. But beyond a certain point an audience cannot go. One recalls the experiments of the brain physiologist, Pavlov, who was working on the capacity of animals to develop conditioned reflexes, that is to say to respond to symbols. If a dog were presented with contradictory symbols he developed a neurosis. A monkey smashed the apparatus – a good illustration of the fact that the advantage of a brain over a computer is that it is attached to a body. Beyond a certain point serious symbols lead to puzzlement, light ones to pantomime. Realism is a method appropriate to a society that is well educated in natural science. Its great virtue is lucidity. There is nothing you can eat which will do you more good than food. The best place for walking is the ground. But when a great dramatist decides to walk somewhere else, we must try to follow him.

Of the symbolism of the second act of *The Silver Tassie* much has been written. Religion hovers over the whole play. But in this act it is flesh, blood and bone. It dominates everything. The chanting, the church music heard off, the juxtaposition of gun and crucifix, and finally the prayer to the gun effect a commentary on something which is largely forgotten now, the universal use of religion to send men to their deaths in the First World War.[8]

But who were to blame for the war? According to Connolly they were the bankers and industrialists of Britain and Germany who were fighting for hegemony over the undeveloped world. That is not the direction in which O'Casey's symbols point. One can imagine the symbols necessary to indict capitalist imperialism of the international crime. Colonial soldiers could be brought on stage carrying intolerable burdens. The scene could have been set in a ruined bank. There could be advertising and symbols of finance, such as O'Casey used on a much smaller scale when he was attacking capitalism in *Time to Go*. But O'Casey in typically ultra-left fashion decided to shift the blame for the war from capitalist imperialism to the church. He had rejected the only possible Irish reaction against the war. He thereby rejected its imperialist origin and the decision of the International that the answer to war was revolution. Whom had he left to blame? The churches, who made themselves the accomplices of imperialism, were blamed, but the play ends with the victims enjoying the solaces of religion. There is a defeatist streak in ultra-leftism.

The Silver Tassie, as Yeats pointed out, lacks memorable characters. It also lacks memorable speeches. Its irony is that of events. Gabriel Fallon seems to suggest that had O'Casey had the advantage of a 'theatre workshop' like the Abbey, he might have more successfully utilized expressionist technique. There is something in this. Somebody in Dublin would have helped him to write a passable verse prayer to the gun. O'Casey had one deficiency which is fatal to verse, a taste for adjectives. In an atmosphere of co-operative give and take he might have held closer to essentials, with what advantages to the Abbey cannot be imagined.

Apart from the paternalistic desire to mould O'Casey's future did any political consideration influence the Abbey reaction? Possibly the directors sensed the implicit attack on religion and thought it best to play safe.

The upshot of the Abbey's rejection was a complete breach with O'Casey. That the theatre behaved shabbily in a number of respects cannot be doubted. It was acknowledged that O'Casey's earlier plays had saved the theatre from bankruptcy. *The Silver Tassie* is not a 'bad play' and it would have been a financial success. And it was his own reputation that O'Casey was risking. Moreover he was made the victim of bureaucratic bumbledoms. Royalties were paid late; rights were claimed that had never been assigned, and it proved impossible to find out who was responsible. If murder is decided on by a committee, nobody will swing. But O'Casey was not accustomed to suffering in silence, and what happened the world knew.

He was particularly bitter against Yeats, less so towards Lady Gregory. But when the play ultimately opened at the Apollo Theatre on 11 October 1929 she sent her good wishes, and announced her intention of seeing it when she was in London. She asked if she could meet him and make the acquaintance of his wife. He refused to see her. She replied in words of deep humility and affection. But he was obdurate, not because he wished to hurt Lady Gregory, but because he felt that the strong emotions he still felt would, if he spoke to her, surge up in recriminations. The ability to hold emotions at red heat was one of the secrets of O'Casey the dramatist. He continued to correspond with her for the few years she was still to live. He never met her again, and then he must keep uncooled for the rest of his life remorse for his rebuff. One of O'Casey's most characteristic traits was the intensity of his personal emotions. When the devil got into him it was exorcized sometimes by a quarrel, sometimes in a play.

The quarrel over *The Tassie* broke old friendships. O'Casey's ties with Ireland were loosened further. The prospect of his return receded. His financial affairs suffered, for the great depression was beginning. His artistic self-esteem was wounded. Characteristically, he responded by jumping holus-bolus into Expressionism. During the years that followed, his political activity reached its nadir, though his interest continued. From time to time he acknowledged a communist outlook but it was the communism of Bernard Shaw. His sense of commitment in Irish affairs diminished. When George Russell refused to publish a letter from him in the *Irish Statesman*, he asked Fallon to offer it indifferently to the Republican party[9] or to the 'treaty' party who were in office. It appeared in *An Phoblacht*. He had become an admirer of the USSR, but in a letter to Carney[10] expressed his pleasure not that the working class were in power but that 'they have put away from them the problems of party and creed and have settled down to solve the problems of life'.

There was confirmed in him at this time a tendency to retreat into artistic élitism, which came partly from the disillusionment of the counter-revolution in Ireland, and partly from the assault of the Abbey directors on his aesthetic judgment. That tendency was expressed just before the rejection of *The Tassie* in a letter to Lady Gregory:

So long as God or nature leaves us one atom of strength we must continue to use that atom of strength to fight on for that which is above and before all governments and parties – Art and literature which are the mantle and mirror of the Holy Ghost, and the sword of the spirit.

Art had become his substitute religion.

NOTES

1. If New York university had had the grace to give Dr Krause copies of 126 letters from O'Casey to Jack Carney, perhaps one could be surer about this. This earliest letter to Carney in the Krause collection is dated September 1931, when Carney was editing Larkin's *Irish Worker*.
2. The Free State Parliament called itself Dail Eireann, a title the right to which republicans denied it. The distinction became difficult to maintain for practical purposes once De Valera abolished the oath of allegiance to the English Crown in May 1932.
3. 'The Silver Tassie', Sean O'Casey, *Rose and Crown*, pp. 33–4.
4. ibid., p. 34.
5. ibid., p. 41.
6. Cowasjee, op. cit., p. 114.
7. For a brilliant exposition of this theme see George Thomson, *Aeschylus and Athens*.
8. Mr George Gilmore, travelling from Amiens Street to the Co. Tyrone in 1916, tore down a poster from a Dublin wall. It showed alleged German atrocities and carried the legend 'protect catholic Belgium'. He took it to the Protestant area of Tyrone where he was to spend a holiday, and pasted it up alongside a similar poster which bore the legend 'Defeat catholic Austria'.
9. One presumes that *An Phoblacht* (*The Republic*) was intended. But Fianna Fail called themselves the Republican Party.
10. D. Krause, *Letters*, p. 238.

[11]

POLITICAL REGENERATION

The existence of the world is justified only as an aesthetic phenomenon
Nietzsche

The task for art to accomplish is to make that feeling of brotherhood and love
of one's neighbour now attained only by the best members of society, the
customary feeling and instinct of all men.
Tolstoy

During the run of *The Silver Tassie* at the Apollo, Gabriel Fallon paid
the O'Caseys a visit. The two men spent an afternoon at Speakers'
Corner, Hyde Park. O'Casey was fascinated by the free-flowing
cockney humour and repartee. Fallon, anxious that he should once
more concentrate on his talent for characterization, remarked that here
in Hyde Park were the counterparts of the people in his Dublin plays. A
year later O'Casey was still impressed and wrote to Lady Londonderry,
'What a place is Hyde Park'.

On 31 December 1930, he wrote to Fallon about a film scenario
which Krause[1] identifies as the first version of O'Casey's next play
Within the Gates, work on which, interrupted by a move to Chalfont St
Giles near Aylesbury, he resumed in the summer of 1932. He sent the
manuscript to C. B. Cochran, but the impresario decided there was
no money to be made out of it. He advised O'Casey to get back to the
method of *Juno. Within the Gates* was published in December 1933 and
opened at the Royalty Theatre on 7 February 1934. In the meantime
O'Casey had eked out a somewhat precarious living with the aid,
among other things, of autobiographical sketches which were later
incorporated in the life story. Relations with Yeats had improved. When
a printer refused on moral grounds to set O'Casey's 'I wanna woman',
the poet protested against this intrusion on the rights of the artist, and
old wounds began to heal.

In years to come O'Casey was to confess that nothing gave him more
pleasure than the writing of fantasy. Perhaps he surrendered to what
Yeats called 'creation without toil', and described as the chief
temptation of the artist. *Within the Gates* indeed is not fantasy but
phantasmagoria. It is set not among the robust plebeian materialisms of
Hyde Park, but in an unnamed park, furnished with a conspicuous war
memorial to show it is in the vale of tears, but without soapbox orators,

gaily dressed holiday makers, families out for the day or vociferous drunks. Every character is one or other species of damaged goods, transmuted, or should we say 'tollerized', by the dramatic imagination.

The opening scene is a chorus of boys and girls dressed to look like flowers. This is to show it is spring. The seasons play an important part in the structure of this play. The first scene is scheduled on a spring morning, the second at a summer noon, the third on an autumn evening and the last on a winter night. The perspicacious audience will thus deduce that the action is spread over a period of about nine months, the characters assembling in the park at approximately quarterly intervals, at the right time, in order to proceed with their assignments, but seemingly having no truck with each other in the meantime. There is little reason why the action should not be compressed into a single week. This would not matter if the characters had nothing to do but symbolize the seasons. But unfortunately, the most important of them are charged with strong emotional purposes, and particularly the two of them who have names, though the names are tossed to us more or less in parenthesis.

The central figure, Jannice, is a spiritualized form of a figure which occurs elsewhere in O'Casey. She is an ailing prostitute determined to die gamely. She was begotten by a student sowing wild oats, dumped in a religious institution where she learned of the existence of hell fire, and finally rescued by an atheist who lives with her mother and pretends to be her father. Guilt and religion haunt the two women. The home is broken up. The mother becomes a drunkard, the daughter a prostitute, still pursued by visions of perdition. She is in a state of pious remorse when the play opens. But the atheist refuses to have her back home and at the end of the scene she is arrested for soliciting. Krause[2] thinks her arrest results from her asking a gardener to marry her. But the text does not require it. Possibly her return to her profession is a reaction to the rebuff. Or possibly the prospect of a spell in jail helps to explain her unavailability for scene two before the sun has entered the appropriate sign of the zodiac.

In the second scene a Bishop, whom we saw earlier in casual conversation with cardboard characters as he tried to 'get close to the common people', reappears. He is no romantic for all his spiritual slumming, for he refuses the eleëmosynary role in which the park attendants have cast him by explaining that his sister manages his charity for him. He repulses Jannice when she requests his pastoral good offices in persuading the gardener. But then her mother appears and recognizes in the Bishop the erring student of long ago. He denies that he is the man. But as he departs he hands the Dreamer three pounds to give to the girl he now recognizes must be his daughter. The Dreamer is wide enough awake to pocket one of them but passes on the other two. He sits with her while she recovers from a heart attack, revealing that he is an impecunious poet and song-writer. Indeed he composes a song to her on the spot. But she declines to sell her charms for a song. He offers her the note he stole from her. But though she responds to him as a person, for some reason she decides to retire with a Salvation Army Officer, not in the way of business, but of piety.

In the next scene the Bishop returns. It is now an autumn evening. He has put the intervening time to good use, for he has arranged for Jannice to enter another institution. She rejects this proposal and this time goes away with the Dreamer whose charity is thus shown to be the warmer. In the last scene the Bishop returns again, determined in spite of all the protestations of his sister, to help Jannice in some undefined way. He meets the mother and changes his mind. When Jannice appears again, elated and slightly drunk from a bed of joy with the Dreamer, he consigns her to the 'down and outs' who crowd round threatening like the Eumenides of old. The Dreamer urges her to 'sing them silent, dance them still, and laugh them into an open shame'. His well-meant advice proves fatal. He and she dance together for a minute. Then she falters, falls and dies, but not before the Bishop has guided her hand in the sign of the cross.

The superficial moral is that all a poor devil will get from religion is a valedictory gesture. The above synopsis does not of course take account of the amusing sub-plots. O'Casey's difficulty is, however, that he does not know how to endow English people with amusing or endearing qualities. It is on the whole a dreary, depressing, pessimistic play and easily O'Casey's weakest. George Jean Nathan, the American critic who so much admired O'Casey, declared on reading the manuscript that it had 'overwhelming beauty'. He must have been easily overwhelmed. George Beckles, writing in the London *Daily Express*, challenged O'Casey to explain what it was about, and when O'Casey declined to contribute to his education, pronounced it 'ranting socialistic nonsense'. The *Daily Express* had a keen nose for heresy. It could smell what was not there. James Agate used the expression 'pretentious rubbish', and likened the mingling of symbol with reality, to interleaving *Alice in Wonderland* with *Euclid*. He incidentally put his finger on one of the play's more irritating weaknesses. There is no Irish accent, but there is Irish idiom. For anybody who knows his Hyde Park (or for that matter even a park with a war memorial) the solecisms stick out like the quills of a porcupine.[3]

If O'Casey had nothing to say to Beckles, at least he tried to reveal to Agate something of what was in his mind. It was that 'force and power must be created out of what we have. That only the brave and wise should govern and all the rest must serve.'⁴ But what character in *Within the Gates* is both brave and wise? Certainly not the Bishop who would probably have been wiser if he had kept out of the park altogether. Presumably O'Casey meant the Dreamer. But there is no suggestion in the play that the Dreamer should govern. But perhaps there were other dreamers not in the play who would be prepared to attempt it. For O'Casey explained further that he was calling for 'active life through the Dreamer'. Now a dream is the antithesis of active life. Elsewhere he declared, 'The first dreamer is the Holy Ghost.' One would have imagined that an avowed atheist would have considered himself precluded from offering this explanation. But not O'Casey. Obviously one must search further for his meaning. It cannot have been clear to himself or he would have been more explicit.

It is tempting to recall the remark already quoted, namely that art and literature are 'the mantle and mirror of the Holy Ghost'. O'Casey had rejected Father and Son, but retained the Holy Ghost as providing a transition to his substitute religion, the worship of art. If this is relevant, then the Dreamer represents the new religion. He is the artist whom the society of the nineteen-thirties rejected, but who alone can 'govern' in the sense of giving purpose and meaning to the lives of others. Of course the Dreamer effects no permanent change. He is prostitute enough himself to appropriate Jannice's pound. He enjoys her body free of charge and finally dances her to death. But he is interested in her, makes her a song, and is always kind and even generous when he has money. He is the first character in which O'Casey incarnates the anti-commercial principle he had once sought in religion.

O'Casey obviously held that Jannice had not made a bad bargain. There is no question that in the middle thirties such would be the judgement of thousands of gifted and artistic young people whose prospects had been blighted by the slump. Many of them abandoned organized religion and substituted art. It is a matter of opinion whether they were well or ill served, when the *ars meretricia* of radio and television lined their pockets and put an end to their casuistries.

It was the virtue of such magazines as *Left Review*, founded in 1934, that they tried to give the alienated artist a sense that his work could be significant in a material sense, that it was more than the object of an occult worship. It was not a matter of the discordance between blind faith and empty scepticism being resolved in art. It was one of ending the separation of the artist from the forces which were trying to remould society, by recognizing art as a function necessary to the process of social evolution. All capitalism could do was to lock him in a rainbow coloured box on a full belly, and let him *entertain*. O'Casey was one who could not be caught.

While *Within the Gates* prompts these reflections, it delivers nothing clearly. It was a transitional work both artistically and politically. We can discern the problems it reflects. There was always a streak of artistic élitism in O'Casey, but only for a brief period in the thirties was it dominant.

In February 1935 he published in the *New Statesman* a devastating review of the play *Love on the Dole*.[5] In it he quotes with approval Toller's dictum that it is not the artist's duty to 'serve the tastes of the day, but to serve the eternal powers of life, truth, joy, beauty, freedom, the mind and the spirit'. O'Casey goes even further. The artist 'is above the kings and princes of this world, and he is above the Labour Leaders and Proletariat too'. Indeed, he goes on, 'Under the patronage of the Proletariat we have got so far . . . such things as *Singing Jailbirds*, a terrible thing from Upton Sinclair, *Love on the Dole* from Ronald Gow and Walter Greenwood, and seven Soviet plays from Russia.' To make matters clear beyond peradventure he declares: 'The artist is answerable only to himself, and his work is for those finer minds among men who hold varying views upon all other things.'

The logic of this position was, as Tolstoy so clearly saw, to deny the common people the right to art, and to salute the intellectual *Uebermensch*. With O'Casey it led to a kind of classless socialism redolent of the early nineteenth century. 'This social system,' he wrote, 'inadequate to the need of the worker, is just as inadequate to the need of the rich.' When Gow and Greenwood had replied to him, he wrote to Lady Astor with engaging innocence, 'two organizations that can't bear criticism, the church and the so-called Labour movement'.

Next month, angry at the banning of *Within the Gates* by the Mayor of Boston, forgetting syntax, he wrote, 'Good taste never has and never will spring from the majority. Man in the mass is vulgar,'[6] and again, 'If the statesmen and bureaucrats can't set the world to rights, then the Dramatist must set the bureaucrats and statesmen to rights.' Those who believe O'Casey was at this time a fully-fledged socialist of years' standing should ponder this incredibly naïve statement. In 1913 he acquired a strong but essentially emotional sympathy with the working class and became a 'Labour man'. In 1919 he acquired a sympathy with socialism. Under Shaw's influence he felt himself in tune with a somewhat vague communism. And with all this went a sympathy with the USSR which was trying to base human relations on something superior to the cash nexus. But he imagined that class distinctions could be ignored between 'finer minds'. (Perhaps if the minds were fine enough this might be possible.) And he thought that statesmen concerned with interests could be swayed by precept. Either O'Casey had regressed, or he had never understood the class struggle apart from its crude manifestation in industrial disputes.[7] This would explain his political ultra-leftism, which is, after all, in essence an exaggerated concern with objectives that cannot be immediately attained, to the neglect of the course of action that could if followed attain them. Ultra-leftism is a phenomenon of untrained emotions and common in those whose socialism is insufficiently educated to be scientific. O'Casey had, however, come to share the feeling that was very widespread in the early thirties, that there was something radically wrong with society in general.

The world counter-revolution was carried over from the twenties into the thirties, but met ever-increasing resistance. In Ireland the first break came in 1932. Fianna Fail was returned to office. The political prisoners were released. De Valera started to dismantle the machinery of the 'treaty', though its worst consequence, partition, remained. He was resisted by enemies within and without. The 'treaty' party donned blue shirts and changed their name to Fine Gael. They began provocative parades in republican areas. The republicans defended themselves so effectively that the government stepped in, taking action against both sides, but removing the danger of a slide towards fascism. The English National Government declared an 'economic war' when De Valera breached the financial provisions of the 'treaty'. The Irish economy was seriously injured, and doubt arose over Ireland's capacity to supply England with food in the event of a war. In the settlement with Chamberlain in 1938, De Valera obtained everything he wanted, including the return of the 'treaty' ports, Berehaven and Lough Swilly, and the renunciation by England of all claim to sovereignty in the twenty-six counties. As a result the twenty-six counties were not dragged into the holocaust that the western powers prepared for themselves. O'Casey did not react strongly to these events. The reason may be that fascism failed to gain a hold in Ireland because it was pro-British, and was defeated by precisely those republican forces which O'Casey had mentally written off.

At the same time, if reaction could not fly the national flag, it was still able to masquerade as religion. Thus, when the quarrel with Yeats was finally made up, and *The Silver Tassie* was played at the Abbey in August 1935, a campaign was waged against it by a Father Gaffney of the Catholic Youth Movement in Galway. His denunciations were taken up by the entire Catholic press. Here was an outrage on religion and morality. This opposition must on no account be confused with that of 1926. It came from the right, while that to *The Plough* came from the left. Frank Ryan and Hanna Sheehy-Skeffington wished to see the completion of the national revolution. Father Gaffney's supporters knew as much about the national revolution as they knew about *The*

Silver Tassie. They nevertheless reflected the thinking of the propertied classes who felt that piety among the masses could only benefit them, and cared little how that piety was induced.

O'Casey defended himself in his usual forthright manner. But he became highly receptive to the notion that his native land was groaning under a clerical yoke. He grew increasingly anti-clerical.

Meanwhile events in England took another course and it was to these that O'Casey responded. A labour movement stunned by the treachery of MacDonald and Snowden who had joined the Tories in the National Government, was shocked out of its apathy by the victory of 'National Socialism' in Germany in January 1933. Refugees flocked to Britain and recounted the barbarities of Hitler's regime. The mighty German working-class movement, apple of Marx's eye, pride of three internationals, previously thought indestructible, was annihilated in a matter of months. In February 1933, gaining access through the underground passage from Goering's palace, the nazis burned the Reichstag. The world watched with rising admiration the defendant Dimitrov, who exposed his accusers and turned them into accused. News came of the establishment of concentration camps and the brutalities practised behind their fences. The most oppressive regime in world history had established itself in an advanced European country. And its spokesmen proclaimed unequivocally they were bent on war.

From the first, the Conservatives favoured Hitler. When, at the election before he was handed power, the nazis lost two million votes, the Tory press engaged psychologists to speculate upon what subconscious complexes inhibited Hitler from seizing it. There was only one enemy to the thinking of such people. That was the USSR. Hitler, they thought, was going to smash the USSR, Germany sustaining in the process sufficient damage to disembarrass England of her competition for some time to come. Tory policy was therefore aimed at breaching the *cordon sanitaire*, established to bar Russia from the West and now barring Germany from the East. *Fag an bealach* was the slogan. Make way for the anti-Soviet crusader!

There was a strong anti-war sentiment in Britain. This speedily became an anti-fascist sentiment. There was also a distrust of Germany, deriving from the First World War. This, in wide sections of the labour movement and among the liberal intelligentsia, became a cautiously pro-Soviet tendency. There were on the other hand those who would have liked to deal with these 'lefties' as Hitler had dealt with his. The British Union of Fascists, headed by Sir Oswald Mosley, conducted provocative parades and their challenge was accepted. The part played by the British communists, in initiating a broad movement against fascism, is not often recalled today. Thousands attended the vast public meetings at which Tom Mann, William Gallacher and, above all, Harry Pollitt, called for a united front of all right-minded citizens against the new danger. The first theoretical exposure of the base of fascism in monopoly capital was provided by R. Palme Dutt in his *Fascism and Social Revolution.*

English fascism was imperialist, anti-communist, pro-German, but above all anti-Jewish. This last has lately been denied, but a glance at the newspapers of the time should satisfy any doubter. At the same time it suffered from the deficiency of fascism in Ireland. It was implicitly anti-national, though Union flags floated aloft at all its gatherings. Naturally enough Jews resented being insulted in their own ghettoes. Ex-servicemen objected to what almost amounted to praise of those who had given them their wounds. Having brought upon themselves hostility by the unpopularity of their opinions, which were expressed in extravagant language, the fascists disgraced themselves by the violence they meted out to those who disagreed with them. After the disturbances at Olympia in June 1934 doctors had to treat many cases of serious injury. The average citizen began to take alarm. The police, who had first shared the anti-popular prejudices characteristic of their upper echelons, began to turn against the fascists. The decisive conflict was probably that on 9 September 1934 when it was estimated that half a million Londoners turned out to 'drown fascism in a sea of working-class activity'.

Italy invaded Abyssinia on 3 October 1935. The Tory press immediately produced evidence of slavery in that country. This was intended to justify the Italian fascists in an attempt to enslave the entire population. In April 1936 a Popular Front won an overwhelming victory in the Spanish general election. On 18 July a number of generals revolted and brought over Moorish troops to slaughter their own countrymen. The same press designated the legally elected government of Spain 'the reds' and quickly produced examples of the burning of churches and the ill-treatment of priests and nuns. There was a Popular Front government in France. This was not attacked but subverted. On 23 July the British government persuaded its leader, Leon Blum, to announce a policy of non-intervention. All preceding international law was to go for nothing. The legitimate government of Spain was to be denied arms with which to put down a revolt.

On 24 August, Hitler introduced military conscription based on a minimum of two years. In October, the Rome–Berlin axis, or alliance between nazi Germany and fascist Italy, was established. The 'anti-Comintern pact' with Japan followed in November. The Italian and German intervention in Spain began. The arrival in Madrid on 8 November of the first volunteers of the International Brigade to counter this intervention, aroused world-wide enthusiasm. Throughout the next two years a number of Irishmen served in the Brigade and some of them O'Casey knew well. At an enormous rally of women, Dolores Ibarruri, the great Basque orator and communist leader said, 'Better to be the widows of heroes than the wives of cowards.' History was repudiating the philosophy of Nora Clitheroe and the fact cannot have been lost on O'Casey.

The Spanish Republicans held out for two-and-a-half years. While the British government refused to sell arms, the anti-fascist movement organized a network of committees which sent civilian supplies and food through the military blockade. There were demonstrations and meetings. The publication of left-wing literature reached unprecedented levels. At the same time, the malicious identification of the Spanish Republic with communism, tended to obscure the fundamental democratic issue. With each territorial advance on the part of the nazis, the tempo of political activity accelerated. Hitler took Austria. The British Prime Minister gave him the only defensible part of Czechoslovakia in September 1938. He quickly acquired the rest. France was now reduced to a second-class power. Hitler's rhetoric grew ever more strident and bombastic. Public opinion in Britain was thoroughly aroused. There were sometimes as many as three demonstrations outside 10 Downing Street in one week.

Indeed, in the spring of 1939, Mr Chamberlain seems to have feared that his policy was succeeding too well. Hitler had been given a license to drive to the East. But what if he were now strong enough to drive to the West? The British government hastened its rearmament. This being feared insufficient, negotiations were opened with the USSR, but were pursued at an ostentatiously leisurely pace. The purpose was not to establish an alliance against fascism, which would have made war impossible, but to set Hitler pondering on the relative advantages of a war on one front, with benevolent neutrals on the other, and a war on two fronts. Hitler pondered well. On 24 August Britain's bluff was called. Russia and Germany signed a non-aggression pact. One might think that all that was necessary was for Britain to sign another, and thus restore collective security at the last moment. But Britain's 'men of Munich' were as intent on war as the nazis. Emergency powers were rushed through Parliament. Children were evacuated from the big cities. On 1 September Hitler invaded Poland. But he was pledged to proceed no further. The British Commons revolted at the collapse of Chamberlain's policy, for now there was set in train the process which was to reduce Britain as well as France to a second-class power. War was declared on 3 September. But Chamberlain's purpose was not to destroy fascism. It was to compel Hitler to renew his drive to the East.

It was of course impossible to escape the political turmoil in England. During the years immediately preceding the war, the country was divided into opposing camps. People previously indifferent to politics were drawn into them. But the two camps did not enjoy internal unanimity. The crudities of Mosley embarrassed the finesse of Chamberlain. Within the anti-fascist camp the leaders of the Labour Party and trade unions constantly eased the government's path for the sake of minor concessions. Perhaps the most revolting spectacle was that of the *News Chronicle*. This newspaper wished to retain the radical readership it had inherited from the *Daily News*. It justified every move of the government while it was being prepared, and condemned it as a mistake from the day it was performed.

There were also the professional ultra-leftists, who displayed their customary inability to grasp the essence of a practical issue. For example, in Spain there were those who were not content to defend a democratically elected government against rebellion and invasion, but must choose this time for an uprising aimed at establishing the dictatorship of the proletariat. And in Britain, just as there were those who refused to support the Spanish republic because they had been told that it was communist, so there were others who held aloof from it because it was not communist. There were people in the nineteen-thirties, and the breed is not extinct today, who thought that once socialist revolution had been invented, no other political issue was even entitled to existence.

It is natural to ask at what point O'Casey was caught up in the rising movement. There is little in the life story to help us. *Sunset and Evening Star* has a chapter on the war, but only a few lines on the political fight against fascism that preceded it. There is more material in the letters. If, using Dr Krause's admirable index, we count the number of pages on which 'Communism' is mentioned before December 1933, we find three. The number of pages containing references to 'Communism' in successive years thereafter is as follows; 1934, nil; 1935, 5; 1936, 9; 1937, 14; 1938, 14; 1939, 9; 1940, 8; 1941, 5. If we count the references to the USSR on a similar basis, we find up to December 1933 four only, and thereafter as follows: 1934, nil; 1935, 2; 1936, 3; 1937, 1; 1938, 28; 1939, 13; 1940; 3; 1941, 13. Now in each case the value is zero for 1934, the period of *Within the Gates* and artistic élitism, the time when O'Casey was not seeking solutions through politics. In each case the references for the years 1937–39, are more numerous than all the others put together. It therefore seems reasonable to conclude that the Spanish civil war was the decisive political event impelling O'Casey's abandonment of artistic élitism, and his adoption of the frankly partisan and, some have said, crudely propagandist method of his next play, *The Star Turns Red*, which he began in London early in 1937 and completed at Totnes in January 1939. But the change was beginning in 1935 and was hastened by the outbreak of the Abyssinian war.

In November 1935 he told Lady Astor that 'there was something in Communism'. In March 1936 he was admitting that *Within the Gates* contained many faults. In May he wrote a letter to *Time and Tide* in which he showed a shrewd grasp of political essentials. 'Every anti-communist in England, France and America, is asking for a German hegemony in the West, and a Japanese one in the East.' He warned that if their wishes were granted their countrymen might regret it. He denounced the hypocrisy of the British imperialists who, while condemning Mussolini for dropping poison gas on the Ethiopians, were storing tons of it in England. He advocated an understanding with the USSR as the basis of collective security.

As his interest in politics revived, he began to make comments on the Irish question. He recognized that Ireland was not free while partition remained. He explained that he had stood for an alliance of labour and republicanism, not nationalism (that is to say the Redmond party). He declared that he was more 'national' than ever.[8] At the same time his knowledge of world politics was not profound and his speculations were often wide of the mark, for example his opinion that Japan would be the next communist country.

In March 1937 he finally declared himself in relation to socialism and communism. He described as 'our creed', the *Communist Manifesto* of Marx and Engels. It was from this understanding of communism therefore that he wrote *The Star Turns Red*.

During the summer of 1937 he spent a holiday in North Wales and became interested in Welsh nationalism. He attended gatherings of the nationalist movement and there is no doubt that his old blood was stirred by memories of Sinn Fein. 'National independence must, unfortunately, come before Communism', he wrote to Harold Macmillan.[9] It is remarkable that, while he ignored this principle in considering Ireland where it applied, he should affirm it so definitely in Wales, where it was in dispute. In recognizing the popular character of the Welsh movement, he was of course a generation ahead of his time. But it is just possible that he may have met Mr Roose Williams, a Welsh communist then resident at Bangor, less than ten miles from where he was staying. At this time Mr Williams, whose mother came from Dun Laoire, was secretary of the North Wales district of the Communist Party. He had strong nationalist connections and would certainly have made contact with O'Casey if he knew he was there. O'Casey was now in touch with the British communists, and excluded them alone from his unflattering description of the English – 'ready to laugh, ready to weep, at the least thing, but never moved.'

Before long, under the influence of the British 'left' he was beginning to reconsider the Irish scene. In March 1938 he wrote of 'semi-independence', and in April of the 'curse of partition'. When the *Daily Telegraph* declined to print one of his letters, he sent it to the *Daily Worker*. All his family were registered as Irish citizens and, in defending himself against some animadversions that had been directed at him in the United States, he declared: 'I am as loyal to Ireland as any man alive.'[10]

O'Casey moved to Totnes in September 1938. He was thus cut off from the increasingly feverish life of the capital. But his political evolution continued. He started corresponding with *International Literature* in Moscow and sent material for publication at the suggestion of its representative in England, Jack Lindsay. In December he spoke of making an 'odd dash into politics for Communist, Irish Front and Democratic activities'.

Irish Front was a duplicated quarterly founded by Charles Donnelly and Leslie Daiken in 1934. It was published by the London Branch of the Republican Congress. When the parent organization in Ireland was disbanded the London organization became the Connolly Club. Similar clubs were established in Birmingham, Liverpool and elsewhere, and a few years later they were amalgamated into the Connolly Association, *Irish Front* becoming a monthly and changing its name first to *Irish Freedom* and later to *Irish Democrat*.

The Star Turns Red was completed after the Munich agreement but before the great disasters of 1939 and 1940. O'Casey had completely recovered from the political demoralization which occasioned his departure from Ireland. In what is probably his most ambitious play, he tackled the issues of fascism and social revolution at a time when they were white-hot in Western Europe. By the very attempt he places himself in a unique category.

The action takes place in the 'future'. But it is a future containing many familiar things and the place is a slightly stylized Dublin. O'Casey did not expect a performance in Ireland, and advised non-Irish players not to attempt an Irish accent. He employs standard English spelling, but Dublin idiom abounds, for example in such expressions as 'bowsey', 'the time that's in it', 'Jasus!' 'aself', not to mention occasional Kiltartanisms like 'the way he'll be kept' (meaning *so that* he'll be kept) and the 'Lord Mayor does be angry'. There are references to history which would be comprehensible only to an Irish audience, and fascism is presented in the Irish aspect of the Christian Front, an organization which combined ostentatious piety with opposition to all forms of socialism and republicanism and support for General Franco in Spain. Needless to say it was never in a position to engage in mass intimidation as it does in the play.

The first act shows a working-class family whose two sons, Jack (O'Casey's name) and Kian[11] are so bitterly divided over politics that the old cynic who has fathered them swears that they are agreed only in one thing, their willingness to murder each other. Jack is a dedicated but somewhat dogmatic communist. His younger brother is as decided a fascist. He swaggers in wearing blue dungarees, and swaggers out gorgeously arrayed in saffron shirt, black breeches and jackboots. The time is Christmas Eve, and carol singers are already busy with *Adeste fideles* in the street. But we gather that the members of 'Red Jim's' union are engaged in a stay-in strike (a comparative novelty in 1937) and that they have selected this unusual time for armed action of some kind, whether offensive or defensive is not clear. And it emerges that the fascists have chosen the same time for a 'great procession that is to declare once and for all the utter end of Communism'. Red Jim is of course identified with Larkin, though it was to the younger Larkin that this sobriquet was in fact applied.

Jack's fiancée, Julia, has been dressing for a dance, and at first declines to follow him to the hall which is presumably the union premises. She changes her mind after seeing the 'large shining silver star' that has been visible through the window since the act began. This simultaneous outrage upon optics and astronomy, persuades her to 'face and fight' the saffron shirts who are raiding suspect houses under the instructions of the 'Red priest of the politicians'. They soon arrive. The Red Priest is accompanied by the 'Brown Priest of the poor' who backs him up, but with increasing hesitation. The fascist leader permits himself to disparage Julia's fancy dress and receives a retaliatory slap across the face. For this reason she is dragged out to be whipped. It is then made clear that the visit is intended as a warning. The act ends with the entry of Julia's father, one of the lieutenants of Red Jim, who, enraged at his daughter's treatment, rushes at the fascist leader and is mortally wounded by a shot from Kian. He refuses the Brown Priest's ministrations and dies as Jack lifts up his fist in the communist salute.

The second act is set in the headquarters of the General Workers' Union where the Red Priest and union officials are hatching a plot to depose Red Jim and bring the struggle to an end. They include Sheasker (*seascoir*, well-heeled), Brallain (*breall*, a blot, mistake) Eglish (*Eaglais*, a church perhaps using the first vowel of the Welsh *Eglwys*), Caheer (*cach fhiar*, every defect) and an anonymous secretary. The Red Priest leaves them to perfect their plans, but before Red Jim arrives there are two diversions. Brannigan, a union member with a taste for alcohol, comes in to demand payment of a maternity claim. He is refused, but being armed he exacts the payment of twenty-five shillings which he goes out to spend on drink. The Brown Priest then brings warning of a

Saffron-shirt plan to arrest Red Jim, to execute which mounted police and soldiers are mustering.

The officials are delighted, but not for long. Red Jim appears. After some hesitation they break the news of his deposition, and say that the red funeral he had planned for Julia's father has been cancelled and a religious service substituted.[12] They refuse his request for money to give to Julia and accuse him of the wanton dispersal of union funds. The committee has decided that no money shall in future be dispensed without written permission. To this Red Jim replies, 'I'm the committee now. I'm the union. I march with the men and women.' He then particularizes his colleague's past. Sheasker was an undertaker's debt collector (shades of the coffin in 1918?). Caheer was a defalcating insurance agent. Brallain was little more than a tramp. Now who chose these individuals and had them appointed as union officials? Red Jim declares: 'I did.' He gets his money. But when Brannigan comes in drunk, he refuses to pay him the maternity benefit which he says is due to his wife, and insists on a promise that he will give up drink.[13] He then leaves the officials under armed guard, with the miraculously sobered Brannigan in charge.[14]

In the third act the setting is once more the home of Jack and Kian. The body of the dead man lies on a raised platform. Neighbours come to pay their last respects. Most of them are impoverished, some sick. The question is of course the possession of the body. Jack arrives first with four armed men, then come the priests and confraternity men. The Red Priest demands the removal of the communist emblems. The four guards fidget uneasily. But Red Jim arrives and, after a brief dispute with the Red Priest, bears off the corpse.

For the last act the scene is 'a large room in the residence of the Lord Mayor', where a Christmas party is in preparation. A rumour is about that police have gone to the union hall to arrest Red Jim. As the carols begin again factory sirens sound. The star, visible near some factory chimneys, suddenly changes from silver to red. There are rifle shots. Mounted police[15] are reported in full retreat. The telephone exchange is seized by the workers. Red Guards enter and take over the Mayor's house. The message comes that the army have refused to fire on the workers. Kian and the Red Priest arrive under a flag of truce, the Brown Priest having by now joined the workers. But Jack has been killed in the fighting. Kian refuses to go back with the Red Priest and, as the curtain falls, is seen standing mesmerized by the corpse of his brother.

The Star Turns Red has attracted little praise, even from O'Casey's most committed admirers. Dr Krause[16] considers it obvious that it was written as a 'piece of anti-fascist propaganda'. A generation has grown up lacking acquaintance with the political atmosphere of the thirties. Propaganda is designed to make converts. But anti-fascist propaganda at the time this play was written would have been superfluous. By 1939 those who did not believe that fascism was an evil were beyond redemption. The issue before the people was not its evil nature, but the means by which it could be defeated. At that time every politically literate person with an ounce of liberalism in his constitution, was interested in one thing only, and that was trying to prevent the central disaster of the twentieth century, the unnecessary and avoidable Second World War.

O'Casey was concerned with the best means of defeating fascism, but not by winning a war, for the war had not begun. His proposal was 'proletarian revolution'. He went for communism. Now the communists advocated a popular front, to defend democracy where it survived, and to restore it where it had been destroyed. He was adopting the ultra-left position. Apart from siting the struggle in the one country where fascism was no great danger, he depicts an Ireland from which the struggle for national independence has disappeared, and where it is not even possible to discern the defensive nationalism of Fianna Fail. Workers and employers seem to confront each other in the absence of intermediate classes. In the choice of saffron (not orange which in effect it is) for the colour of the fascists' shirts, O'Casey seems to suggest that the Gaels, who wore saffron kilts, have joined the counter-revolution, something highly improbable.

Kian is of course depicted as an empty-headed young fellow who likes dressing up. Jack on the contrary is O'Casey's fantastic self. In 1916, O'Casey, for reasons already given, failed to take part in a national insurrection. We have traced the evolution of his recollection of it. Now in 1939 he tells his conscience, 'Look what I would have done if it had been a proletarian revolution. Not only would I have fought. I would have died.' The Covey has come into his own.

Though the hero loses his life, *The Star turns Red* is the first of O'Casey's plays in which his principles are victorious. And victory does not come from the star, which is after all only one of O'Casey's expressionistic trappings, which would, if it were omitted, lose the play only its title. The decisive event is the refusal of the soldiers to fire on the workers. It is Russia over again. The workers have won. This in itself most critics would find objectionable. It is a settled convention among the literary establishment that 'artistic reasons' demand the failure of any struggle directed against authority. But that is not the point. The point is that proletarian revolution was not what was required in Ireland in 1916, or in Britain in 1939. O'Casey would probably have agreed that other questions would insist on getting themselves settled first. He was not a political child. Why then show the wrong solution in his play? From his own inner necessity.

According to Goldstone,[17] *The Star Turns Red* was first written as a realist drama and O'Casey added the expressionist drapery during revision. He draws this conclusion from an examination of successive drafts in the New York public library. These extraneous decorations include the songs and chants and, one takes it, the passages where purple prose makes the transition into gruesome blank verse. There is also evidence that at a late stage he made significant modifications of two important characters. Kian was at first conceived as a simple embodiment of the evils of fascism. He was changed into an example of a decent backward worker led away by fascism and finally rueful of the consequences. Julia was first portrayed as a gad-about who, for the sake of a dance, misses the revolution in which she has promised to join her fiancé. She was to be a weakling like Nora Clitheroe. She was, however, given a stauncher role in keeping with the sturdy political optimism which was characteristic of O'Casey at this period of his life.

There were further revisions after the first performance. The Red Priest became the Purple Priest. The new colour has Unionist associations. In saffron and purple we almost hear the song 'Give 'em a dose of the orange and blue!' Does this revision mean that it struck O'Casey that the Dublin he had depicted in the future was not dissimilar to Belfast in the present? This is an example of the suggestiveness of symbolism. But unfortunately we have no means of knowing if it was intended. If red was to be rejected as confusing the priest with Red Jim, perhaps purple was regarded as the imperial colour. But it is impossible to guess the reason for the original choice of red, unless it symbolizes the shedding of blood. The Brown Priest is of course a Franciscan.

In later editions of the play the blank verse was rewritten as prose, and when the Brown Priest announces the plot to arrest Red Jim, he says the intention is to send him to a 'concentration'. What is a 'concentration'? If we are expected to supply the word 'camp', then it may be guessed that in revising the play after the war had been in process some time, O'Casey came to expect that proletarian revolution would overthrow Hitler. This opinion was quite widespread at a certain period, when it was common for people to talk of appealing to the German people over the heads of their government.

Much historical material is woven into the play. That Red Jim represents Larkin there can be no doubt. His capacity for handing out union funds was well known. In 1913 his colleagues concealed a sum of £7,000 from him, so that there would be something left when the settlement came. O'Casey believed that he left for the USA because he had used insurance funds in the industrial struggle. His brother Isaac was involved in one of the resultant inquiries. O'Casey depicts Larkin's egotism in a way that in one less venerative would have been deemed satirical. What are we to say of a leader who chooses trash for his subordinates and then has to become the committee himself?

The play is full of biblical language and a Russian correspondent[18] asked for an explanation. O'Casey replied that though he had long ago given up any attachment to any form of constitutional religion, religious beliefs still held 'fast sway' in Britain. Militant Labour was up against the church. The faithful were becoming bewildered by the church's support for Franco. His object was to make them more bewildered. He therefore used their own language to criticize and denounce it.

There could of course be something in this explanation, though it would hardly seem a complete one. From the time of *The Silver Tassie*, when O'Casey mentally transferred responsibility for the war from imperialism to religion, he used biblical language against itself. But it was surely more for his inward satisfaction than for its effect on an audience. One would hardly recognize his description of the piety of 'pagan England', for even in 1939 only a fraction of the population attended a place of worship. The biblical texts he quoted would be unknown to most of his audience. Moreover, during the Spanish Civil War, many Anglican clergymen supported the campaign of food for Spain. At this time boy scouts used to help to make the collections. If O'Casey had the Catholics in mind, then his technique could be of little avail. For one thing they might fail to recognize texts from the Protestant Bible. For another they would not accept the authority of the Bible as Protestants did. Again and again in studying O'Casey we are thrown back on his inner necessity, which is at the one time the root of his idiosyncrasy, and the rock of his greatness.

The transfer of responsibility from state to church is one part of O'Casey's ultra-leftism, according to which he sees socialism as the outcome not of historical but of intellectual causes. *The Star Turns Red* takes the process a stage further. While the Bishop in *Within the Gates* is a Catholic, in the first draft he was an Anglican, and the sister was then his wife, thus making sense of her antagonism to Jannice. There is nothing in the play inconsistent with his being an Anglican. But in *The Star turns Red*, after Julia has denounced the Red Priest in the third act, she apostrophizes a crucifix in words reminiscent of some stout Lutheran spurning the intercessor and speaking directly to God: 'Against you, dear one, we have no grudge; but those of your ministers who sit like gobbling cormorants in the market place, shall fall and shall be priests no more.' Leaving aside the habits of cormorants, who ought undoubtedly to eat the fish they catch with a knife and fork, especially when sitting in the market place, there is an implication that not Christianity as such, but the Catholic church is now seen as the enemy. And O'Casey could not see that, however reactionary the church had been in Spain, by singling it out in this way in Ireland, he was in danger of encouraging anti-Irish prejudice in the English working class.

The last important question is the significance of the title. If it is

Christmas Eve, then the star is the star of Bethlehem. It is thus a symbol of Christianity, peace and humility. But what when it turns red? It becomes the star of communism, the doctrine that the workers must forget their former docility and fight to become the ruling class. In *The Star Turns Red* O'Casey celebrates his conversion to communism. He had passed from religion, through the intermediate stage of the worship of art, to a materialist philosophy. So perhaps when Dr Krause detected a special emotionalism in O'Casey's communism, what he was sensing was its origin as a substitute belief for a substitute religion. For one of O'Casey's necessities was something to believe in, whether a religion or a cause.

Of points of style little need be said. O'Casey's mannerisms have become fixed. The parallel alliterative adjectives are now used in Swinburnian fashion, not for what they mean, but for general effect. We read 'bothering and blasting', 'ripe red drunken ruffian', 'long lingering hinderer', 'red and rowdy emblem'. They are not only enemies of their noun but enemies of each other. There are attempts to create solemnity through archaism. It would be interesting to know whether these were absent from the first draft. But O'Casey's exuberance can carry most things off. It might be thought that a realistic treatment of his subject might give a clearer political picture. But that was not O'Casey's object. He was celebrating his conversion in the present by negating his part in the past.

NOTES

1. D. Krause, *Letters*, p. 424.
2. D. Krause, *O'Casey, the Man and his Work*, p. 149.
3. In the second scene (p. 152) the nursemaid says 'Why wouldn't he?', which is Irish usage. The Londoner would use the emphatic 'Why shouldn't he?'. O'Casey has not mastered the cockney accent. He changes the quality of unaccented vowels and those protected by a post-vocalic r. A Londoner will say 'fly' for 'flay', but never 'flier' for 'flare'.
4. D. Krause, *Letters*, p. 501.
5. D. Krause, op. cit., p. 537.
6. D. Krause, op. cit., p. 552.
7. Connolly's contemporaries seldom understood the depth of his political understanding. I remember Tom Johnson telling me that though he considered himself a Marxist, he was seventy years old before he understood what Connolly meant by the class struggle, namely an antagonism that revealed itself in every aspect and issue of social life no matter how far refined and removed from its economic basis. In taking part in the Easter Rising Connolly was prosecuting the class struggle. And the English imperialists knew it.
8. D. Krause, op. cit., p. 649.

9. D. Krause, op. cit., p. 677. See also Eileen O'Casey, *Eileen*, p. 158, for a denial of involvement in Welsh nationalist activities.

10. D. Krause, op. cit., p. 740.

11. Kian may be the simple personal name Cian, taken from ancient mythology, or it may be the word *cian* meaning grief. *The Star Turns Red* is the first play in which O'Casey uses Gaelic words for the names of characters.

12. When his brother, Peter, died in 1931, Jim Larkin gave him a red funeral which excited much comment in Dublin at the time. Anti-clericalism was very strong among Larkin's supporters. Shortly after Larkin's death I attended a memorial Mass in the pro-Cathedral in Marlborough Street, Dublin. There were about fifty men, mostly middle aged or elderly, who stood throughout the service.

13. Larkin was a strong supporter of the temperance movement and a total abstainer.

14. This Brannigan would not of course be the Belfast man Braithwaite. But O'Casey may have had in mind Barney Conway, a splendid character, though fond of his drop. In the case before the Master of the Rolls in which Larkin challenged the union, Barney Conway arrived to give evidence in a state of undue cheerfulness, if not of complete intoxication. Larkin ignored the judge and ordered him out of court. But Conway was always one of Larkin's most stalwart supporters. It is highly probable that O'Casey was in court.

15. There were no mounted police in Dublin since the British withdrawal. But of course who knows what there might be in the future? The anachronism shows how far O'Casey was drawing on past memories.

16. D. Krause, *Sean O'Casey, the Man and his Work*, p. 158.

17. H. Goldstone, *In Search of Community*, p. 118.

18. D. Krause, *Letters*, p. 794.

12

THE FINAL POSITION

In January 1939 an unexpected challenge added to the dangers facing British imperialism. The Irish Republican Army which, since the surviving members of the second Dail transferred their authority to it, regarded itself as the legitimate government of Ireland, declared war on England and began a campaign of bombing that lasted over a year. The appellations 'thugs' and 'murderers', readily bestowed by the Tory press, were not the result of investigation. Those who undertook this dangerous work on English soil included some of the most dedicated patriots of the younger generation. Among them were former members of the International Brigade who had fought for the Spanish Republic and now wanted to fight for an Irish one. At their worst, they could not cause the common people of England a fraction of the suffering brought on them by the National Government.

But they were embarked on a folly. They considered it possible to compel the British government to evacuate the six counties. But they had not considered the political pre-requisites for such action. Least of all did they reflect on the danger of contributing to the isolation of the left-wing forces who had had the courage to maintain opposition to partition in English politics. They were on the one hand victims of immature romanticism. On the other hand they were made what they were by the failure of the Irish labour movement to tackle an issue which is bound to loom large in the life of any nation, the integrity of its national territory. Since Labour had opted for 'economism', it was useless to deplore terrorism. Leave a vacuum and something will fill it up.

The six county administration reacted immediately by clapping all known republicans into jail. Early in February the Dublin government introduced a Treason Bill and an Offences against the State Bill. The exaggerated catholicity of the period that followed contained an element of surrogate nationalism. It was the only thing in the national tradition of the south that did not raise the inconvenient question of how, if the young republicans deserved to be locked up, the Irish territorial claim should be pursued. And of course it did not help the process of uniting the Irish people irrespective of religion.

The British left reacted creditably. The Communist Party demanded the end of partition. O'Casey told the Abbey that it could have the *Star Turns Red*, but that it would not be played in Britain until partition was ended. Some among the friends of the left were unhappy, and a controversy followed in which Dr Marie Stopes attacked the censorship of books in the twenty-six counties, forgetting the censorship of plays in England, and suggested that 'Eire' sought to 'place all thoughtful Protestant Britons in Ulster in shackles, and create a form of intellectual slavery new to the British Empire'.[1]

The *Daily Worker* reiterated its dislike of censorship, but suggested that the Special Powers Act in the six counties was somewhat more oppressive. The editor did not think that intellectual slavery was new to the British Empire. Over a period, William McCullogh and others made clear the general consensus of the left in both Britain and Ireland, that partition was the means of aiding reaction in both parts of Ireland, and should be ended for the sake of the peoples of all these islands. O'Casey was entirely at one with this consensus, and despite his antagonism to the Catholic church, never wavered.

When the Spanish war ended, Frank Ryan was serving a thirty-year sentence in Burgos jail. In May 1939 the Connolly Club established the Frank Ryan Release Committee. Among the committee's patrons were Desmond Ryan and Sean O'Casey. O'Casey made efforts to interest the press in Ryan's case and wrote to F. R. Higgins describing him as a 'splendid fellow'. The rift over *The Plough and the Stars* was long healed and indeed O'Casey had moved towards Ryan's position. In July he protested against the length of the sentences imposed on those IRA men who had been caught and convicted, arguing that they would be no deterrent, and that only the ending of partition could put a permanent stop to violence. Of course finding a policy for ending it was another matter.

For the next twenty-five years O'Casey's politics were broadly speaking those of the British Communist Party, though he never became a member. From time to time he made his home available for its gatherings. One of his sons distributed the *Daily Worker*. This is not to say that there were no rifts in the lute. Your dedicated local political worker can sometimes prove insensitive to the demand of the artist to be left in peace during periods of gestation. But undoubtedly he had found his political home as far as England was concerned. As far as Ireland was concerned, he grew increasingly intolerant, and matters were not helped by such absurdities as the banning of the first volume of his autobiography *I Knock at the Door*. His anti-partitionism, however, was essentially external. He wished to see the end of partition because of the international advantages that would follow.[2] This was the position of the British left and a perfectly legitimate one. But it would also have been legitimate for an Irishman to wish the end of partition whether it brought international advantages or not.

When the war broke out, De Valera announced that the twenty-six counties would remain neutral. There had been doubts on this score, but public opinion was overwhelming. If there was no immediate reaction in Britain, this was because instead of the *blitzkrieg* that had been expected, came the 'phoney war' in which everything proceeded normally but for the black-out, and the date for the introduction of food rationing was postponed week by week. For eight months the Chamberlain government tried one expedient after another to undermine the Russo–German accord and instigate a war against the Soviets. All England's ill-chosen military experiments directed towards this end met with disaster. On 10 May 1940, after the fiasco in Norway, Hitler invaded Holland, Belgium and Luxembourg on his way to France. It is impossible today to describe the sense of apocalypse that hung over those days. Chamberlain resigned, Churchill became Premier. In his first speech he told the public that he had nothing to offer but blood, tears, toil and sweat. The Anglo–German war had begun.

When the Polish war ended at the close of September 1939, the Russians and Germans issued a joint statement suggesting immediate peace. There was some feeling in Britain that the offer should be accepted. But seemingly Hitler had second thoughts, for on 6 October he accompanied a further *démarche* with a demand for the return of the German colonies lost during the 1914–1918 war, and the ending of 'inequalities in the extent of British and German colonies'. It was taken for granted in those days that the 'undeveloped' world was at the absolute disposal of the 'developed'.

O'Casey did not share the average Englishman's confidence that the war could be won. Bernard Shaw suggested that as the First World War had led to the end of the Austrian, German and Turkish Empires, so the second might lead to the end of the British and French. O'Casey believed that a German victory was possible as early as Christmas, and wondered about the fate of his play, *The Star Turns Red*, which had not been produced. He was deeply impressed by the Bourbon impenetrability of the English ruling-class mind, and joined with those who supported Irish neutrality and wanted it extended to the whole of Ireland. In a message to the Connolly Club he gave the impression of wanting the Irish government to take an initiative in favour of peace, possibly along the lines of the Dutch and Belgian offers of mediation.

It was during the autumn of 1939 that he began work on his play *Purple Dust*. It is a satire directed against the colonial outlook of the British ruling class. It seems to have been written quickly and easily, presumably for the American market where the 'stage Englishman' is always good for a laugh. It was completed in February 1940, before *The Star Turns Red* had been performed. It was thought to have an anti-English tendency. But its criticism is directed against members of the English ruling class. O'Casey never satirized the English as a people. There is adequate evidence of what he was thinking of the establishment when he was writing it. 'Hypocritical bastards,' he wrote to Fallon[3] of the English censorship. He described it as 'silent, cute, cunning and sinister', whereas the Irish one they were never tired of denouncing was merely ridiculous.

Purple Dust is the story of two wealthy Englishmen, Stoke and Poges, who purchase a decayed mansion in the west of Ireland. The time is the present, that is to say 1939–40, and there are references in the play to the war in progress. There was at this time widespread disgust among the British people at the catastrophic incompetence of the ruling class, although the majority saw nothing for it but to win the war and settle with them afterwards. There was particular indignation at the novelists, entertainers and foot-loose rentiers who discovered the most compelling reasons for visiting America, and if possible remaining there.

Stoke and Poges are running away from the war, but not so far that they cannot keep in touch by telephone with those who are making profits out of it for them. They imagine themselves feudal chiefs in a Tudor arcadia, but bring with them all the ill-assorted bric-à-brac their essentially vulgar minds associate with the life they intend to lead, including Irish mistresses they have picked up in England. They also bring with them their ignorance, arrogance, snobbery, complacency, insensitivity, hypocrisy so complete that it deceives themselves, and that sentimentality that Wilde called the 'bank holiday of cynicism'. All these deficiencies stem from one – their chauvinism.

The play consists of a series of episodes designed to illustrate these endearing qualities, and the conflict between them and the essentially egalitarian values of Irish society. Stoke and Poges have settled in somebody else's country. But they expect that country to adapt itself to them. They have no respect. Poges speaks contemptuously of 'your kings of Tarara'. It is considerate of him not to add the 'boom de ay' but O'Casey could be sure of his audience's adding it. He decides to call the house 'Ormond Manor' and adopt the Ormond crest, never for a moment imagining that the Irish might resent the looting of their tradition. He and Stoke reflect that the Irish are 'quaint and charming'. But they 'need control'. When a workman quotes the old saw about the 'horns of a bull, the hoofs of a horse, the snarl of a dog and the smile of an Englishman', Poges proclaims magnificently, his hand on his heart, that 'every right-minded man the world over knows that wherever we have gone, progress, civilization, truth, justice, honour, righteousness and peace have followed at our heels. In the press, in the Parliament, in the pulpit or on the battlefield, no lie has ever been uttered by us, no false claim made, no law of God ignored, no human law, national or international, broken.'

O'Casey must have enjoyed a rare chuckle, portraying this sublime hypocrisy, when it was precisely the want of these virtues in its ruling class that had brought the English nation to the verge of ruin. And a deserter was an ironical mouthpiece.

In the first act Stoke falls off his horse and loses his mistress to Jack (O'Casey's name) O'Killigain (Coileach, a cock?), the Englishman's building contractor, a young Spanish war veteran who embodies the non-commercial principle of keeping Ireland Irish. The country people have a great time pretending to take literally Stokes's piteous complaint that she has gone off 'naked and unashamed'. It is perhaps a point worth making, as possibly not well known to the present generation, that in the thirties Connacht was the least parochial part of Ireland, even though it preserved the past to a greater degree than the other provinces. Its people were the most travelled. Few townlands, indeed few families, were without some member who had worked in Britain or America. Although O'Killigain is something of a Dublin importation and speaks for O'Casey, there is much recognizable in him of that class of strong, shrewd sophisticated artisans, whose playfulness has a deliberation born of centuries of peasant tradition. It has been suggested that O'Casey drew his material from Shaw and Synge. One would suggest rather the literature of the Gaelic League, including the writings of Canon Hannay.

In the second act the town-lubbers are terrified by an invading cow they imagine to be a bull. Obviously in their colleges and counting houses they have never seen a bull. The women smash Poges's expensive oriental ornaments (made in Derby) in fright at the appearance of rats. Poges embeds an outsize lawn roller in a crumbling wall. Stoke completes the confusion by shooting the cow. All this may not amount to much in philosophical terms, but the point is constantly made that the Englishmen bring trouble on themselves because they regard themselves as superior to the natives. In the final act the slapstick proceeds against a more serious background. The house has been built on a site liable to flooding. Following days of continuous downpour the river begins to rise. The play ends with the Englishmen abandoning their expensive dreams and making for the roof.

Though the technique of the play is superficially realist, in the sense that it is not necessary to assume that the main characters are anything more than they appear, the result is an elaborate allegory comparable to *Kathleen Listens In*. The house symbolizes, not the free state, but the British Empire about to be swept away by the stream of history. At one time there were Stokes and Pogeses all over the world. Critics have thought that the names Stoke and Poges refer to Gray's elegy, written in Stoke Poges churchyard, and are therefore symbols of death. That seems very likely. But the Christian names are even more significant; both are taken from the Greek. Basil means a king, and Cyril is derived from the word for lord. They symbolize the ruling class. *Purple Dust* contains amusing dialogue, but it is marred by the wordy euphuism which O'Casey had by now made an essential element of his style.

On 12 March 1940, *The Star Turns Red* was performed at Unity Theatre, London. James Agate described it as a masterpiece, and there is no reason to suppose, though some have supposed, that he did so in fear of O'Casey's vitriolic pen. In the atmosphere of early 1940, he had much more to fear from the displeasure of his anti-communist employers than from anything O'Casey might say of him. Agate appreciated the strength of its unashamed partisanship, and was no doubt helped to this by the enthusiasm of an audience composed of people not accustomed to favourable mention. These followed the international allusions, were somewhat puzzled by the Irish, but were disinclined to look a gift horse in the mouth.

Agate's enthusiasm was not echoed throughout the left. In the *Daily Worker* the regular reporter acclaimed the play as the best thing Unity had done. But a few days later Randall Swingler, in a special article, complained that Red Jim's communism was 'not that of Marx and Lenin'. He wrote of 'elated poetry' and suggested that O'Casey gave 'a very distorted picture of trade union organization and practice'. One remarks that it was not an unrecognizable portrait of one aspect of Larkin's practice. But O'Casey was not seeking to give a picture of trade union practice but of social revolution, which neither he nor his critic had personal experience of. Swingler excused O'Casey's inadequacies in industrial matters. He appreciated his indignation against 'the degradation of poverty' but suggested that his weakness was that though he might understand the street and the home, he knew nothing about the factory. Of course neither did Swingler. His dissatisfaction may however have had its origin in the fact that O'Casey had depicted proletarian revolution (somewhat in the manner envisaged by syndicalists) when that was not in fact politically on the agenda.

With the replacement of Chamberlain by Churchill the content of the British war effort began to change. There was now no question of a compromise with fascism. Britain was defending herself, but she was also defending her empire. The overrunning of France had handed her the French colonies to administer as well as her own. The communists concluded that the war remained imperialistic and the *Daily Worker* continued its vigorous criticism. It was naturally feared that the government might try to suppress it, and with a view to broadening its basis of support, in June 1940 an editorial board was established under the chairmanship of that brilliant but irascible old mechanist J. B. S. Haldane whose popular science articles were one of the glories of the paper. O'Casey was invited to serve on this board and agreed to do so. In his letter of acceptance he wrote: 'Had the *Daily Worker*'s policy of some years ago been followed or even listened to, we should have had to face far less loss of sweat, less toil, and far less sacrifice than we are called on to face today.'

When the nazis reached the Atlantic, fresh strategical questions arose and in early July there were consultations between the British and Irish governments. Throughout the summer and autumn the demand was voiced for the return of the treaty ports and even the abandonment of Irish neutrality. The January 1941 issue of *Irish Freedom* concentrated on this question and among those who contributed was Sean O'Casey, who wrote:

I can see no reason on God's earth, or man's earth, why Irish bodies should mingle with the mangled squirming mass wriggling in pain here and in Germany. One would imagine that this war had gone far enough.

He dissented from Shaw's opinion that De Valera should hand the ports back to England. He concluded:

Guarding England is the trinity of rent, interest and profit, and I'm afraid the same powers stand watch over Ireland. Till socialism strangles these three evils, there will be war and men women and children will be mangled senselessly.[4]

The *Daily Worker* had been taking up soldiers' grievances, and on occasion would publish half a page of letters from members of the forces. Its success in this field was doubtless a cause contributing to its suppression. The occasion was the publication of an editorial headed 'We accuse the government', on 21 January 1941. The ban remained in force until September 1942, and during this time O'Casey was tireless in his efforts to have it withdrawn.

After two spectacular raids on London in early May 1941, German bombing suddenly ceased. Throughout a month of resplendent summer weather rumours multiplied of an impending German invasion of the USSR. Disregarding his non-aggression pact, Hitler invaded on 22 June. The British sighed with relief; their isolation had come to an end. But so utterly sceptical had they become of politicians and their promises, that Churchill in his broadcast announcing the Russian alliance, went to great pains to assure the public that he intended to go on fighting fascism.

The war was being transformed into a world struggle against fascism.

The decisive turning point had come with Hitler's new aggression, though the United States was not to come in until she was herself attacked by Japan. At the same time imperialist elements remained. The British communists adjusted themselves fairly easily to the change. It brought them no opprobrium to be supporters of the war. For the Irish it was not so easy. For one thing it meant supporting Churchill whose part in the counter-revolution was not forgotten. It might lead to accepting the conscription of Irish people in Britain despite De Valera's negotiation of exemption. It might even lead to supporting the clamour in some quarters that the twenty-six counties should abandon their neutrality. There was much heart-searching. Ultimately *Irish Freedom* adopted the principle of supporting the war against fascism without prejudice to the national rights of the Irish.

O'Casey wrote no play during 1941. When he resumed work in December of that year, it was on the highly significant autobiographical work *Red Roses for Me*. The logic of purely political events would have taken him straight to his pro-war *Oak Leaves and Lavender*. Perhaps when Dr Krause publishes his second volume of O'Casey letters we shall know the reason for the interruption. Part of the explanation may be that during 1941 O'Casey was getting *Pictures in the Hallway* through the press and reflecting on his early life. The subject matter of *Drums under the Windows* was agitating in his mind. But before he could write it, there were attitudes to be decided. These demanded the composition of another play. Thus *Drums Under the Windows* is in a sense derived from *Red Roses for Me*, for it is there that St Barnabas is first called Burnupus. Life was made to imitate art. The new play was completed and published in 1942 and performed at the Olympia Theatre in Dublin in March 1943. *Drums under the Windows* was not published until 1946.[5]

The central character in *Red Roses for Me* is Ayamonn Breydon, a Protestant railway labourer who lives alone with his widowed mother. He is interested in books, enthusiastic about Shakespeare, and becoming interested in secularist criticism. He is in love with the daughter of a sergeant of the Royal Irish Constabulary, whom he ingenuously supposes will be prepared to live on 'water and a crust' for the sake of their romance. The opening of the first act shows him rehearsing for a concert. Its purpose is to raise money for a strike fund which will be necessary if the employers decline to pay the railwaymen an extra shilling a week.

Ayamonn's problems are quickly communicated. His mother upbraids him for wishing to marry a Catholic and a policeman's daughter to boot. She points out that he has made no financial provision for her. The girl herself, Sheila, arrives and presses precisely the same argument. She tells him: 'You lead your life through too many paths instead of treading the one way of making it possible for us to live together.' She is worried about the strike and asks him why he should 'meddle' in such things. The representatives of his 'many paths' then present themselves one after another; Brennan o' the Moor who has set an air to Ayamonn's lyric 'Red Roses for Me'; the singer who is to perform it; Mullcanny, the mocker of sacred things (the name compounded of *magadh* and *beannuightle*?) who promised to bring a copy of Haeckel's *Riddle of the Universe*, one of the most popular expositions of Darwinism in the early years of this century; Roory O'Balacaun the Gaelic enthusiast; and some Catholic neighbours who report that their holy statue of 'Our lady of Eblana'[6] has mysteriously disappeared from its niche.

In the second act, Brennan of the Moor brings back the statue, explaining that he had taken it away for repainting. He returns it to its place, and the neighbours thereupon proclaim a miracle. This episode gave rise to criticism in Dublin. For just as O'Casey gratuitously transforms St Brigid into St Frigid, so he has Catholics shamelessly inventing stories of seeing the statue returning of its own accord. They are either hysterically credulous or pious frauds. Not of course that there is nothing to satirize. O'Casey knew well of visions that had been seen and had given rise to more commerce than edification. But the *bona fides* of the seer was not in question.

Sheila returns with what amounts to an ultimatum. She conveys the news that the masters have rejected the workers' demands, and offers a suggestion that Ayamonn should remain at work in return for being made a foreman. He replies that he has a soul to save as well as she. The rector of St Burnupus and a deputation of railwaymen arrive. They say the strike will take place, and ask Ayamonn to address a public meeting that has been proclaimed. In spite of Sheila's objections, he agrees and burns the proclamation forbidding the meeting. Sheila seeks the clergyman's support, but fails to secure it, and she is too considerate to awaken Mrs Breydon.

The third act is largely symbolic. The Catholic neighbours are revealed as impoverished flower-sellers, bunched up on the Liffey quay. Roory has nothing to say to them. Police Inspector Finglas, the rector's churchwarden, treats them with insolent contempt. The rector himself is made uneasy by them and hastens away. Brennan o' the Moor sings them a song but receives little thanks for it. But Ayamonn tells them 'our strike is yours,' and declares 'we who have known and know the emptiness of life shall know its fullness.' He is saved the necessity of explaining how this follows from the circumstances by the sudden illumination of the scene as 'bright and lovely colours are being brought to them by the caress of the setting sun.' Everybody who has been in Dublin around the equinox, when the sun sets due west up the Liffey, will recognize this phenomenon, which often occurs after a shower, but it was left to O'Casey to make it a symbol of social regeneration.

The last act is set in the grounds surrounding St Burnupus. Orangemen are objecting to Ayamonn's gift of a wreath of daffodils formed into the shape of a Celtic cross. They are also objecting to his politics. It is the day of the proclaimed meeting. Both Sheila and Mrs Breydon try without success to delay him. After a while comes the news that he has been shot dead when police dispersed the strikers. The body is brought to the church. Sheila places a bunch of red roses on the bier. The Inspector pays attentions to her, but she listens half-heartedly. Suddenly she thinks of the roses, and runs away from him. Her conclusion is that Ayamonn must have seen the shilling a week 'in the shape of a new world'. The workers say: 'he died for us'.

Goldstone[7] states that the character finally given the name of Ayamonn Breydon was called Sean O Casside in the first drafts. There is thus no doubt that O'Casey was dramatizing himself. He calls himself Casside in the early volumes of the life story. At first sight Breydon strikes one as an ordinary Protestant name, and indeed there are Braydons in Ireland. But there is an Irish word *bréid* which means a length of cloth or canvas, and can be used to signify a sail. The title first intended for *Red Roses for Me* was 'Afloat in a Gold Canoe'. Ayamonn was thus envisaged as a motive force. In the first act[8] when his mother complains about the multifariousness of his activities, the threatened strike and the Catholic girl he replies: 'I am drifting away from you, mother, a dim shape now, in a gold canoe, dipping over the far horizon.' He is separating himself from family tradition and creating his own in which the 'fullness' of life will have its part. But that requires a revision of its economic base.

The name Ayamonn is of course Eamonn pronounced in the manner of the Dublin working class. Who has not heard the intrusive vowels of the sellers of 'musharooms' in Moore Street? Protestant parents would be unlikely to christen a child Eamonn in the eighteen-nineties. One is to suppose therefore that he was named Edward and, like O'Casey his Jack, translated it into Irish for political or cultural reasons.

The play shares four other characters with the autobiography: the mother, the rector, Sheila Moorneen (Muirnin, sweetheart, Nora Creena) and Roory O'Balacaun (O'Farrell). O'Casey's mother helped him with Shakespeare in 1892. He was dismissed from the railway after a strike in 1911. In 1913 Larkin burned the proclamation which forbade the famous meeting in O'Connell Street. During the lock-out a girl, Alice Brady, died after being shot by an armed blackleg. But the police did not use firearms. The first shooting of unarmed workers was at Bachelors Walk, following the Howth gun-running. O'Casey thus transfers to the labour struggle a degree of violence which properly belongs to the national. Two other discrepancies should be noted. O'Casey did not live alone with his mother except for the three years 1915–18. And until she fell ill over Christmas 1917, Isabella was constantly in and out. And at no time did Maire Keating have an opportunity to dissuade O'Casey from taking part in a strike. Historical persons are placed in relations which are contrary to history.

In *The Star Turns Red* Julia is with Jack from the start. In *Red Roses for Me* Sheila confronts Ayamonn with a completely distinct philosophy, the prudential as opposed to the idealist. His mother also pleads the cause of discretion. O'Casey himself is the anti-commercial character. But every objection to the Rising of 1916, raised in *The Plough and the Stars* is equally valid against defying the authorities by speaking at a proclaimed meeting. In *The Plough* dying for an Irish republic is attributed to vanity. In *Red Roses* dying for a shilling a week signifies heroism. But if a shilling a week can be seen 'in the shape of a new world', why cannot national independence? Certainly Connolly so saw it and Lenin complimented him for it. And the very least politically educated 1916 Volunteer had a vision of a new world where armed police and troops would not club or shoot defenceless people in their own country. Whether that hope was fulfilled or not, is no more material than whether the railway workers got their shilling a week. Moreover it is not possible to ascribe to all O'Casey's work an 'anti-heroic vision'. That vision was confined to the issue of national independence. There was heroism in fighting for the dictatorship of the proletariat, and even in relatively minor economic struggles.

At the risk of tiresome repetition, one must note once more that O'Casey was living alone with his mother in 1916. He took no part in the Rising and the fact rankled. He had quarrelled with the Citizen Army. But many estranged forgot their estrangement. Not many of them would of course have an aged mother on their hands. There was a compelling reason why O'Casey should stay at home. In *The Star Turns Red* O'Casey implied that the fight for the dictatorship of the proletariat cannot be approached in an anti-heroic manner. In *Red Roses for Me* he seems to say, 'Even if it had been merely a railway strike, I would have still risked my life.' The heart of the matter was 1916 again. The dead men were still hammering at the door. The unfortunate girl friend was dragged anachronistically into the mental fight, and no wonder she burst into tears in the middle of the play's performance. Her refusal to marry O'Casey was based solely on the difference of religion. It in no way signified incomprehension of, still less antagonism to, the finer aspirations which O'Casey possessed, denied to Jack in *The Star Turns Red*, but so touchingly conferred on young Ayamonn.

The war over religion is part of the background of the play. The Catholics are depicted as backward and credulous when they are poor and philistine when they are prosperous. They need Protestants to support, comfort, educate and transfigure them. It is to the Protestant church all repair and the rector shows the liberalism of the reformed religion by his dignified dismissal of the Orangemen.

Red Roses for Me has been praised as widely as *The Star Turns Red* has been condemned. For one thing its hero has the propriety to die with his object unaccomplished, in accordance with the best aesthetic conventions. It is, however, undeniable that in *Red Roses*, drawing on past experience rather than visualizing a future that was really anybody's guess, he works with a surer and more delicate touch, and apart from his use of the sunset and the accompanying dance, his method is realist throughout. But once again parts of the dialogue are couched in inflated and improbable language which O'Casey seems to have considered fine writing.

After *Red Roses for Me* O'Casey dramatized himself no more. The cathartist was cathartized and the fact that the final emotional position was not the historical one need disturb nobody, not even the historian, once he knows what happened. The deepest function of art is the creation of new consciousness, and this takes place in the author during composition even more profoundly than in the audience during performance. The creation of new consciousness implies that what was previously considered the natural order is compelled by means of a ritual to accept new elements.

Perhaps this principle is seen in its simplest and starkest clarity in the structure of the classical sonata. Here the new, the additional material representing the principle of change or negation, is exposed in the key of the dominant, or some readily recognizable substitute for it. But it can only be admitted into the natural order by recapitulation in the key of the tonic.

The greatness of a work of art is thus measured precisely by the amount of new consciousness it confers. By new consciousness is not meant new information. It is rather a rectification of consciousness, and the process is analogous to dreaming, where purposeful reality is revalidated by involuntary imagination.

Red Roses for Me was a turning point, the last play of his second period which had begun with *Within the Gates*, where his own relation to the world was never far from his canvas. At this point he adopted the emotional position that as a life-long socialist, he had always been prepared to die for the workers, but would not take part in a national revolution. From this standpoint he completed the autobiography. Students fell under the spell of the emotion and from materials supplied by the master, created the myth. But for all that, O'Casey remained an Irish patriot, and who will grudge him the means by which he came to terms with his enforced non-involvement in Easter week? When Cyril Cusack visited him in Devonshire he said that O'Casey at seventy-five struck him as a man 'whose one obsession was Ireland'. He was passionately patriotic to his dying day.

It has already been pointed out that his contemporaries in the movement thought the centre of his politics the reaction to 1916. The phenomenon is not unique. One recalls the case of the young student who went with the republicans to fight on the border in 1956. He found he was not the man for freezing in ditches at midnight. He left the zone of operations, changed his name, went to England, became a rabid anti-national Trotskyite, and finally committed suicide – all the time insisting on speaking his fluent Irish. O'Casey with his tons of intellectual ballast, could not be capsized by a psychological storm. But he had to win the inward peace that comes from justification of oneself to oneself. The fool or the criminal does not trouble. But the man of genius must. And he achieved this by projecting his ultimate position backward. He could then sit comfortably in judgement on contemporary Ireland from the standpoint of an independent socialist critic. He had done the impossible that everybody longs to do. He had gone back into the past, changed what happened there, and then come back into the present to enjoy the improvements. Such is the power of art. But such is the power of life that when a man has done this, the conflict is over, and his works of compelling emotional power are now behind him. After the recapitulation there is only the coda.

It has already been explained that to the British left the war had three distinct phases, the 'phoney war', the Anglo-German war, and the international war against fascism. During the first two there was little feeling that the twenty-six counties should join in, because the war was held to be predominantly imperialist. Ireland's right to be neutral was vigorously defended, and indeed was defended throughout. In the last phase, when the war was regarded as a liberation struggle, there were those who thought that De Valera should come in, though how far the allied governments really wished this is open to question. O'Casey's next play, *Oak Leaves and Lavender*, was completed just before the end of the conflict, but was set in the earliest phase of the Anglo-German war, during the Battle of Britain. It thus brings to events in retrospect an attitude which O'Casey did not have when they were happening. Like *Within the Gates* it must be classified as weak O'Casey. But it was the first of a series of plays in which the interest was not personal but social. Its analogue from the earlier period is *Purple Dust*, but it was also an attempt to break new ground.

The action takes place in Dame Hatherleigh's manorial house in the west of England. She has made it available as a local centre for civil defence. O'Casey is thus enabled to present a series of typical aspects of war-time life which are handled with characteristic lightness of touch. Those who lived through the Second World War remember well the Home Guard, the Land Girls, the black-out wardens, air raids and endless news bulletins. O'Casey provides many vivacious secondary characters who provide the typical war-time background.

There are two fundamental political ideas, first the need to win the war, second the fact that Ireland is not a belligerent. The two are linked in the character of Feelim O'Murragun (*margadh*, a bargain?), the Dame's Irish butler. On the one hand he is her general factotum who keeps the civil defence machinery running. On the other he has no interest in the work beyond what he is paid for it, though he gives value for money. He typifies the thousands of Irishmen who poured into Britain during the war because war meant work.

The fact that he is essential to the working of the centre, does not prevent the local people from throwing Ireland's neutrality in his face. Repeatedly he rebuts arguments founded on ignorance of history and uses those that would be used in 1945, when the exploits of Irish servicemen had become known through the decorations lists.

His son, like Dame Hatherleigh's, is a member of the Royal Air Force. But Drishogue (*driseog*, a thorn) is a communist who insists that he is not fighting for England but against fascism. The two boys part from their girl friends, go to their units, and in the last act they are killed, together with one of the girls, in a defence operation, coming down close to the manorial house. Another girl explains to Feelim that she is secretly married to Drishogue and carries his child.

The moral is thus that whatever the losses, life must go on, the war must be won. On the other hand Drishogue has answered the critics of Ireland who say the Irish are not in the fight against fascism. When he has lost his son moreover, Feelim becomes emotionally identified with the war and in a sense takes Drishogue's place.

But it is hard not to concur with Dr Krause's opinion that this play gives the impression of propaganda. Whether it would have done so in 1945 amid the interminable and universal propaganda, one can not be sure. The trouble is that the symbolism creaks. The play begins with a prologue in which ghostly figures predict dire dangers for England. An unearthly odour of lavender presages a death in the family. A radio plays 'Deutschland über alles' without being switched on.[9] At one point the time is jerked forward by a complete year by nothing more convincing than 'a voice'. Moreover this burst of acceleration takes place while Drishogue and Edgar are dramatically, if not physically, 'in the air'.

It might be thought that a war-time play would be best handled in a strictly realistic fashion and introduce no distortion of the time-sequences which were written on everybody's memory. The struggle over Ireland's neutrality could have taken place in the mind of Drishogue, for the most politically conscious republicans were torn between two loyalties. But possibly O'Casey did not wish to reopen questions that had been closed by *Red Roses for Me*.

It may not be appreciated today that despite the offence of 'spreading alarm and despondency' which included the disparagement of Britain's allies, there were those who contrived to make anti-Soviet statements during the war. In April 1943 the *Catholic Times* reported statements made at the Sunderland Conservative Women's club that 'free love' was practised on collective farms in the USSR. O'Casey replied scathingly in the *Daily Worker*. He seems to have been persuaded that anti-Sovietism was of Catholic origin and in March 1944 wrote a full length article in the *Daily Worker* entitled 'The Shadow of the Vatican'. It began: 'Everywhere there is a Vatican community there is a shadow . . . creeping everywhere it can, and bringing with it an icy wind of opposition to blow on every hot heart-beat in the workers' movement.' He continued, 'Not only in things that they call spiritual, but in literature, art and politics, every cardinal, bishop, priest or deacon thinks he, and he alone, is the final judge. Indeed they will soon regulate what the husband will say to the wife . . . and will show them how the house should be furnished.' He quoted the Archbishop of Westminister who had expressed support for the censorship of books and concluded: 'Is it any wonder that Marx thought religion to be the dope of the workers.' On Marx's behalf let it be said that he was here misquoted and his meaning vulgarized.

At the end of October 1944, he wrote an Open Letter to the *Daily Worker*, which was a hymn of hate against the Germans. Lady Gibbs had written to Ehrenburg, who was then advocating revenge unlimited, suggesting that too strict a vengeance might 'lead to sorrow in the future'. O'Casey brushed aside any such contention. The Germans despised the 'soft answer'. The German people were as responsible for Hitler as the Americans were for Roosevelt. This was of course historically untrue. O'Casey continued by saying that Lady Gibbs said, 'Leave them to God', but Cromwell when he left it to God, drilled his Ironsides. He concluded, 'The Germans are not fit to govern, and many and many of them are not fit to live.' But an Irishman was fit to quote Cromwell!

The following March, 1945, he described Archbishop Griffin's complaint that the Yalta agreement had brought the USSR too far west in Poland, as 'clericalism gone loony', and commented: 'These ecclesiastical boyos speak about everything as if what they said had been divinely revealed to them.' It is clear that during 1944 and the early part of 1945, O'Casey felt that Catholic influence was being directed in favour of a soft peace with Germany, with the object of weakening the post war position of the USSR.

This no doubt explains the insertion in the play of the altercation between Drishogue and the anti-Soviet Deeda Tutting who appears in the life story[10] as Creda Stern. Her arguments were of course drawn from the phoney war period when British policy was directed towards turning the Germans eastward.

At the time of writing *Oak Leaves and Lavender*, O'Casey may have seen himself in the role of a western Ilya Ehrenburg, watchdog against weaknesses in the resolve of Britain and America to proceed to the complete extirpation of fascism.

NOTES

1. *Daily Worker*, 17 April 1939. Dr Stopes was a delightful person but she was susceptible to that peculiar class-determined 'dottyness' which sometime affects bourgeois intellectuals. She was, I think, a convert to the views of Sir Peter Chalmers Mitchell, and I remember her once at a scientific dinner announce that she knew how to live to be a hundred and fifty, and intended to do so.
2. D. Krause, *Letters*, pp. 806–9.
3. ibid., p. 837.
4. I remember writing a protest against this statement on the grounds that it was not right to present Britain and Ireland as equivalent capitalist countries, when one was imperialist and the other was not. O'Casey had, however, made the point that 'the civilization of England as Ireland has known it, has been a bitter, blushing and vulgar one from the day they first landed. . . . England gains no points on the score of civilization.' My protest was not published, but I was invited to join the editorial board of *Irish Freedom*.
5. D. Krause, *Sean O'Casey and his World*, p. 112, gives the date October 1945. Possibly this was the English date. The difference is not great enough to affect the argument.
6. Eblana is popularly identified with Dublin, though the Ptolemaic Eblana at the mouth of the Bovinda corresponds to Drogheda, which seems to have been the main population centre in antiquity.
7. Goldstone, op. cit., p. 134.
8. O'Casey, *Collected Plays*, vol. 3, p. 135.
9. While one had not the time to monitor German radio, my recollection is that the Nazis never played Haydn's fine tune, but repeated the undistinguished ditty that commemorated Horst Wessel, with a rubato reminiscent of their goose step.
10. O'Casey, *Sunset and Evening Star*, Macmillan, New York, 1955, p. 125.

13

ECONOMIST IN ARCADIA

Could commodities themselves speak, they would say: our use-value may be a thing that interests men. It is no part of us as objects. What, however, does belong to us as objects, is our value. . . . In the eyes of each other we are nothing but exchange values.

Karl Marx, *Capital, chap. 1*

Just before the war ended the American government perpetrated the greatest single crime in world history. It ordered the dropping of atomic bombs on Hiroshima and Nagasaki. Here was cold-blooded devilishness corresponding to the productive forces of a new age. Against this the perverted bestialities of the nazis appeared almost recognizably human, in the sense that there is a psychopath hidden in all of us. But the men who took this decision wore striped trousers not jackboots. The victims were 'Asiatics'. And the world was crying out for peace, peace at any price, no matter who paid it.

There can have been only one object. The world's new management was to declare itself. In future, business was to be done under the aegis of a *Pax Americana*. The explosions announced an age of technical development in which economic forces tore through the fabric of traditional society with similar savagery and ruthlessness. It has been estimated that in the period 1945 to 1975, world production rose every year by three times the total output of British industry. Never had so much 'wealth' been created in so short a time. But granted the unprecedented wealth, how was it to be distributed? The capitalist world replied 'according to precedent'. And this was the core of the politics of the post-war world.

The British people were in a mood for sweeping changes. In his election campaign of 1945, Clement Attlee, who did not expect to be returned with a majority, declared that the Labour Party was socialist. He undertook to do away with the dictatorship of capitalist interests which had gambled with the lives of the ordinary people for the sake of profit. He promised to maintain the war-time friendship with the USSR so as to guarantee a secure peace. His party was returned with one of the largest majorities on record.

The Tories received belated recompense for the crimes and follies that had caused the war. Yet within no time they were back to their vomit. Encouraged by the new government's obsequiousness towards the interests they had undertaken to control, on 5 March 1946, at Fulton, Missouri, Winston Churchill delivered a speech he had discussed with President Truman. It called for a grand alliance against the USSR, and, if necessary, war to effect a revision of the Yalta settlement. The scandalous thing was that it was not immediately repudiated by those who had been entrusted with the making of British foreign policy.[1] The cold war had begun.

In 1939 Britain had not been strong enough to push Germany into mutual annihilation with the USSR. Churchill can never have believed that the much weaker Britain of 1946 could jockey the United States. He had told Roosevelt that while he appreciated the American desire to fall heir to the British Empire, he relied on that country to prop it up as a bulwark of reaction. Now he had come to the conclusion that American enthusiasm for this worthy cause would be strongest under conditions of chronic antagonism to the USSR. As Chamberlain with Germany, so Churchill with America. History repeated itself as a farce. Mr Attlee refused to dissociate himself from the Fulton speech. As part of the resultant accord, the USA exacted a level of arms expenditure which precluded the re-equipment of British industry. The imperial assets, under challenge by colonial liberation movements, inevitably passed, if not into American possession, into effective American control, and within ten years Britain had become a second class power.

O'Casey's stand in the new situation was unequivocal. He supported the USSR and opposed the Cold War. At the same time, as he explained to Jack Lindsay[3], he felt too old to work in the new movement. He gave moral support in the form of political statements issued over the years and in financial contributions. In December 1946 he attacked 'Vatican support' for the Yugoslavian prelate Stepinak. He attacked Douglas Hyde, the news-editor[4] of the *Daily Worker* when he left the Communist Party on becoming converted to Catholicism. He accused the famous philosopher Bertrand Russell of 'baboonery' when in November 1948 he told school children: 'Either we must have a war with Russia before she has the atom bomb, or we will have to lie down and let them govern us.' He sent a message of support to the international peace conference held in Paris in April 1949, to the British Peace Committee the following September, and to the demonstration in favour of the abolition of nuclear weapons held in Trafalgar Square in July 1950.

In March 1953 he gave permission for the production of three short plays at a function connected with the Communist Party conference. He was giving money to the *Daily Worker* at least until 1957, although the editorial board had been disbanded for technical reasons. He remained an ardent admirer of the USSR, and supported its intervention in Hungary. At the same time, when his son Niall objected, he unreservedly accepted the youngster's right to his opinion. He was independent in his own views and recognized the independence of others. He told Jack Lindsay[5] that he 'wrote some sharp things to Apletin the time Zhdanov was bullying writers into his narrow shell of literature'. He also wrote criticizing Soviet estimates of English writers. He was thus not an active politician but a steady political influence. There is no justification for the opinion that his communism was more emotional than his nationalism or Protestantism had been. It was his political creed for the last three decades of his life and was held steadily. He was neither over hot nor lukewarm.

Within the Irish community in Britain, he gave regular financial support to the Connolly Association, though when he was invited to become president he replied that he thought Larkin and not Connolly the great inspirer of Irish socialism. He was active in the movement for the release of the Republican prisoners and was jubilant when in 1948 they were finally freed.

It is in relation to internal Irish affairs that we find the old ambivalence. He kept in touch with the Gaelic League. He regularly donated to Labour causes. He sent a message of support to Mr Michael O'Riordan when he offered himself as Irish Workers' League candidate in the 1951 election. And whereas all the socialists in his early plays were unpleasant fellows, the communists in his late work are invariably drawn sympathetically, if somewhat woodenly. But to the national question he seemed to have become insensitive. In part this was due to the isolation of the twenty-six counties during the war, and the suspicion that those who were raising the demand for the ending of partition had ulterior motives. Again the six county regime which had been discredited in the thirties had contrived to become respectable again, thanks to the banning of sectarian parades during the international war against fascism. But there were also emotional reasons which have been suggested.

The twenty-six counties were spared the destruction that befell the belligerent countries. They were nevertheless struck a severe blow in their economic life. In three years their imports fell by seventy-four per cent. That industrial production fell by only twenty-five per cent is explained partly by the ingenious makeshifts that were adopted, and partly by wastage of capital. The belligerents' resources were destroyed; Ireland's were consumed. Thus, while cereal production was considerably increased thanks to the policy of compulsory tillage, yields per acre declined through lack of fertilizers and the ploughing up of inferior land. At the end of the war there was acute capital starvation. The situation was aggravated by the partition of the country, but even a united Ireland would have suffered a fuel famine.

As in the economy so in politics. Everything was subordinated to the aim of preserving neutrality. Wages rose very slowly when compared with prices. But nevertheless the government attempted to control the trade unions. Republicanism was discouraged as potentially pro-German. By the same token communism was considered pro-Russian. A people traditionally highly aware of the outside world were asked to ignore it. Restrictions were accepted by belligerent populations as necessary for winning the war. In Ireland they were accepted as a price to be paid for the maintenance of neutrality. There was a strong sense of national purpose. But this purpose was conservative and protective. The church, as was natural, co-operated with the government. Whereas in Britain and the six counties the war resulted in a period of rapid change, in the twenty-six counties it was a period of suspense, enlivened not by invention but by expedient.

It was understandable that observers in the countries that had been fighting the axis powers should associate in their minds the three predominantly Catholic neutrals, Spain, Portugal and Ireland, and imagine that the conservatism characteristic of all three was essentially one. There were many attempts to depict the twenty-six counties as a backward state comparable with Salazar's Portugal. Such propaganda provided beforehand the justification for a possible Anglo-American invasion. It was openly hostile to Ireland and appealed to people with Tory views. The Soviet veto of the Irish application for membership of the United Nations Organisation in August 1947 encouraged similar thinking on the left. Nor did clerical utterances always help. The Archbishop of Cashel's contribution to industrial peace will exemplify. 'Lightning strikes,' he declared, 'and lightning lock-outs, are serious violations of Catholic moral principles, and those who promote them or willingly take part in them are guilty of grave sin.'

What the outside observers did not appreciate was that warnings of this kind were completely lost on potential strikers. There were no such warnings in Spain or Portugal because there strikes were illegal. In Ireland there were capitalists, but no great rural landlords. The church owned no vast estates, and was dependent on the people. The trade unions could be divided and confused, but they were too strong to tame. If standards of living were generally low, especially among the very small farmers, this arose from lack of capital and was a legacy of hundreds of years of imperial robbery.

The swing to the left which took place in Britain was not reproduced in Ireland because there was no previous experience to impel it. If Attlee's government had shown the slightest disposition to open the question of partition, perhaps Irish Labour would have benefited and been enabled to stand on its own feet. Hopes were dashed in Dublin as well as London. What developed during the immediate post-war years was a slow but steadily accelerating current of discontent, which displayed itself in a revival of republicanism, the establishment of Clann na Poblachta as a radical competitor of Fianna Fail, and in a steady increase of trade union membership. In 1946 the number of days lost as a result of industrial disputes was 150,108. In 1947, the year of the Archbishop's lenten warning, the figure rose to 449,438.

In its efforts to overcome the fuel shortage, Fianna Fail had undertaken considerable investment in the turf industry. Large new bogs were opened, for which labour was recruited among the urban unemployed. The work was ill-paid, arduous and uncertain. Many of the men were lodged in hostels. At the same time their city origin predisposed them to organisation. In June 1946 turf deliveries to Dublin were interrupted by a strike of two hundred lorry drivers who were demanding higher rates. The lorry owners association had aligned itself with the Workers' Union of Ireland. In May 1947 two thousand workers in Kildare and Offaly took sudden strike action in protest against the failure of the Labour Court to issue a decision on their wage demand. They were at once locked out and denied canteen facilities.[6]

Cock-a-Doodle Dandy, O'Casey's next play, seems to have been begun in the spring of 1948, but derives from the industrial unrest of the preceding year. According to Eileen O'Casey,[7] the dramatist was excited at the prospect of breaking free from realism not merely for a single act but for a complete play. Robert Hogan[8] describes its genre as 'pastoral' and it is possible that O'Casey decided to borrow and adapt elements from that patrician form, to accomplish his plebeian purposes. Krause called the play a 'morality'. Again it is largely a matter of borrowing elements. But really it is *sui generis* and might perhaps best be described as a fantasy of ideas. The dialogue sparkles with humour and is stimulating to read. But like that of *Kathleen Listens In*, its content is too weighty for its form. When produced at the Abbey in 1977 before charabanc loads of tourists, whose main concern was to be able to say they had been to the Abbey while 'doing' Dublin, it was played as pantomime.

The action takes place outside the house of the central character Marthraun (*martran*, a cripple), a parvenu turf contractor whose sole joy is making money. He is thus the embodiment of capitalism. He lives near the small Irish country town of Nyadnanave (*nead na naomh*, nest of saints). The time is 1947, for Fianna Fail is still in office, and turf workers are threatening to strike. The time is further confirmed by the circumstance that the grass has 'turned a deep yellow hue,' which is what it did at least in England during an exceptionally long, dry and brilliant summer. Marthraun has married a fine young woman who has brought him the bog that is making his fortune. A business associate

Sailor Mahan (*meathan*, a weakling) has called to discuss a higher price for cartage. But Marthraun is anxious to talk about something else, namely the seemingly supernatural events that have accompanied the return from England of his daughter by his first wife. Loreleen is a pretty and vivacious girl, but to him a 'godless and laughing little bitch'. When she passes through the house a mysterious wind blows the holy pictures face to the wall. If her name is connected with Lorelei, then it will mean 'little witch'.

Now it is important to appreciate that the supernatural events, even when visible to the audience, are not always visible to all the characters. O'Casey periodically stops to remind us that what he is portraying are ideas in the heads of Marthraun, Mahan and others. Marthraun's values are those of commerce and in the midst of the thaumaturgical slapstick of the first scene, he is never far away from his bargaining with Mahan.

Loreleen challenges commercial values on her first appearance. She lightly but mischievously throws at the two hard-bitten businessmen, the biblical warning that moth and rust corrupt worldly possessions and thieves break in and steal. She thereby denies the god of wealth and laughs at the accumulation of capital. To Marthraun her statement of a well-known fact of experience is a 'lying hallucination'. We see Marthraun's hallucinations in due course. For the moment one is reminded of Balzac's miser, when the nephew from Paris suggests 'a couple of chickens' for his supper. Two ethical systems come into collision, founded respectively on value in use and value in exchange. At this point two turf workers come in to demand a guaranteed wage. Marthraun refuses and receives warning of a strike.

As they retire they catch sight of Loreleen and follow her with amorous intentions. From their exclamations of astonishment Marthraun learns that she has been transformed into a cock. It is manifestly impossible to perform this miracle in full view of the audience. Yet it is for Marthraun's eyes that it is required. O'Casey solves the problem by using the workmen as a semaphore.[9] He thereby puts the fetishism of commodities on the stage, and while the two old men go on chaffering over the things that are real to them, the principle of use value parades in resplendent plumage.

The two workmen are of course interested in money for what it will buy. But even so their acquisition of use value is mediated by exchange. Their desire for use value is to Marthraun a misuse of the function of money. 'And it's this materialism's doing it,' he wails; his own pursuit of money for its own sake is not materialism. The natural, the normal, the sane and the sensible are seen through the bewitched eyes of capital as products of sorcery. The illusion is encouraged by Shanaar (*sean fhear*, old man) who assures them, however, that a few words of Latin (symbolizing the church) will be efficacious against all the forces of evil. Thus early does O'Casey press his favourite contention that the main prop of capitalism is religion.

A commotion is heard in the house. The cock has got in and is pecking the holy pictures. Marthraun's wife Lorna (the name is connected with Devonshire where O'Casey resided) and the maid-servant Marion are firing cups and saucers at it in an effort to drive it out. That is to say, they are still under the influence of Marthraun's ideology. Shanaar decides not to risk the failure of his hocus pocus, and Marthraun is just about to send for the parish priest when a post office messenger, who answers to the highly pastoral name of Robin Adair, brings the bird under control and the women lose their fear of it. He hands Marthraun a telegram which he stuffs into his pocket unread.

But it now emerges that in the course of his depredations, the cock has pecked to pieces a silk hat that Marthraun intends to wear on the occasion of the visit of 'his brightness' the president. In 1947 this would be Douglas Hyde, no object of O'Casey's admiration. Marthraun decides on a drink before resuming the bargaining. When Marion brings it he playfully pinches her backside. Emboldened by the favourable response, the two men put their arms round her, when, to their horror, they see horns sprouting on her head. Money is their god and the merchants, therefore, see life in the form of the devil. The scene ends with a sad procession headed by the parish priest, Father Domineer. Lorna's sister Julia is going to Lourdes in search of a miracle that will cure her paralysis.

The second scene develops the theme of the first. Further misfortunes afflict Mathraun and Sailor Mahan. Their chairs collapse under them. They regard this as the work of demons, though the women present the material explanation that they have chosen two ricketty chairs that are only for show. Their whiskey changes colour and refuses to be poured out. 'And all the time,' moans the contractor 'my turfworkers and your lorry drivers are screwin' all they can out of us, so that they'll have more to spend on pictures an' the dance halls.' It is a cry like that of Marx's 'freeborn Englishman' who has gone mad and imagines himself to be compelled to dig gold for Pharaoh.

A porter brings in a new silk hat which he says has been damaged by a mysterious shot. A sergeant of the Gardaí explains that he had tried to shoot the cock but that it turned into a silk hat before his eyes. A silk hat is a use value even if its use is to symbolise commercial success. Therefore it is an article of consumption and a subject for bewitchment. At this point the town crier enters ringing his bell and advising all citizens to retreat to their homes. The cock is coming in the shape of a woman. The fetishism is complete. One is reminded of old Grandet in his dotage hoarding not money but *commodities*. But Mathraun and Mahan are afraid to enter the house. There are demons in it. Indeed it is full of them. But remembering that Shanaar's advice has been to 'take no notice' in the presence of demons, Marthraun persuades Mahan to give an appearance of unconcern by singing a song.

It is indeed the shape of a woman that now enters. Loreleen, puzzled to find Mahan entertaining Marthraun, calls on Lorna and Marion to come down and join the party. The women have been 'practising a few steps' completely unconscious of the miracles around them. It is not that they have been in the house and have not noticed what was taking place outside, for the sergeant describes how the silk hat resumed the shape of a bird to the accompaniment of darkness and lightning. Lorna is completely mystified. She tells Marthraun that the new silk hat was delivered an hour ago and is safe upstairs. She brings it out but he jumps away from it in terror. She decides upon a drink and picks up the 'bewitched' bottle. It functions as a normal use value in her hands. And first the sergeant, then Mahan and finally Marthraun succumb to its attraction. The effect is to humanise them. They are back in the real world. But the world of exchange where they are usually sane and normal, is now seen to go mad. Marthraun offers Sailor Mahan twice what he has been asking for the cartage. Mahan refuses to accept a penny. 'What th' hell's money?' he asks. All six begin to dance. But Father Domineer appears to the accompaniment of a thunderclap. The businessmen are struck with terrible remorse. Only Loreleen refuses to apologise. The implication seems to be that even capitalists would cease to be capitalists if the church did not insist on their remaining such.

The priest then tackles Mahan on another matter. He wants him to dismiss a lorry driver who is living in 'sin'. He refuses; the man is his best worker. Marthraun tries to reassure the priest, 'He'll do what your reverence tells him.' But Sailor Mahan replies heatedly, 'He won't do what his reverence tells him.' Reducing the cost of labour power by restricting the consumption of luxuries is one thing. Interfering with the process of making profit is another. The culprit appears in person to report that Marthraun's workers are on strike and that there is no turf to load. This was the message of the forgotten telegram. The priest seizes the opportunity to demand that the man should mend his ways. When he refuses the priest strikes him with such force that he is killed. The power of the yellow slave to knit and break religions is clearly demonstrated. The capitalist who 'outfaces his priest' suffers no ill consequences. The worker dies. Grave sin is grave sin, but much depends on who commits it.

When the third act opens police and soldiers are searching for the cock to the sound of martial music. The fetishism affects the whole of capitalist society from the businessman to the forces of the state. Lorna tells Mahan that the turf workers are entitled to their demands. He replies that that is Marthraun's business. That gentleman is however bent on something else. He brings in Father Domineer who has consented to perform a service of exorcism within the house. While the work is in progress and the tumult threatens to bring the building down, Sailor Mahan, smitten by Loreleen's charms, and learning that she would like to return to England, but has no money, promises to provide it if she will satisfy him in the 'red barn' that night.

Looking at the matter realistically one would imagine that if she could transform herself into a cock, she could translate herself to England. But at a realistic level the play does not function this way. The point is not that a little witch can turn herself into a cock. It is that Marthraun and most other members of the local community suffer under a mass delusion that the principles of life, pleasure and usefulness are demoniacal and that truth reposes in the crazy fetishistic world of money-making, the accumulation of abstract value.

Father Domineer issues from the house tattered but victorious. There is not a demon left in it. But two books have been found, one of them Joyce's *Ulysses*. He wishes to take them away for burning, but Loreleen recognises no censorship and snatches them up. As she runs away her pursuers are rooted to the ground. The cock reappears. There is darkness and thunder and both Father Domineer and the cock disappear. This is Loreleen's last exploit as a cock. Though there are mysterious winds that deprive respectable citizens of their trousers while leaving by-standers unruffled, Marthraun and Mahan resume their bargaining over cartage, even though there is no carting to be done. They have recovered from their charitable aberration.

We see the cock no more. Instead we see Father Domineer give his harsh judgment on a bedraggled Loreleen who is brought in after her adventure in the barn with Sailor Mahan. Marthraun no longer fears her. The mysterious life-forces that tortured his brain have been reduced to something he can affect to despise, adultery. But when Loreleen is packed off to England, Lorna decides to accompany her. Then Marion decides to leave with Robin Adair. They have decided to go to a place 'where life resembles life more than it does here.' Julia returns uncured. The young man says to her: 'Be brave.' Marthraun who is dejected and forlorn in his Pyrrhic victory asks a word of advice for himself. It is the monosyllable 'die'.

If the interpretation given here is correct, while *Cock-a-Doodle Dandy* is set on Irish soil it has universal significance as a satire against capitalism. Marthraun and Mahan represent the commercial principle. This leaves no other nexus between man and man than naked self-interest, callous cash payment. To them the non-commercial, socialist principle represented by the young people, is seen as a dangerous spirit of evil requiring exorcism. So everything is turned on its head. But the play has immense complexity.

The young people are defeated and driven out. Among them the most important is Loreleen. She may more especially symbolise the artist in capitalist society. Though he can exude all the ectoplasm of imagination, he must sell himself in order to escape. The conclusion is thus pessimistic although the young people do escape. O'Casey must have been deeply conscious of the fact that between 1945 and 1949 the highest hopes of a generation were brought to nothing. In so short a time were the wells poisoned. He asked himself what force was responsible, and his reply was a simple one – Stepinak, Mindszenty, the Vatican, the cardinals, bishops and priests, in a word Father Domineer. That Avro Manhattan, the great anti-Catholic polemicist was not a whit more progressive than Cardinal Mindszenty influenced him not at all. His mind was made up. American imperialism was relieved of responsibility for world counter-revolution after 1946, as British had been exonerated a generation earlier.

O'Casey confessed that he could only present universal ideas in an Irish setting. It is of some interest therefore to consider the setting from which he selected his themes. The Irish background of *Cock-a-Doodle Dandy* is the disintegration of a peasant proprietary under the impact of a market economy. The extreme conservatism of such a society arises from the desire to hold property that is slipping away. The clergy do not create this conservatism. They retain their popular support because they resist all change. They, like the small farmers, are the victims of a process over which they have no control. Indeed for twenty years they watched their flocks dwindling as a result of emigration, until at last Dr Lucey was moved to voice a protest. Two influences affected the farmer's ideology, prices and 'luck'. He could do nothing about either. He therefore invested them with mystical significance. Only when prices became a matter for government control and luck was smoothed out by insurance, could conscious action replace dogged conservatism as the farmer's mode of self-protection.

The turf workers were of course not local men. They did not belong to the doomed rural world. Not that this world was unable to suckle revolt. But its natural form was republicanism with which O'Casey had lost rapport. He learned about the emigration and blamed it on capitalism and the clergy. But only economic forces could effect such a transformation. Beginning in Leitrim and Mayo, then spreading to Monaghan and Cavan and finally affecting the more prosperous south-east the denudation of the countryside continued for thirty years. There were townlands with two hundred houses and three or four children. Clusters of empty dwellings dilapidated on Connemara hillsides. Thanks to the stranglehold of partition and the neo-colonial nature of the Irish economy, Ireland was forced to contribute to Britain's development instead of her own. In the new Ireland that came into being when the process ended in 1970, the urban population exceeded the rural and the most numerous class became that of the wage earners. Their mode of self-protection was trade unionism. If they turned to revolt it might well be through communism. Yet the fear of communism was never so universal as during the time when it presented no danger.

The capitalists of Ireland had had the fright of their lives when they lost the leadership of the nation from 1916 to 1922. They had seen both land and factories taken over by men of no property. If the factories were to be insured against another change of hands, the farmers must be made owners of their farms. To this end the most comprehensive of all Land Acts was passed in 1923. When the men without land had wanted to seize it, they had no fear of communism. But now they possesssed property they were anxious to preserve it and, wishing to take no risks, set their faces against anything which appeared to smack of expropriation. The irony was that their fierce possessiveness and fear of a potential expropriator disarmed them in face of the real one. For it was capitalism which carried out one of the severest· expropriations in Irish history, even though it was accomplished without the aid of a single battering ram. The clergy, many of whom came from farming stock, reassured their parishioners that private property was sacred, while invisible economic forces made it valueless to them and depopulated whole dioceses. The fear of communism, however, ensured that they left quietly. Some of the finest people in Europe were driven out of their native environment to slave amid the fumes of Widnes or Huddersfield.

O'Casey's play was thus a product of a period that has passed. It has been suggested that the solution by emigration may have been related to the preparation of *Inishfallen, Fare Thee Well*, which was published in 1949. If so then Loreleen may represent the Irish artist who brings in the light but is driven out for it. But against this stands the fact that more of those who emigrate have Irish names. In *Cock-a-Doodle Dandy* O'Casey achieved his early ambition of a drama of ideas. But he did so by means of fantasy.

As if to answer in advance any who thought far-fetched the suggestion that *Cock-a-Doodle Dandy* might have been indebted at least in part to political economy, O'Casey now wrote *Time to Go*. This seems to be related to the longer play in much the same way as Beethoven's eighth symphony is related to his seventh. There was surplus material to be worked up. But the tensions of the greater work had been resolved. The only mood available was cheerful and valedictory. The one-act play was published in 1951.

It is described by Cowasjee as a 'morality' whose characters are either good or bad, and he not unnaturally wonders why thirteen of them are required for one comparatively short act. The reason is of course the complex class structure of Ireland. The scene is the centre of an Irish country town the day after the fair. A merchant, Bull Farrell and a publican Michael Flagonson are discussing the state of business, the exactions of the clergy and the quietness of the fair. It has been quiet despite all the money they made out of it, because the young people have emigrated to England.

That their sole interest is money and that they are unscrupulous in their pursuit of it, is shown when the first two non-commercial characters come on. They are two young cyclists anxious to visit the ruins of the Abbey of Ballyrellig (town of the graveyard) which contains what is left of the chapel of Saint Kurrakawn (field of the tributes). Flagonson informs them that it is fifteen miles distant, and his wife charges them five shillings for a meal that should have cost one and sixpence.

While they are in the hotel, Widda Machree (*mo chroidh*, my heart) appears. She is dressed in black but for a bright blue cloak, and the man recognises her as the 'fine-looking woman' who sold a cow to an 'up-standing chap' in a saffron kilt and a green shawl. During her appearance coins jingle in the bar as Mrs Flagonson counts her takings. The widow is troubled in her conscience. She has 'lost her virtue for a few lousy coins.' It is made clear that the businessmen have no virtue to lose, but have gained many coins. She is seeking the man in the kilt to whom she sold the cow. She shows so clearly her contempt for the two capitalists, that they suspect she is a 'red' and one is for calling in the priest, the other the Gardaí.

There follows a passage in which a large and a medium farmer strike a bargain over the sale of cattle. The richer man has the advantage and the smaller man believes he has received too little for his beasts. Scarcely have they begun to drink the difference they were haggling over, when the man in the kilt appears. His name is 'Kelly from the Isle of Mananaun'. He complains in words that echo Widda Machree that his conscience is troubling him. He 'gave too little for what he got'. The businessmen ask whether perhaps he 'bet the lady's price down too low'. But he replied that he gave what he was asked, but it was too little. He would like to find her and make restitution. The medium farmer thinks that Kelly is quite right to denounce not giving enough for what you buy. 'Because it suits yourself,' says the richer man. Kelly and the medium farmer agree formally, but they are contradicting each other. Kelly says that a man should give more than he is asked. Cousins says that the other man should do so. Conroy the strong farmer accuses Kelly of inciting discontent and after Kelly has thrown doubt both of Farrell's morals and Conroy's piety, decides to run for the police. Kelly shows that he is a wizard by pointing his finger at him and rooting him to the spot.

The poor man is speedily released and goes on his way. The jingling of coins continues. A sergeant enters. There is some spell on him, but he is able to explain the new mercantile principle that he has heard. It is 'ask less than you'd like to get for the thing you're selling'. Cousins reacts impatiently. That is not what the kilted person said. It becomes clear that the sergeant is pursuing not Kelly but Widda Machree, who shortly enters followed by Kelly. Kelly offers to return the cow. She offers the money. Instead of buyer and seller in selfish confrontation we have the two offering gifts. Police reinforcements arrive. Both Kelly and the widow are handcuffed and borne off. But soon it is clear that they have escaped by magical means. Two blasted trees burst into sudden blossom, but quickly fade. The play ends with the merchant's refusing credit to the smallest farmer, who remarks that what he thought was a miracle must have been a hallucination.

This play, like *Cock-a-Doodle Dandy* is obviously a satire against capitalism. But the emphasis is different. In *Cock-a-Doodle* the distinction between use-value and abstract value is presented in conjunction with productive processes. In *Time to Go* we see the process of exchange where the dominant capital is merchant capital. The latter is more typical of rural Ireland. O'Casey's three farmers with respectively five, twenty-five and a hundred and fifty acres are completely typical and one would suspect the dramatist of consulting the Statistical Abstract to make sure his agrarian categories were correctly chosen. The unequal bargaining powers of the strong and the middle farmers and the subjection of the small farmer to merchant capital are also completely typical of the situation that prevailed in 1950.

The two young cyclists quite obviously symbolize the Gaelic enthusiasts who look longingly for Ireland's dead past, and whom O'Casey considered Irish capitalism had both exploited and betrayed. But what do Kelly and Widda Machree represent? In a sense of course they represent exchange freed from the law of value. This explains why the altruistic character is duplicated and the result polarised as man and woman. The law of value cannot express itself unless every transactor strives to gain the maximum for himself. To abandon this principle is to convert a commodity into a use-value or a gift. But the essence of a commodity is precisely that it cannot be a gift. We have already noted its own observations on this subject at the head of the chapter. It is moreover the effort of the exchanger to secure the greatest possible amount of value that stabilises the relation between price and value, and in the last analysis determines the distribution of capital throughout the various fields of economic activity. It is therefore perfectly understandable that the guardians of law and order should wish to take into custody the subverters of a principle without which capitalism cannot function. But the matter can be pushed further if we ask under what conditions products would remain use-values while industrial investment was governed by qualitative decision. The answer can only be, under full-fledged communism. O'Casey has thus made his main point clear.

But there is a Celtic residuum. Kelly wears the highly symbolical green and saffron of the Irish Irelander. Yet he is called 'Kelly from the Isle of Mananaun'. The accent here is that of Irish, falling on the last syllable. In the Isle of Man it is usual to stress the penultimate. There may be nothing worth pursuing here, since Manannán mac Lir of the Tuatha de Danann (people of the goddess Dana, deities of ancient Ireland frequently credited with a historical existence), is represented as a prince or merchant from the Isle of Man, who is endowed with magical powers. He is also the son of the sea god and was no doubt originally conceived as a god himself, but 'euhemerised' by Christian writers who disposed of the Celtic deities by converting them into ancient heroes. The question is not of course what the name Manannán means to Gaelic scholars, but what O'Casey intended it to convey in the context of his play. In the absence of any throughgoing examination of O'Casey's Irish language sources it is only possible to speculate. Why did O'Casey choose as a symbol of the replacement of capitalist values by socialist values a figure from Ireland's mythological past? Was it a tribute to Ireland's long centuries of 'primitive communism' free from the curse of commodity production?

The *Tuatha de Danann* were supposed to have invaded Ireland and Manannán was closely identified with shipping. Had O'Casey reached the melancholy conclusion that Ireland's salvation from men like Farrell and Flagonson could come only from abroad? Does this imply that the Irish exiles would take back communism into Ireland? The supposition is not outrageous. From 1941 onwards there was a succession of speeches and questions in the Dail expressing fears, usually highly exaggerated, of precisely this possibility.

Of Widda Machree there seems even less to be said. If the cow was the sweet, brown, white-back that represents Ireland, then the returning exile wearing Gaelic colours felt he paid too little for her. Possibly

Widda Machree also stands for Ireland. The same ambiguity and duplication (Kathleen and the family cow) occur in *Kathleen Listens In*. But she also challenges the principle of commerce and feels she demands too much. Is it too much to regard her as the symbol of the indestructible Irish people whose former national colour was blue? So when O'Casey returns in imagination to unchanging Ireland, with a sense of guilt because he has done too little for her, Ireland welcomes him home and says she has asked too much.

For those who have failed to notice the influence of Marxism in O'Casey's writings, it should be stated that to acquire the knowledge of political economy which I have postulated, he would need to read only the first chapter of Volume One of *Capital*. It seems most unlikely that having embraced communism he would omit to do that. And a man of his imagination could not have failed to admire the dialectical *tour de force* by which Marx establishes that the value with which commodities are popularly assumed to be endowed by nature is in fact conferred on them by society.

There are several levels of symbolism present simultaneously in O'Casey's fantasies of ideas. His method of retouching, adding decorative symbols to the essential ones facilitated such plurality. But if some enterprising student would make a study of the Irish language sources much at present unknown might be revealed.

NOTES

1. Junior staff of the Foreign Office were soon touting among the old school ties. I remember the visit of one of them to the head office of a company of which I was a technical executive. When I dissented from the policy of preparing for war against Russia, the colleague who had introduced me and who had Irish connections and knew my views, warned me with great solemnity: 'What *you* don't understand is that Russia is now imperialist power number one.' 'Think they are!' said the civil servant, completely destroying his friend's point, 'As a matter of fact we're still imperialist power number one.' With such blockheads advising them what government would require any incompetence of their own. In a few years they were busy 'jebbing' the country into European union.
2. For a detailed account of the politics of the first post-war years, see D. N. Pritt, *The Labour Government*.
3. Letter dated 1 May 1945, published in *Sean O'Casey Review*, vol. 1, no 2, Spring 1975.
4. Mr Hyde has sometimes been referred to as editor of the *Daily Worker*. He did not hold this position.
5. *Sean O'Casey Review*, loc.cit.
6. I happened to be in Bord na Mona's head office when the news came through. The officials could not have been more excited at an announcement of armed rebellion. I

remember one engineer, probably the kindliest person in daily life, shouting over the telephone 'Smash them! Finish them! Starve them out!' No doubt there was a histrionic element, but if there was 'grave sin' on one side there was not 'grave virtue' on the other.

7. Eileen O'Casey, op. cit., p. 200.
8. In Ayling, op. cit. p. 167.
9. In the Dublin performance referred to, people who were not familiar with the play missed the message of the semaphore, and with it much of the point of the play.

14

THE LAST PHASE

Those whom the gods love die young.

O'Casey had little fresh to say after *Time to Go*. The old man's soaring brain cannot rise for ever. Yet to the last he was shaping and re-shaping his past experience and following current events. He would almost certainly have reacted to any new political development that was close enough. The Chinese revolution, whilst it pleased him, was too far away. The situation in Britain and Ireland provided no grounds for enthusiasm. It was not that O'Casey was incapable of saying anything new. There was nothing new to say.

It was the deplorable achievement of the Attlee government to dam the flowing tide of popular democracy and drive it back along the course it had followed. Elected to build a new world order in concert with the USSR, it participated in an arms race directed against that country. During the international war against fascism, communists had been accepted into many key positions. Some of them had performed indispensable services, for example Desmond Bernal, the Tipperaryman whose scientific skill facilitated the landing of the allied troops in France. Services rendered were forgotten in the new political climate. The first dismissal of a communist from the civil service took place in 1948. The purge was later extended to government factories and finally to nationalized industries. There were even cases where the purge was applied in academic institutions. There was no reason to suspect that people of left-wing views would not loyally perform their duties. The purpose of the witch-hunt was to strengthen the atmosphere of fear and suspicion in the interests of the Cold War. Yet with characteristic ingratitude the United States chose this very time to push Britain aside and talk tête-à-tête with the USSR. The independent honest broker became the special poor relation. It must be said that not once did O'Casey moderate his statements in favour of peace and friendship with the USSR. When many were flying for cover he stood in the open.

In Ireland, De Valera was defeated in the general election of January 1948. Most observers forecast a return to 1932 when Fianna Fail held office by grace of the Labour Party. They might have been warned by a pre-election speech by Mr Sean MacBride, then the leader of Clann na Poblachta. He threw doubt on the general principle of party government. He had belonged to the right wing of the republican movement, but his subsequent development should cause no surprise. While the right wing has always shown itself more durable than the left, it has never lost its capacity for differentiation and the consequent production of a new left wing within it. It was, however, no victory for the left when MacBride persuaded Labour and Clann na Talmhain, a small agrarian party, to join with Clann na Poblachta in an 'inter-party government' headed by the former blue-shirt, John Costello. O'Casey was disgusted by the action of the Labour deputies and commented, 'Their backsides were itching for the plush seats of office.'

In the new government Sean MacBride agitated the issue of partition, but not in a way that would arouse the interest of the British labour movement. There was no response from official London. The world was then treated to the spectacle of the annulment of the 'treaty' by a member of the party which had killed seventy-seven men to enforce it. The twenty-six counties withdrew from the Commonwealth. But the procedure had something in common with the behaviour of those lizards which make their escape by leaving their tails in the hands of their captors. To make sure that the tail remained where it was, Mr Herbert Morrison introduced the retaliatory Ireland Act which conferred on the six-county administration the right, though of course not the power, to veto the reunification of Ireland. The bill was passed thanks to Tory votes, but it is likely that the Labour backbench rebellion would have been greater, but for the way in which the twenty-six county state had been traduced. The most vigorous opponent of the bill was Ireland's old champion, William Gallacher.

By its action the British government made politically impossible the incorporation of the twenty-six country Republic in the western alliance. This had been suggested as the price of ending partition. But the rulers of England were determined not to depend on the goodwill of their western neighbour. General MacEoin, no doubt for the sake of saying something when he had nothing to say, declared that the next war would be a 'holy war', and that there would be no shortage of young Irishmen ready to fight. He was a simple man, but sophisticated people suspected him of flying a kite. The assumptions of the Cold War were the more easily accepted in Ireland from its previous neutrality, though action upon them was blocked by partition. This fact illustrates the way in which the continuing demand for national independence places the Irish, whatever right-wing political theories may be in vogue, objectively on the left.

The coalition reaped the advantages of the previous government's fuel policy. But within a few years the Labour and Clann na Poblachta gilt had worn off the Fine Gael gingerbread. By 1952 De Valera was back.

O'Casey wrote his next play in a pessimistic mood. It was completed in 1954, and though he regarded it as within the genre of *Cock-a-Doodle Dandy*, it lacks that play's complex allegory. *The Bishop's Bonfire* is concerned with the preparations for the visit of Bishop Mullarkey[1] to his home town of Ballyoonagh.[2] He is to stay at the house of Councillor Reiligan (*reilig*, a cemetery), and that worthy, who has just been appointed a papal Count, is lavishing money on the occasion. He is advised by Canon Burren (*borr*, grand, proud)[3] and amusingly obstructed by lazy drunken and incompetent work-people. He has two daughters, both of whom have been brought up as 'ladies'. One of them, Keelin (*ciall*, commonsense) is the general manager and is in love with a workman, Daniel Clooncoohy.[4] Her sister, Forawn (*fuar*, cold) has stifled her love for a 'spoiled priest', Moanroe, and vowed life-long celibacy. The arrival of the Bishop is to be celebrated by the consignment of all immoral books and pictures to the flames of a bonfire. O'Casey does not imply great efficiency on the part of the censorship, for the books and pictures have to be in the country before they can be burned. But the reference is to the notorious 'burning of the books' by the nazis. It was a reference likely to have an unfortunate effect in England where the left were quite unaware that political books were not subject to censorship in Ireland, and that copies of Marx's *Capital* could be borrowed from the libraries of provincial towns. The suggestion was that the Republic was a fascist state.

Everything goes wrong, much as in *Purple Dust*, and good entertainment is provided. But Reiligan is not a superstitious weakling like Marthraun. He is no jumped-up peasant cashing in on the turf boom. He is more like Poges. He respects the Canon, but is his social equal. For he owns the dance hall, the public house, a shirt factory and a slice of land which, we are allowed to know, is not well worked. He thus embodies the principle of monopoly which was beginning to affect Irish capital in the fifties, as the drain of population led to the concentration in fewer hands of the enterprises left behind. The only workers we are introduced to are Reiligan's domestic staff, and these typify the unorganized and down-trodden who can only wriggle and cheat. When they do pluck up courage to object to the menial chores demanded by the Bishop's visit, the Canon has little difficulty in persuading them that working for the Bishop is working for God. The implication is thus clear. The capitalists and the church are in a conspiracy to keep the workers in subjection and the workers are credulous enough to accept the position.

Reiligan's daughter, Keelin, is prepared to elope with Daniel, but he lacks the courage to claim her, and prepares to emigrate alone. Moanroe, surprised by Forawn in the act of stealing his fare, shoots the girl with a revolver conveniently abandoned during a previous episode. The desire to emigrate is so strong that people are prepared to commit murder for it. Forawn has time before she dies to write a note exonerating Moanroe, and it is said that in the early versions she took as long to die as the lustiest prima donna breathing her last on top C. The point O'Casey is making is that religion has stultified not a casual liking but a deeply felt passion.

Despite the occasional somewhat arbitrary sounding of a magical horn (the 'buckineeno' of Saint Tremolo) the form of the play is realist. That is not to say that it bears the slightest resemblance to Irish reality. After *Time to Go* O'Casey seems to have begun a retreat from fantasy. But the total effect is not realist and he was right to classify it with *Cock-a-Doodle Dandy*, though the breadth and complexity of that play are lacking. There is a reference to the cold war in an episode which introduces the capitalist's son as an army officer. But its only significance seems to be in supplying the gun. There is no revolt by the factory workers, nor a breath of republicanism. The minor characters conclude with whiskey and revelry as the bonfire blazes. O'Casey seems to be saying 'Ireland is finished'. In 1948 he had given an interview to the journalist Terry Ward. He told him: 'All the good men in Ireland are dead. I take no further interest in the Dail until there are fifty communists there.' Somebody else, however, must contrive to get them elected.

The Bishop's Bonfire was a huge success when it was played at the Gaiety Theatre in Dublin in February 1955. There were occasional booes and hisses, and much controversy in the press, but packed houses for weeks. Gabriel Fallon justly commented on the irresistibility of O'Casey to Dublin audiences, even weak O'Casey. But one should also see in the play's success another example of the profound commonsense of 'statistical man'. In a famous presidential election a Fianna Fail government hoped to enlist the great prestige of De Valera in an effort to abolish proportional representation. The electors had two questions to answer – whom they wished for president, and whether they wished to continue to elect their representatives in the old way. They elected De Valera president and ignored his advice on the constitutional issue. The Dublin audiences knew that O'Casey's picture was both coloured and distorted. They did not recognize it as a reality. But there was sufficient truth in it for them to be pleased that somebody was saying it. The boss may not in fact be a blood-sucker, bed-breaker or body-snatcher, but it is pleasant to hear him abused.

There was something more also, which goes closer to the root of the O'Casey question. The audience felt, and could not but feel, that O'Casey was intensely concerned with Ireland and the Irish people. Cyril Cusack, who visited him in Devon to discuss the Dublin production wrote:[5] 'I sometimes think that O'Casey's egomania . . . comes from an identification of himself with Ireland.' O'Casey laughed at De Valera when he said that to know what the Irish people wanted he looked into his own heart. But he said the same himself, 'I know the mind of Ireland because I am within it; I know the heart of Ireland because I am one of its corners.'[6]

It was to this deep solicitude that audiences responded, forgiving the iconoclasm for the breath of healthy epicureanism. He wanted the plain people of Ireland to enjoy the good things of life. But to him these good things were simple things, things of the heart and imagination, love, friendship, song, dance and gaiety, the delights of nature and of literature, not Jaguars, gin and hemp. He liked to think of the way of a lad with a lass. But he was a thousand miles removed from the degenerate hedonism in promoting which publishers achieve their astonishing economies of scale, thanks to the identity of the human anatomy throughout the world. He was a permissive puritan.

At the end of 1956 a dreadful misfortune befell the O'Casey family. The younger son, Niall, intelligent, artistic, politically aware and of more than average scientific ability, died of leukaemia. To see how O'Casey could write under the concentrating influence of a simple emotion, it is only necessary to read his commemorative essay 'Under a Greenwood Tree he died'.[7] Here there is a complete absence of gratuitous ornamentation. Here is direct strong prose, free from all mannerisms that are not part of the man. It is a tribute to O'Casey's remarkable resilience that after this blow, when he was nearing eighty, nearly blind and suffering constant pain and irritation, he was able to produce a completely cheerful play, *The Drums of Father Ned*, in which he recognized the existence of regenerative forces in Ireland.

In 1955 there was a fundamental change in the policy of Irish capitalism. The principle of Sinn Fein was abandoned. From 1921 to that year, a weak bourgeoisie, constrained within limits imposed by imperialism, threatened as they believed by both republicanism and communism, tried to generate capital for national development within their truncated territory. Mr Lemass decided to give up the unequal struggle. Foreign capital must be brought in. In the long run this meant the subjection of native capital to the transnational companies, the progressive loss of national sovereignty and an increasing threat to the cultural values of the nation. After all, if crispy-whispies from Kalamazoo were to sell 200 million breakfast packs on the world market, people must not be encouraged to sing about bacon and eggs. But the inflow of foreign funds ended the culture of poverty. It freed the worker from dependence on the local employer, and over the years was bound to change the political function of the church, which might resume its old role, and participate in the defence of the nation. The most immediate means of bringing in foreign finance was the encouragement of tourism. The government decided to promote an international festival of music and drama, the *Tostal* (pageant).

Encouraged by the success of *The Bishop's Bonfire*, O'Casey started to write a play about a *Tostal*, which he obviously regarded as a means of infusing new international blood into the body of Irish culture and breaking what he regarded as the strangle-hold of the church. The promoters of the *Tostal* required plays that would attract tourists and, for the 1958 season, bethought them of the famous names of O'Casey and Joyce, whose work was already providing raw material for the dissertation industry. Joyce had achieved some small reputation for bawdiness. O'Casey had been banned. But when the plays arrived, one of them *The Drums of Father Ned*, they began to glance anxiously from the box office to the clergy. Instead of keeping the saints and the devil separate, they invited Archbishop McQuaid to open the *Tostal* with a solemn votive mass. They hoped thereby to justify new-fangled things to the less adventurous part of the population. The archbishop refused. The committee were thrown into consternation and the *Tostal* collapsed.

O'Casey's reaction was to forbid the production of his plays in Ireland. The result was to penalise an entirely innocent party, the Abbey Theatre which had been producing his three Dublin plays for years. It also led English workers who knew nothing about Ireland to think 'there must be something wrong with it'. At this time the IRA was fighting on the border. Over thirty times it tried to bring the British army into action, but the British government was able to rely on the RUC. The myth of six county independence was preserved. The false belief that the Republic was a backward priest-ridden state lent a spurious justification to the intransigence of the six county authorities, and concealed the important fact that whether the IRA offensive was good, bad or indifferent, it should never have been necessary. The British aggression upon which the whole position rested went unnoticed.

The play itself did not deserve the treatment it received. The action takes place in the small Irish coastal town of Doonavale ('shut your mouth'). The capitalist figures are two, Aloysius Binnington, solicitor, mayor and owner of the general store, and Councillor McGilligan, deputy mayor, building contractor and builders' provider. It is clear from the dialogue that Binnington is a supporter of Fianna Fail, for the other sneers at him for swearing an oath of allegiance to the king of England while protesting that he was only signing his name on a piece of paper. This is a reference to De Valera's entry into Parliament in the summer of 1927.

The two men are rivals and their enmity goes back far beyond 1921. This is shown in a prelude set in the days of the black-and-tans, that is to say in 1920 or 1921. At this time they have not spoken to each other for ten years, although they were born in the same street, attended the same school, and went to mass at the same church. We are given no clue to the origin of the quarrel. But it is so embittered that when the black-and-tans who are interrogating them order them to shake hands or be shot, they still refuse. They could hardly be worse friends than that.

It would of course be natural for men who were keeping up a family feud to take up opposing positions on the 'treaty'. The Irish countryside was famous for such feuds. But they always had some material foundation such as land-grabbing, fencing or turbary. O'Casey's purpose in depicting this exaggerated but groundless hatred is to make the point that despite their preferring death to reconciliation, they still do business. 'Business is business.' At a later stage he gives the impression that they not only symbolise capitalists in general, but in particular the two capitalist parties, Fianna Fail and Fine Gael, who hate each other like poison but nevertheless do business. If this is so he obfuscates matters by placing their quarrel in 1910 instead of 1922 when Ireland was divided into warring camps and the distinction between Fianna Fail and Fine Gael was created. Possibly he did not wish to obtrude the special symbolism at the expense of the general.

The theme 'business is business' runs through the play. Although they have mellowed and will now speak to each other, the two leading citizens are still enemies when preparations begin for the celebration of a *Tostal*. They resent the fact that these preparations are throwing together Binnington's son and McGilligan's daughter. They are finally reconciled, however, thanks to a business deal with a Portadown Orangeman who brings in a shipload of 'red timber'.

The people are rehearsing for the *Tostal* under the mysterious but benign influence of Father Ned. At the appropriate time a drum roll is heard which is an indication of his approval. Here we have a symbolism similar to that of the star that turns red, the transfiguration on the quay, the cock, and the 'buckineeno'. O'Casey has no *policy* for social transformation and it is always symbolised by a magical effect.

The first act shows the invasion of the Binningtons' drawing room by young people rehearsing a play about 1798 and a *Tostal* song, the local church organist at the piano. Binnington resents the intrusion but allows it. The parish priest, Father Fillifogue, demands that they sing hymns, but they take no notice of him. The second act is set in the almost identical drawing room of the McGilligans. Workmen are busy making window boxes to hold the flowers with which the town is to be decorated. Bernadette, the maid, tells Tom Kilsalligan the foreman, that

Father Ned has said 'that within the timid stir of this dull town would come laughter and a song or two, that girls who hurried off from boys and boys from girls, would linger close together now.' Kilsalligan thinks the prophecy dangerous but not distasteful.

Father Fillifogue (the name recalls the proverb '*Fillean an feall ar an feallaire*'[7][a] – the treachery rebounds on the traitor) alarmed at the change that is coming over his parish, circulates fussily in pursuit of Father Ned but cannot find him. He protests at the painting of the lamp posts in gay colours, only to discover that the *Tostal* flag has been unfurled over his presbytery, and his own door has been coloured bright red.

In the third act Binnington's son, Michael, and McGilligan's daughter, Shillaley, announce their intention of opposing their parents in a forthcoming election. 'We're fighting what is old and stale and vicious,' says Shillaley, 'the hate, the meanness their policies preach.' The Orangeman, Skerrigan, who has called for his cheque, becomes infected with the *Tostal* spirit and even goes the length of declaring 'to hell with partition', while reserving his political and theological position. Father Fillifogue tries to gather a mob to burn the 'atheistical timber'. Nobody can be found to help him. The play ends with the total discomfiture of Father Fillifogue, Binnington and McGilligan who can only repeat 'Oh, dear! What can the matter be?' to the sound of the drums of Father Ned.

What has happened is that the people have withdrawn their moral support from the alliance of priests and capitalists which, according to O'Casey's conception, ruled Ireland. There is a sense therefore in which the *Drums of Father Ned* was prophetic of the great change which came over Irish public opinion in the late sixties and above all in the seventies. The Irish people might be sufficiently comfortable under capitalism not to wish to revolt against it, but they no longer felt any duty to preserve it. In the face of declining numbers of vocations and difficulty in financing its institutions the Catholic church, especially since the days of Pope John, presented a more liberal aspect than previously. It was now concerned with a population which was predominantly urban. How far O'Casey foresaw or had a sense of coming changes it is difficult to say. His hint that a party of young people might confront Fine Gael and Fianna Fail at the polls, might have been inspired by the successes of Sinn Fein in local elections, successes which were reversed after the outbreak of hostilities on the border. Granted the more optimistic conclusion, however, policy is still lacking. A change takes place. But by what means? Social problems are solved through 'joy'. But it has been suggested that when Schiller penned his famous ode to *Freude*, the daughter of Elysium was really *Freiheit*. Joy is a consequence not an agent.

O'Casey was of course bitterly disappointed that 'an idle laughing play, about things encumbring Ireland's way' should succumb to the Archbishop's displeasure. He became more anti-clerical than ever. His last important work, *Behind the Green Curtains*, is a bitter satire against the cowardice and hypocrisy of certain Catholic intellectuals. It was inspired by the refusal of some of them to attend the funeral service of the Protestant Lennox Robinson. It was published in 1961.

In the first scene we see the hesitations, self-deceptions and manœuvres of Chatastray[8] a manufacturer in a small Irish town, and a group of writers who are his hangers on, as they stand outside a Protestant church where Lionel Robartes (the surname from Yeats) is being buried. They are afraid to enter. But a Protestant communist Beoman (*beo*, life), and a catholic girl Reena (*rion*, noble), go in.

The second act shows Chatastray and his cronies behind the green curtains of the house where he lives alone with Noneen (*Nóinín*, a daisy). The assembled literati have such names as Basan (*bas*, death) and Horawn, which I take to be English. At Chatastray's factory in Ballybeedhust ('Bally be dust'), the girls have been persuaded by a Catholic demagogue, Kornavaun (*cornuighim*, I tonsure), to threaten to strike if a Protestant engineer who is anxious to marry a catholic forewoman, is not dismissed. Kornavaun is a journalist. He calls on Chatastray on the pretext of asking for a statement on Mindszenty, but the manufacturer and the intellectuals beat a retreat into the office while Noneen gets rid of the visitor by throwing a glass of whiskey in his face.

There is to be a great anti-communist demonstration the following day under the slogan 'free thought in the world'. After Kornavaun has gone, the writers discuss their course of action. The performance outside the church is repeated, yes and no, if and whether, could and might. O'Casey's satire is withering. When Reena appears with yellow and white rosettes, they all put one on. But Beoman refuses saying, 'I happen to be a red.' This was of course never a crime in Ireland.

When Kornavaun appears with a deputation demanding the dismissal of those attempting a mixed marriage, Chatastray argues that such a marriage is permitted by law. O'Casey here shows the church as more reactionary than the capitalist state, which he concedes is not at fault. But to settle matters a group of hoodlums enter armed with sticks. Beoman seizes one of the sticks and successfully defends himself. Chatastray is taken away.

The third scene takes place on the 'day of the marching souls'. Chatastray is back in his room covered in bandages. Reena enters and tells him that Noneen has been stripped and left all night tied to a telegraph pole. 'We're a huddled nation,' she says, 'frightened under the hood of fear.' She tidies up the room which appears in disorder though there has been no struggle in it.

Reena has decided not to attend the demonstration. Chatastray cannot make up his mind, but supposes he will go. But Kornavaun sends a coat of sack-cloth in which he is to display his penitence. His manhood revolts for once and he decides to stay at home. But when the band passes the door playing 'Faith of our Fathers', he seizes his papal rosette and rushes after his cronies. Beoman exclaims 'Let's go from this dead place' and with Noneen and Reena' who has agreed to marry him, he leaves for England.

With the exception of some buffoonery outside the church, the method of this play is realist. But as with all O'Casey's late plays its total effect is not. When it was played in Dublin in 1976 its intense bitterness and pessimism, together with the slightness of the content, was too much for even a Dublin audience. There was much disappointment. The implication is that Catholics are priest-ridden, cowardly and ineffectual, and will always be so and that the only way to deal with Ireland is to leave it. It was regrettable that this one-sided opinion should have been let loose in England, where it corresponded to the prejudices of the most backward sections of the people. In the middle fifties there were ultra-leftists, some of them Irish, who argued that Irishmen should not be encouraged to join the trade union because of the backward Catholic influence they would exert. Such a proposition would be laughed at today, but it had its time. O'Casey's position also fostered the belief that the most progressive Irishman was the one who broke free from all traditional associations and proclaimed himself the emancipated internationalist.

That was not the classical Marxist position. Writing to Kautsky in 1882[9] Engels put the matter thus:

I therefore hold the view that *two* nations in Europe have not only the right but even the duty to be nationalistic before they become internationalistic: the Irish and the Poles. They are most internationalistic when they are genuinely nationalistic.

This principle is illustrated today not only in Ireland and among the Irish community in Britain, but in the children of Irish immigrants. Where the parents cut off their children from their ancestral tradition, they leave them powerless to repel the reprobations their English schoolfellows cast on their origins. They are compelled to become more English than the English; and from this process have come not a few members of the so-called National Front who bear Irish names. When on the other hand the parents bring their children up to know, respect and understand the struggle of their forbears for independence, these children have no difficulty in becoming international and fitting into the organised Labour movement. His failure to understand that no matter how distorted it might be within special historical circumstances, the

Irish genius was always a rebel one, inevitably gravitating to the side of progress, was the principal lacuna in the intellectual equipment of a very great man.

O'Casey began as a Unionist. As such he came to Irish nationalism from the outside. He was attracted first by its cultural aspects. Then he was captured by the romance of Fenianism. His was not the 'bread and butter nationalism' of the Dublin trades council which kept watch and ward over the principle that work that could be done in Dublin should be done in Dublin. O'Casey's was the nationalism of the splendid dream. And where there is dreaming, there you find excess, and excess which in progressive politics can give rise to the phenomenon of ultra-leftism.

But the romantic Fenian was suddenly showered with the cold water of victimization, unemployment and industrial war. The dream gave way to reality. But it was a reality in which he did not know his way. The extraordinary ambivalence of his writings between 1913 and 1919 illustrates this.

He took no part in the Rising of 1916 for reasons which were probably more personal than political. He glorified it in 1917, but in 1919, partly in reaction to the failure of the Dail to implement its own programmes, and partly under the influence of the 'Larkinites', he decided to repudiate it. He condemned it however from the ultra-left point of view, because it was concerned with the tasks that confronted Irish people at the time, and paid no attention to the more advanced tasks O'Casey now wished to see undertaken.

Now because the national revolution was not completed – because, indeed, a counter-revolution supervened – the conditions in which these more advanced tasks were called for, never materialised. Instead of returning to what was historically necessary, O'Casey demanded them all the more insistently. But the possibility of performing them did not exist. O'Casey reacted by turning on the immediate tasks, which had been attempted with only partial success, and declaring them irrelevant. There was then nothing for him in Irish politics. He left for England where he wandered awhile as a politically rootless person and dabbled in artistic élitism. But the necessities of the struggle against fascism, and the increasing prestige of the USSR, drew him back into practical affairs. Politics are shallow without a vision of the future. They are non-existent without what can be done now. During the period of the struggle against fascism he became a convert to communism. It is no accident that the play which is completely free from the influence of ultra-leftism, *Purple Dust*, was written at the conclusion of a period of considerable involvement in politics.

This play was sandwiched between two highly personal plays,

The Star Turns Red and *Red Roses for Me*. The first substitutes for the fight for national independence, proletarian revolution. The second which is almost a revision of it, substitutes an industrial dispute. In each case proletarian tasks are attempted, democratic tasks being ignored. But in the case of *The Star Turns Red* the tasks are impossible of achievement, in the case of *Red Roses for Me* they are achievable but not achieved. And instead of working class aims' being attained with the aid of democracy, they are attained, where they are attained, by magical means.

After the war *Cock-a-Doodle Dandy, the Bishop's Bonfire and Behind the Green Curtains* show how hopeless it is to attempt socialist tasks in Ireland when the essential basis in democracy has not been laid. But though O'Casey shows this, he does not understand it, and draws the conclusion that Ireland is hopeless, except in *The Drums of Father Ned*.

Leaving aside the two weak plays, *Within the Gates* and *Oak Leaves and Lavender*, it remains now to consider the three early plays. These were written during the counter-revolution and each is more pessimistic than the last. But all have the merit that they do not deal with problems of the future, and there is no need of resolutions by magical means. They show problems of the present which people are attempting to solve in the wrong way. If there is a wrong way, then by implication there is a right way, whether the playwright knows it or not. For this reason, whilst the three Abbey plays show no way forward, their power to move an audience remains far superior to that of O'Casey's later work.

And yet O'Casey remains throughout a 'progressive' artist. The reason is simple. Though he presents Ireland with questions that have not yet been raised in practice, as the relative numbers of the votes of Fianna Fail and Labour clearly show, issues of socialism and working-class power, and the remodelling of the economic basis of society, are highly relevant on a world scale. It is unfortunate that O'Casey did not understand that the national liberation of Ireland through *democratic* change is part of the world *socialist* revolution. O'Casey retains his place as a foremost revolutionary dramatist, not because he understood the part, for he did not, but because all his work was informed by the vision of the whole.

NOTES

1. It is improbable that this name has any special significance, except perhaps to emphasize the Bishop's humble origins.
2. *Ounagh* in Irish place names is usually derived from abhnach, meaning watery, marshy, even boggy. If this is the meaning O'Casey intended, it explains the poor

state of Reiligan's cattle. He had shrunk from the outlay involved in drainage. But John Jordan (Ayling (Ed.), op. cit., p. 157) equates oonagh with *ionadh* making the meaning of Ballyoonagh Wondertown.

3. The name corresponds to that of a barren upland in the Co. Clare, now bare limestone, but centuries ago one of the most populous parts of Ireland.

4. *Clooncoohy* might mean meadow of the cuckoos. *Moanroe* in a place name would mean red bog. But whether O'Casey had some deeper meaning in mind, is not immediately ascertainable.

5. Gabriel Fallon, op.cit., p. 181.

6. Sean O'Casey, *The Green Crow*, p. 137.

7. Sean O'Casey, *Under a Coloured Cap*, pp. 100–33.

7a. I am indebted for this suggestion to Mr Maolsheachlain O Caollai.

8. I can at present suggest no origin for this curious name, but presume it is English, possibly a modification of Chattaway.

9. Marx and Engels, *Ireland and the Irish Question*, Progress Publishers, Moscow, Lawrence and Wishart, London 1971, p. 332.

SELECT BIBLIOGRAPHY

1. O'Casey's Works
   AUTOBIOGRAPHIES
   I Knock at the Door, London, 1939.
   Pictures in the Hallway, London, 1942.
   Drums under the Windows, London, 1945.
   Inishfallen, Fare Thee Well, London, 1949.
   Rose and Crown, London, 1952.
   Sunset and Evening Star, London, 1954.

   PLAYS
   Collected Plays, 4 vols, London, 1949–51.
   The Bishop's Bonfire, London, 1955.
   The Drums of Father Ned, 1960.
   Behind the Green Curtains, 1961.

   OTHER WRITINGS
   Windfalls (stories, poems, plays), London, 1934.
   The Flying Wasp (essays), London, 1937.
   The Green Crow, London, 1957.
   Under a Colored Cap, London, 1963.
   Feathers from the Green Crow (ed.) R. Hogan, London, 1963.
   Blasts and Benedictions (articles and stories selected and introduced by Ronald Ayling), London, 1967.
   The Letters of Sean O'Casey, vol. 1, 1910–1941 (ed.) David Krause, London, 1975.

   as P. O Cathasaigh
   The Story of the Irish Citizen Army, Dublin, 1919.

2. Biography and Criticism
   Ayling, Ronald (ed.), *Sean O'Casey, Modern Judgements*, London, 1969.
   Ayling, Ronald, Preface to: O'Casey. *Blasts and Benedictions*, London, 1967.
   Benstock, Bernard, *Paycocks and Others*, Dublin, 1976.
   Cowasjee, Saros, *Sean O'Casey. The Man Behind the Plays*, London, 1966.
   Hogan, Robert, *The Experiments of Sean O'Casey*, New York, 1960.

Goldstone, Herbert, *In Search of Community: The Achievement of Sean O'Casey*, Cork and Dublin, 1972.

Fallon, Gabriel, *Sean O'Casey, The Man I Knew*, London, 1965.

Krause, David, *Sean O'Casey. The Man and his Work*, London, 1960.

Krause, David, *Sean O'Casey and his World*, London, 1976.

Lowery, Robert G. (ed.), *Sean O'Casey Review* (half-yearly journal of O'Casey criticism).

McCann, Sean (ed.), *The World of Sean O'Casey*, London, 1966.

O'Casey, Eileen, *Sean*, London, 1972.

Mikhail, E. H., and O'Riordan, John, *The Sting and the Twinkle. Conversations with Sean O'Casey*, London, 1974.

Pauli, Manfred, *Sean O'Casey, Drama, Poesie, Wirklichkeit*, Berlin [East], 1977.

Margulies, Martin B., *The Early Life of Sean O'Casey*, Dublin, 1970.

3. Irish History

Blaghd, Ernan de, *Trasna na Boinne* (Across the Boyne), Dublin, 1957.

Boyd, Andrew, *Irish Trade Unions, 1729–1970*, Tralee, 1972.

Connolly, James, *Labour in Ireland*, Dublin, 1951.

Coogan, T. P., *Ireland since the Rising*, London, 1966.

Fox, R. M., *History of the Irish Citizen Army*, Dublin, 1943.

Greaves, C. Desmond, *Life and Times of James Connolly*, London, 1961.

Greaves, C. Desmond, *Liam Mellows and the Irish Revolution*, London, 1971.

Hurley, Michael (ed.), *Irish Anglicanism, 1869–1879*, Dublin, 1970.

Macardle, Dorothy, *The Irish Republic*, London, 1937.

McDowell, R. B., *The Church of Ireland, 1869–1969*, London, 1975.

Martin, F. X., and Byrne, F. J., *The Scholar Revolutionary. Eoin MacNeill, 1867–1945*, Dublin, 1973.

Marx, K., and Engels, F., *Ireland and the Irish Question*, London, 1971.

Mitchell, A., *Labour in Irish Politics, 1890–1930*, Dublin, 1974.

Nowlan, K. B. (ed.), *The Making of 1916. Studies in the History of the Rising*, Dublin, 1969.

O'Shannon, Cathal (ed.), *Fifty Years of Liberty Hall*, Dublin, 1959.

Robbins, F., *Under the Starry Plough. Recollections of the Irish Citizen Army*, Dublin, 1977.

Robinson, Lennox (ed.), *Lady Gregory's Journals, 1916–1930*, London, 1946.

Ryan, Desmond, *The Rising*, Dublin, 1949.

Ryan, W. P., *The Pope's Green Island*, London, 1912.

Van Voris, Jacqueline, *Constance Markievicz*, University of Massachusetts, 1967.

4. Criticism

Corkery, D., *Synge and Anglo-Irish Literature*, Cork and Oxford, 1947.

Hogan, R., *After the Irish Renaissance. A critical History of the Irish Drama since the 'Plough and the Stars'*, London, 1968.

Kavanagh, Peter, *The Irish Theatre*, Tralee, 1946.

McCann, Sean, *The Story of the Abbey Theatre*, London, 1967.

Mercier, Vivian, *The Irish Comic Tradition*, Oxford, 1962.

Thomson, George, *Aeschylus and Athens. A Study in the Social Origins of Drama*, London, 1941.

INDEX